The Moody Collection

That Gospel Sermon on the Blessed Hope

Sovereign Grace

Sowing and Reaping

The Way to God and How to Find It

Men of the Bible

The Moody Collection

Insight and Wisdom from D. L. Moody

That Gospel Sermon on the Blessed Hope

Sovereign Grace

Sowing and Reaping

The Way to God and How to Find It

Men of the Bible

©2010 Bottom of the Hill Publishing

All rights reserved. Printed in the United States of America. No part of this book may be used or reproduced in any manner without written permission except for brief quotations for review purposes only.

This book was written in the prevailing style of that period. Language and spelling have been left original in an effort to give the full flavor of this classic work.

Bottom of the Hill Publishing
www.BottomoftheHillPublishing.com

First Edition

ISBN: 978-1-935785-94-1

10 9 8 7 6 5 4 3 2 1 0

Contents

That Gospel Sermon on the Blessed Hope	6
Sovereign Grace	17
Sowing and Reaping	105
The Way to God and How to Find It	181
Men of the Bible	275

THAT GOSPEL SERMON ON THE BLESSED HOPE

CONTENTS

But How Is He Going to Come   9

Christ is the Prince of Life   10

The Church is the Lambs Wife   12

Christ Will Save His Church   14

A Sermon delivered by D. L. Moody, the Evangelist, at the Great Chicago Tabernacle, Jan. 5, 1877. Repeated in the Boston Tabernacle, April 29th.

In 2 Timothy, 3:16, Paul declares: "All scripture is given by inspiration of God, and is profitable for doctrine, for reproof, for correction, for instruction in righteousness;" but there are some people who tell us when we take up prophecy that it is all very well to be believed, but that there is no use in one trying to understand it; these future events are things that the church does not agree about, and it is better to let them alone, and deal only with those prophecies which have already been fulfilled. But Paul does not talk that way; he says: "All scripture is ... profitable for doctrine." If these people are right, he ought to have said: "Some scripture is profitable; but you can not understand the prophecies, so you had better let them alone." If God did not mean to have us study the prophecies, he would not have put them in the Bible. Some of them are fulfilled, and he is at work fulfilling the rest, so that if we do not see them all completed in this life, we shall in the world to come.

I do not want to teach anything to-day dogmatically, on my own authority, but to my mind this precious doctrine--for such I must call it--of the return of the Lord to this earth is taught in the New Testament as clearly as any other doctrine is; yet I was in the church fifteen or sixteen years before I ever heard a sermon on it. There is hardly any church that does not make a great deal of baptism, but the New Testament only speaks about baptism thirteen times, while it speaks of the return of our Lord fifty times; and yet the church has had very little to say about it. Now, I can see a reason for this: the devil does not want us to see this truth, for nothing would wake up the church so much. The moment a man takes hold of the truth that Jesus Christ is coming back again to receive his friends to himself, this world loses its hold upon him; gas-stocks and water-stocks, and stocks in banks and horse-railroads, are of very much less consequence to him then. His heart is free, and he looks for the blessed appearing of his Lord, who at his coming will take him into his blessed kingdom.

In 2 Peter 1:20, we read: "No prophecy of the scripture is of any private interpretation." Some people say: "O yes, the prophecies are all well enough for the priests and doctors, but not for the rank and file of the church." But Peter says: "The prophecy came not by the will of man, but holy men spake as they were moved by the Holy Ghost," and those men are the very ones who tell us of the return of our Lord. Look at Daniel 2:45, where he tells the meaning of that stone which the king saw in his dream that was cut out of the mountain without hands, and that broke in pieces the iron, the brass, the clay, the silver, and the gold. "The dream is certain and the interpretation thereof sure," says Daniel. Now we have seen the fulfillment of that prophecy all but the closing part of it. The kingdoms of Babylon and Medo-Persia and Greece and Rome have all been broken in pieces, and now it only remains for this stone cut out of the mountain without hands to smite the image and break it in pieces till it becomes like the dust of the summer threshing floor, and for this stone to become a great mountain and fill the whole earth.

BUT HOW IS HE GOING TO COME?

We are told how he is going to come. When those disciples stood looking up into heaven at the time of his ascension, there appeared two angels, who said Acts 1:11: "Ye men of Galilee, why stand ye gazing up into heaven? This same Jesus which is taken up from you into heaven shall so come in like manner as ye have seen him go into heaven." How did he go up? He took his flesh and bones up with him. "Look at me; handle me; give me something to eat; a spirit hath not flesh and bones as ye see me have; I am the identical one whom they crucified and laid in the grave. Now I am risen from the dead and am going up to heaven," Luke 24:39,43. He is gone, say the angels, but he will come again just as he went. An angel was sent to announce his birth of the virgin; angels sang of his advent in Bethlehem; an angel told the women of his resurrection; and two angels told the disciples of his coming again. It is the same testimony in all these cases.

I do not know why people should not like to read the Bible, and find out all about this precious doctrine of our Lord's return. Some have gone beyond prophecy, and tried to tell the very day he would come. Perhaps that is one reason why people do not believe this doctrine. He is coming, we know that; but just when he is coming we do not know; Matt. 24:36, settles that. The angels do not know; and Christ says that even he does not know, but that is something the Father keeps to himself. If Christ had said: "I will not come back for 2,000 years," none of his disciples would have begun to watch for him, but it is the proper attitude of a Christian to be always looking for his Lord's return. So God does not tell us just when he is to come, but Christ tells us to watch. In this same chapter we find that he is to come unexpectedly and suddenly. In the twenty-seventh verse we have these words: "For as the lightning cometh out of the east and shineth unto the west, even so shall also the coming of the Son of Man be." And again in the forty-fourth verse: "Therefore be ye also ready, for in such an hour as ye think not the Son of Man cometh."

Some people say that means death: but the Word of God does not say it means death. Death is our enemy, but our Lord hath the keys of death; he has conquered death, hell, and the grave, and at any moment he may come to set us free from death, and destroy our last enemy for us; so the proper state for a believer in Christ is waiting and watching for our Lord's return.

In the last chapter of John there is a text that seems to settle this matter. Peter asks the question about John: "Lord what shall this man do? Jesus said unto him, If I will that he tarry till I come, what is that to thee? Follow thou me. Then went this saying abroad among the brethren that that disciple should not die." They did not think that the coming of the Lord meant death; there was a great difference between these two things in their minds.

CHRIST IS THE PRINCE OF LIFE

There is no death where he is; death flees at his coming; dead bodies sprang to life when he touched them or spoke to them. His coming is not death; he is the resurrection and the life, when he sets up his kingdom there is to be no death, but life forevermore.

There is another mistake, as you will find if you read your Bible carefully. Some people think that at the coming of Christ everything is to be done up in a few minutes; but I do not so understand it. The first thing he is to do is to take his Church out of the world. He calls the Church his bride, and he says he is going to prepare a place for her. We may judge, says one, what a glorious place it will be from the length of time he is in preparing it, and when the place is ready he will come and take the church to himself.

In the closing verses of the fourth chapter of 1 Thessalonians, Paul says: "If we believe that Jesus died and rose again, even so also them which sleep in Jesus will God bring with him.... We which are alive and remain unto the coming of the Lord shall not prevent them which are asleep. For the Lord himself shall descend from heaven with a shout, with the voice of the archangel, and with the trump of God, and the dead in Christ shall rise first. Then we which are alive and remain shall be caught up together with them in the clouds to meet the Lord in the air, and so shall we ever be with the Lord. Wherefore, comfort one another with these words." That is the comfort of the church. There was a time when I used to mourn that I should not be alive in the millennium; but now I expect to be in the millennium. Dean Alford says--and almost everybody bows to him in the matter of interpretation--that he must insist that this coming of Christ to take his church to himself in the clouds is not the same event us that to judge the world at the last day. The deliverance of the church is one thing, judgment is another. Now, I cannot find any place in the Bible where it tells me to wait for signs of the coming of the millennium, as the return of the Jews, and such like; but it tells me to look for the coming of the Lord; to watch for it; to be ready at midnight to meet him, like those five wise virgins. The trump of God may be sounded, for anything we know, before I finish this sermon--at any rate we are told that he will come as a thief in the night, and at an hour when many look not for him.

Some of you may shake your heads and say, "Oh, well, that is too deep for the most of us; such things ought not to be said before these young converts; only the very wisest characters, such as ministers and professors in the theological seminaries, can understand them." But my friends, you find that Paul wrote about these things to those young converts among the Thessalonians, and he tells them to comfort one another with these words. Here in the first chapter of 1 Thessalonians Paul says, "Ye turned to God from idols to serve the living and true God, and to wait for his Son from heaven whom he raised from the dead, even Jesus, which delivered us from the wrath to come," To wait for his Son; that is the true attitude of every child of God. If he is doing that he is ready for the duties of life, ready for God's work; aye, that makes him feel that he is just ready to begin to work for God.

Then in 1 Thessalonians, 2:19, he says: "For what is our hope, or joy, or crown of rejoicing? Are not even ye, in the presence of our Lord Jesus Christ, at his coming?" And again, in the third chapter, at the thirteenth verse, "To the end that he may establish your hearts unblamable in holiness before God, even our Father, at the coming of our Lord Jesus Christ with all his saints." Still again, in the fifth chapter, "For ye yourselves know perfectly that the day of the Lord so cometh as a thief in the night. But ye, brethren, are not in darkness, that that day should over take you as a thief." He has something to say about this same thing in every chapter, indeed I have thought this Epistle to the Thessalonians might be called the gospel of Christ's coming again.

There are three great facts foretold in the word of God: First, that Christ should come; that has been fulfilled. Second, that the Holy Ghost should come; that was fulfilled at Pentecost, and the church is able to testify to it by its experience of his saving grace. Third, the return of our Lord again from heaven--for this we are told to watch and wait "till he come." Look at that account of the last hours of Christ with his disciples. What does Christ say to them? If I go away I will send death after you to bring you to me? I will send an angel after you? Not at all. He says: "I will come again and receive you unto myself." If my wife were in a foreign country, and I had a beautiful mansion all ready for her, she would a good deal rather I should come and bring her unto it than to have me send some one else to bring her.

THE CHURCH IS THE LAMB'S WIFE

He has prepared a mansion for his bride, and he promises for our joy and comfort that he will come himself and bring us to the place he has been all this while preparing.

My friends it is perfectly safe to take the word of God as we find it. If he tells us to watch, then watch! If he tells us to pray, then pray! If he tells us he will come again, wait for him! Let the church bow to the word of God, rather than trying to find out how such things can be. "Behold, I come quickly," said Christ. "Even so, come, Lord Jesus," should be the prayer of the church.

Take the account of the words of Christ at the communion table. It seems to me the devil has covered up the most precious thing about it. "For as often as ye eat this bread and drink this cup ye do show forth the Lord's death till he come." But most people seem to think that the Lord's table is the place for self-examination and repentance, and making good resolutions. Not at all; you spoil it that way; it is to show forth the Lord's death, and we are to keep it up till he comes.

Some people say, "I believe Christ will come on the other side of the millennium." Where do you get it? I cannot find it. The word of God nowhere tells me to watch and wait for the coming of the millennium, but for the coming of the Lord. I do not find any place where God says the world is to grow better and better, and that Christ is to have a spiritual reign on earth of a thousand years. I find that the world is to grow worse and worse, and at length there is to be a separation. "Two women grinding at a mill, one taken and the other left; two men in one bed, one taken and the other left," Luke 17:34,36. The church is to be translated out of the world, we have two examples already, two representatives, as we might say, of Christ's kingdom, of what is to be done for all his true believers. Enoch is the representative of the first dispensation, Elijah of the second, and, as a representative of the third dispensation, we have the Saviour himself, who is entered into the heavens for us, and become the first fruits of them that slept. We are not to wait for the great white throne judgement, but the glorified church is set on the throne with Christ, and to help to judge the world.

Now, some of you think this is a new and strange doctrine, and that they who preach it are speckled birds. But let me tell you that most of the spiritual men in the pulpits of Great Britain are firm in this faith. Spurgeon preaches it. I have heard Newman Hall say that he knew no reason why Christ might not come before he got through with his sermon. But in certain wealthy and fashionable churches, where they have the form of godliness, but deny the power thereof,—just the state of things which Paul declares shall be in the last days,—this doctrine is not preached or believed. They do not want sinners to cry out in their meeting, "What must I do to be saved?" They want intellectual preachers who will cultivate their taste, brilliant preachers who will rouse their imagination, but they do not want the preaching that has in it the power of the Holy Ghost. We live in the day of shams in religion. The church is cold and formal; may God wake us up! And I know of no better way to do it than to get the church to looking for the return of our Lord.

Some people say, "Oh, you will discourage the young converts if you preach that doctrine." Well, my friends, that has not been my experience. I have felt like working three times as hard ever since I came to understand that my Lord was coming back again. I look on this world as a wrecked vessel. God has given me a lifeboat, and said to me, "Moody, save all you can." God will come in judgment and burn up this world, but the children of God do not belong to this world; they are in it, but not of it, like a ship in the water. This world is getting darker and darker; its ruin is coming nearer and nearer; if you have any friends on this wreck unsaved, you had better lose no time in getting them off.

But some will say: "Do you then make the grace of God a failure?" No, grace is not a failure but man is. The antediluvian world was a failure; the Jewish work was a failure; man has been a failure everywhere, when he has had his own way and been left to himself.

CHRIST WILL SAVE HIS CHURCH

But he will save them finally by taking them out of the world. Now, do not take my word for it; look this doctrine up in your Bible, and if you find it there, bow down to it and receive it as the word of God. Take Matthew 24:48,50: "But and if that evil servant shall say in his heart, my Lord delayeth his coming ... the Lord of that servant shall come in a day when he looketh not for him, and in an hour that he is not aware of, and shall cut him asunder and appoint him his portion with the hypocrites; there shall be weeping and gnashing of teeth." Take 2 Peter 3:4,5: "There shall come in the last days scoffers, walking after their own lusts, and saying, where is the promise of his coming? for since the fathers fell asleep all things continue as they were from the beginning of the creation." Go out on the streets of Chicago and ask men about the return of our Lord, and that is just what they would say: "Ah, yes, the Lord delayeth his coming!"

"Behold, I come quickly," said Christ to John, and the last prayer in the Bible is, "Even so, come Lord Jesus, come quickly." Were the early Christians disappointed then? No; no man is disappointed who obeys the voice of God. The world waited for the first coming of the Lord; waited for 4,000 years, and then he came. He was here only thirty-three years and then he went away; but he left us a promise that he would come again; and as the world watched and waited for his first coming and did not watch in vain, so now to them who wait for his appearing shall he appear a second time unto salvation. Now let the question go round, "Am I ready to meet the Lord if he comes to-night?" "Be ye also ready, for in such an hour as ye think not the Son of man cometh."

There is another thought I want to call your attention to, and that is this: Christ will bring all our friends, with him when he comes. All who have died in the Lord are to be with him when he comes in the clouds of heaven. "Blessed and holy is he that hath part in the first resurrection: on such the second death has no power, but they shall be priests of God and of Christ, and shall reign with him a thousand years," Rev. 20:6. "But the rest of the dead lived not again until the thousand years were past; this is the first resurrection" (verse 5). That looks as if the church were to have a thousand years with Christ before the final judgment, when Satan shall be cast out, and there shall be new heavens and new earth wherein dwelleth righteousness.

Now, I want to give you some texts to study.

When we eat the Lord's supper we show forth his death, until he come. 1 Cor. xi. 26.

We are using our talents, until he come. Luke xix. 13.

We are fighting the good fight of faith, until he come. 1 Tim vi. 12-14.

We are enduring tribulation, until he come. 2 Thes. i. 7.

We are to be patient, until he come. James v. 8.

We wait for the crown of righteousness, until he come. 2 Tim. iv. 8.

We wait for the crown of glory, until he come. 1 Pet. v. 4.

We wait for re-union with departed friends, until he come. 1 Thes. iv. 13-18.

We wait for Satan to be bound, until he come. Rev. xx. 3.

And so let us watch and wait till he comes.

D. L. Moody, who is perhaps the most popular and efficient preacher of the gospel of Christ in the world, to-day, is evidently fully committed to a belief in the speedy coming of our Lord Jesus Christ, to judge the world and establish his eternal kingdom. Looking over the published reports of his sermons in Great Britain and in this country, since the beginning of 1874, I give extracts which go to show in a plain light the man's inner love and hope as relates to the last things, and his warm, bold, consistent manner of expressing the same. Thousands pray, God bless D. L. Moody.

1. Mr. Moody proclaims that the grand symbols of Daniel's, second and seventh chapters, announce four dominant world empires, and but four, to cover all centuries of human probation.

2. That these kingdoms are and were Babylon, Medo-Persia, Greece and Rome.

3. That these have had their day of earthly supremacy and the last has nearly passed away.

4. That the fifth kingdom of Daniel is God's, to come in its order as the fifth, to overthrow all previous kingdoms, to be a visible and eternal kingdom, and to be established by Christ in person at his second coming.

5. That the stone cut from the mountain denotes "Christ himself," "at his appearing and kingdom," whose advent "is not far distant," and for whose advent "the whole creation groans." Rom. 8:19-22.

6. That the last days, described by our Saviour in Matt. 24:37-39 as resembling the days of Lot and Noah, are already here; observing, "I do not think the day is far distant when our Lord will return." And again, "just as judgment overtook Belshazzar carousing at his feast, so will judgment come suddenly and swiftly upon the world revelling in its sins."

The foregoing he preached in the City Hall, Glasgow, March 15th, 1874, before three thousand people. On the same day he preached on "Christ's Second Coming" in the Free church (Pres.), telling the churches that every thirtieth verse in the New Testament bears on that glorious coming; and says the London Christian, "With his usual power he showed what a mighty motive this doctrine is to all who are winning souls. He himself had found it rousing him to ten-fold more effort to save all that could be rescued from the coming wreck."

In Philadelphia, in a discourse on Daniel's second chapter, he said: "This dream has been nearly fulfilled as Daniel interpreted it. In the present age the prophecy is nearly completed, and the hour of the Lord's second coming is close at hand." D. T. T.

Sovereign Grace
Its Source, Its Nature and Its Effects

By

D. L. Moody

"By Grace are ye saved."—Ephesians II:8

With Three Gospel Dialogues

PREFATORY NOTE

IN the exercise of his high calling, the faithful ambassador of Christ must not scruple to declare the whole counsel of God—"rightly dividing the word of truth," to all classes of hearers. He must warn the openly wicked man that if he persists in his evil courses, the just judgments of God will inevitably overtake him; he must unmask the hypocrite; he must utter no uncertain protest against the crooked and devious ways of the self-seeker and the time-server. But if he enters into the Spirit of his Master, no part of his public work will be more congenial or delightful than the proclamation of the full, free, and sovereign grace of God, manifested towards sinful men in the gift of His Eternal Son, to be the Saviour of the world. It has been my happy privilege in years past to tell out, as best I could, this wonderful story of redeeming grace. The following pages record the addresses I have given on the various aspects of this great subject. I pray God that in their printed form they may serve to deepen in the mind of the reader the appreciation of this grace, at once so infinite and so undeserved.

The chapter entitled "A Chime of Gospel Bells," though not strictly flowing out of the general subject, is in perfect harmony with it; every note in the chime is intended to ring out the gracious invitation to "Come" to the God of all grace and be blessed. The Dialogues which form the latter part of the book were heard with much interest and profit at some of the London meetings; I think the perusal of them will be helpful in removing many of the hindrances that prevent anxious inquirers from accepting without delay the salvation that God in His grace has provided for the sinful children of men.

D. L. Moody.

CONTENTS

The Fountain of Grace	21
Saved by Grace Alone	25
Possessing, and "Working Out"	31
Grace Abounding to the Chief of Sinners	36
Law and Grace	48
Grace for Living	56
Grace for Service	61
"A Chime of Gospel Bells"	67
GOSPEL DIALOGUES:	
I. What It Is to be a Child of God	82
II. How to Become a Christian	91
III. What It Is to be Converted	101

"Grace! 'tis a charming sound,
Harmonious to the ear;
Heaven with the echo shall resound,
And all the earth shall hear.
'Twas grace that wrote my name
In life's eternal book;
'Twas grace that gave me to the Lamb,
Who all my sorrows took.
Grace taught my wandering feet
To tread the heavenly road;
And new supplies each hour I meet,
While pressing on to God.
Oh let that grace inspire
My soul with strength divine.
May all my prayers to Thee aspire,
And all my days be Thine."
Dr. Doddridge.

CHAPTER I
THE FOUNTAIN OF GRACE

THERE are some words with which we have been familiar from our infancy up, and probably there are few words in the English language that are so often used as this word "GRACE." Many of you at your table "say grace" three times a day. You seldom go into a church without hearing the word mentioned. You seldom read any part of the New Testament, especially the Epistles, without meeting the word.

There is probably not a word in the language so little understood. There are a great many who have received the grace of God into their heart, but who, if they should be asked what the word means would be troubled, and confused, and unable to tell. I experienced the grace of God a good many years before I really knew the true meaning of the word.

Now, grace means unmerited mercy—undeserved favor. If men were to wake up to the fact, they would not be talking about their own worthiness when we ask them to come to Christ. When the truth dawns upon them that Christ came to save the unworthy, then they will accept salvation. Peter calls God "the God of all grace."

Men talk about grace, but, as a rule, they know very little about it. Let a business man go to one of your bankers to borrow a few hundred dollars for sixty or ninety days; if he is well able to pay, the banker will perhaps lend him the money if he can get another responsible man to sign the note with him. They give what they call three days' grace after the sixty or ninety days have expired; but they will make the borrower pay interest on the money during these three days, and if he does not return principal and interest at the appointed time, they will sell his goods; they will perhaps turn him out of his house, and take the last piece of furniture in his possession. That is not grace at all; but that fairly illustrates man's idea of it. Grace not only frees you from payment of the interest, but of the principal also.

ITS SOURCE.

In the Gospel by John we read, "The Word was made flesh and dwelt among us, and we beheld His glory, the glory as of the Only-begotten of the Father, full of grace and truth . . . For the law was given by Moses, but grace and truth came by Jesus Christ." Now you know that for many years men were constantly trying to find the source of the Nile. The river of grace has been flowing through this dark earth for six thousand years, and we certainly ought to be more anxious to find out its source than to discover the source of the Nile. I think if you will read your Bible carefully you will find that this wonderful river of grace comes right from the very heart of God.

I remember being in Texas a few years ago, in a place where the country was very dry and parched. In that dry country there is a beautiful river that springs right out of the ground. It flows along; and on both sides of the river you find life and vegetation. Grace flows like that river; and you can trace its source right up to the very heart of God. You may say that its highest manifestation was seen when God gave the Son of His bosom to save this lost world. "Not as the offense, so also is the free gift. For if through the offense of one many be dead, much more the grace of God, and the gift by grace, which is by one man, Jesus Christ, hath abounded unto many."

A FREE GIFT.

Notice, it is the free gift of God. "Grace be unto you, and peace, from God our Father, and from the Lord Jesus Christ. I thank my God always on your behalf, for the grace of God which is given you by Jesus Christ." Paul wrote fourteen Epistles; and every one of them is closed with a prayer for grace. Paul calls it "The free gift of God." Thousands have been kept out of the kingdom of God because they do not realize what this free gift is. They think they must do something to merit salvation.

The first promise given to fallen man was a promise of grace. God never promised Adam anything when He put him in Eden. God never entered into a covenant with him as He did with Abraham. God told him "of the tree of the knowledge of good and evil thou shalt not eat of it: for in the day that thou eatest thereof thou shalt surely die;" but when this came to pass then God came and gave him a gracious promise. He dealt in grace with him. As he left the Garden of Eden he could say to Eve, "Well, God does love us, though He has driven us out." There was no sign that Adam recognized his lost condition. As far as we know there was no cry for mercy or pardon, no confession of sin. Yet we find that God dealt in grace with him. God sought Adam out that he might bestow His grace upon him. He met Adam in his lost and ruined condition, and the first thing He did was to proclaim the promise of a coming Saviour.

For six thousand years, God has been trying to teach the world this great and glorious truth—that He wants to deal with man in love and in grace. It runs right through the Bible; all along you find this stream of grace flowing. The very last promise in the closing chapter of Revelation, like the first promise in Eden, is a promise of grace: "Whosoever will, let him take the water of life freely." So the whole revelation, and the whole history of man is encircled with grace, the free favor of God.

Some years ago when I was speaking on this subject, a friend sent me the following: "By the grace of God I am what I am!" This is the believer's eternal confession. Grace found him a rebel—it leaves him a son. Grace found him wandering at the gates of hell—it leads him through the gates of heaven. Grace devised the scheme of Redemption: Justice never would; Reason never could. And it is grace which carries out that scheme. No sinner would ever have sought his God but 'by grace.' The thickets of Eden would have proved Adam's grave, had not grace called him out. Saul would have lived and died the haughty self-righteous persecutor had not grace laid him low. The thief would have continued breathing out his blasphemies, had not grace arrested his tongue and tuned it for glory.

"'Out of the knottiest timber,' says Rutherford, 'He can make vessels of mercy for service in the high palace of glory.'"

"'I came, I saw, I conquered,' says Toplady, 'may be inscribed by the Saviour on every monument of grace.' 'I came to the sinner; I looked upon him; and with a look of omnipotent love, I conquered.'"

My friend, we would have been this day wandering stars, to whom is reserved the blackness of darkness—Christless—hopeless—portionless—had not grace invited us, and grace constrained us.

RESTRAINING GRACE.

It is grace which, at this moment, keeps us. We have often been a Peter—forsaking our Lord, but brought back to him again. Why not a Demas or a Judas? 'I have prayed for thee that thy faith fail not.' Is not this our own comment and reflection on life's retrospect? 'Yet not I, but the grace of God which was with me.'

Oh, let us seek to realize our continual dependence on this grace every moment! 'More grace! more grace!' should be our continual cry. But the infinite supply is commensurate with the infinite need. The treasury of grace, though always emptying is always full: the key of prayer which opens it is always at hand: and the almighty Almoner of the blessings of grace is always waiting to the gracious. The recorded promise never can be canceled or reversed—'My grace is sufficient for thee.'

Let us seek to dwell much on this inexhaustible theme. The grace of God is the source of minor temporal as well as of higher spiritual blessings.

It accounts for the crumb of daily bread as well as for the crown of eternal glory. But even in regard to earthly mercies, never forget the channel of grace through Christ Jesus. It is sweet thus to connect every (even the smallest and humblest) token of providential bounty with Calvary's Cross—to have the common blessings of life stamped with the print of the nails; it makes them doubly precious to think this flows from Jesus. Let others be contented with the uncovenanted mercies of God. Be it ours to say as the children of grace and heirs of glory—'Our Father which art in heaven, give us this day our daily bread.' Nay, reposing in the all-sufficiency in all things, promised by 'the God of all grace.'

CHAPTER II
SAVED BY GRACE ALONE

I WANT to call your special attention to the fact that we are saved by grace alone, not by works and grace. A great many people think that they can be saved by works. Others think that salvation may be attained by works and grace together. They need to have their eyes opened to see that the gift of God is free and apart from works. "For by grace are ye saved through faith; and that not of yourselves, it is the gift of God. Not of works, lest any man should boast." Many people would put it thus: "For by your works are ye saved,—or by your tears, or your prayers, or your fastings, or your trials, or your good resolutions, or your money!" But Paul tells us plainly that it is "not of works, lest any man should boast." If we could be saved by works, then of course Christ's mission to this world was a mistake. There was no need for Him to come.

What had Paul ever done that could merit salvation? Up to the time that Christ called him he had done everything he could against Christ and against Christianity. He was in the very act of going to Damascus to cast into prison every Christian he could find. If he had not been stopped, many of them would probably have been put to death. It was Paul, you remember, who cheered on the mob that stoned Stephen. Yet we find that when Christ met him He dealt in grace with him. No apostle says so much against salvation by works before the cross, as Paul; and none says so much about works after the cross. He put works in their right place. I have very little sympathy with any man who has been redeemed by the precious blood of the Son of God, and who has not got the spirit of work. If we are children of God we ought not to have a lazy drop of blood in our veins. If a man tells me that he has been saved, and does not desire to work for the honor of God, I doubt his salvation. Laziness belongs to the old creation, not to the new. In all my experience I never knew a lazy man to be converted—never. I have more hope of the salvation of drunkards, and thieves, and harlots, than of a lazy man.

WHAT THE THIRTY-NINE ARTICLES SAY.

I find some people have accused me of teaching heresy, because I say salvation is all of grace. I remember once, a clergyman said I was teaching false doctrine because I said salvation was all of grace. He said that works had as much to do with our salvation as grace. At that time I had never read the Thirty-Nine Articles; if I had I should have been ready to meet him. I got the Prayer Book, and looked through the Thirty-Nine Articles; and I found, to my amazement, that they put it a good deal stronger than I had done.

Let us hear what they say—

"XI. Of the Justification of Man. We are accounted righteous before God, only for the merit of our Lord and Saviour Jesus Christ by Faith, and not for our own works or deservings: Wherefore, that we are justified by Faith only, is a most wholesome doctrine, and very full of comfort."

"XII. Of Good Works. Albeit that Good Works, which are the fruits of Faith, and follow after Justification, cannot put away our sins, and endure the severity of God's judgment; yet are they pleasing and acceptable to God in Christ, and do spring out necessarily of a true and lively Faith; insomuch that by them a lively Faith may be as evidently known as a tree discerned by the fruit."

"XIII. Of Works Before Justification. Works done before the grace of Christ, and the inspiration of His Spirit, are not pleasant to God; forasmuch as they spring not of faith in Jesus Christ, neither do they make men meet to receive grace, or (as the school-authors say) deserve grace of congruity: yea rather, for that they are not done as God hath willed and commanded them to be done, we doubt not but they have the nature of sin."

That is stronger than I ever put it. These Articles say of works before justification that "they have the nature of sin." I never called them sin! So you see this is not any new doctrine that we are preaching. When the church and the world wake up to the fact that works before salvation go for nought, then—and not till then, I believe—men will come flocking into the kingdom of God by hundreds. We work from the cross, not to it. WE work because we are saved, not in order to be saved. We work from salvation, not up to it. Salvation is the gift of God.

You have heard the Prayer Book: now hear paul; "Abraham believed God; and it was counted unto him for righteousness. Now to him that worketh is the reward not reckoned of grace, but of debt. But to him that worketh not, but believeth on Him that justifieth the ungodly, his faith is counted for righteousness." Notice what the Apostle says: "To him that worketh not." That is plain language, is it not? I may perhaps startle some of you by saying that many of you have been kept out of the kingdom of God by your good works. Nevertheless it is true. If you put works in the place of faith, they become a snare to you. It is "to him that worketh not, but believeth."

I freely admit salvation is worth working for; it is worth a man's going round the world on his hands and knees, climbing its mountains, crossing its valleys, swimming its rivers, going through all manner of hardship in order to attain it. But we do not get it in that way. Paul went through all the trials and hardships he had to endure, because by the grace of God resting on him he was enabled to do so.

PENANCE FOR SIN.

Would you insult the Almighty by offering Him the fruits of this frail body to atone for sin? Supposing your Queen were to send me a magnificent present, and I said to the royal messenger: "I certainly should not like to accept this from Her Majesty without giving her something in return." Suppose I should send her a penny! How would the Queen feel, if I were to insult her in that way? And what have we that we can offer to God in return for His free gift of salvation? Less than nothing. We must come and take salvation in God's way.

There is no merit in taking a gift. If a beggar comes to my house, and asks for bread to eat, and I give him a loaf of bread, there is no merit in his taking the bread. So if you experience the favor of God, you have to take it as a beggar. Some one has said: "If you come to God as a prince, you go away as a beggar: if you come as a beggar, you go away as a prince." It is to the needy that God opens the wardrobe of heaven, and brings out the robe of righteousness.

Paul says again: "If by grace, then is it no more of works: otherwise grace is no more grace. But if it be of works, then is it no more grace: otherwise work is no more work." Paul is reasoning in this way: that if I work for a gift or attempt to give money for it, it ceases to be a gift. The only way to get a gift is to take it as a gift.

An old man got up in one of our meetings and said, "I have been forty-two years learning three things." I pricked up my ears at that; I thought that if I could find out in about three minutes what a man had taken forty-two years to learn, I should like to do it. The first thing he said he had learned was that he could do nothing towards his own salvation. "Well," said I to myself, "that is worth learning." The second thing he had found out was that God did not require him to do anything. Well, that was worth finding out too. And the third thing was that the Lord Jesus Christ had done it all, that salvation was finished, and that all he had to do was to take it. Dear friends, let us learn this lesson; let us give up our struggling and striving, and accept salvation at once.

A FREE PARDON.

I was preaching in the Southern States a few years ago; and the minister called my attention to one of the elders in his Church. He said: When the civil war broke out, that man was in one of the far Southern States, and he enlisted into the Southern army. He was selected by the Southern General as a spy, and sent to spy out the Northern army. As you know, armies have no mercy on spies, if they can catch them. This man was caught. He was tried by court-martial, and ordered to be shot. While he was in the guard-room, previous to the time of execution, the Northern soldiers used to bring him his rations. Every time they came to his cell he would call Abraham Lincoln by every vile epithet he could think of. It seemed as though he "lay awake nights" trying to study such names. At last the soldiers got so angry that they said they would be glad when the bullet went through his heart. Some of them even said they would like to put a bullet through him; and if they were not obliged by military order to feed him, they would let him starve in the prison. They thought that was what he deserved for talking so unjustly of Lincoln.

One day while he was in the prison, waiting to be led out to execution, a Northern officer came to the cell. The prisoner, full of rage, thought his time was come to be shot. The officer opened the prison door, and handed him a free pardon from Abraham Lincoln! He told him he was at liberty; he could go to his wife and children! The man who had before been so full of bitterness, and malice, and rage, suddenly quieted down, and said, "What! has Abraham Lincoln pardoned me? For what? I never said a good word about him." The officer said, "If you had what you deserved you would be shot. But some one interceded for you at Washington and obtained your pardon; you are now at liberty." The minister, as he told me, said that this act of undeserved kindness quite broke the man's heart and led to his conversion. Said the minister, "You let any man speak one word against Abraham Lincoln now in the hearing of that man, and see what will happen. There is not a man in all the Republic of America, I believe, who has a kinder feeling towards our late President than he."

Now that is grace. The man did not deserve a pardon. But this is exactly what grace is: undeserved mercy. You may have been a rebel against God up to this very hour; but if you acknowledge your rebellion, and are willing to take the mercy that God offers, you can have it freely. It is there for every soul on the face of the earth. "The grace of God that bringeth salvation to all men hath appeared." Thank God for that! Salvation by grace is for all men. If we are lost, it will not be because God has not provided a Saviour, but because we spurn the gift of God—because we dash the cup of salvation from us.

What says Christ? You remember that when He was on earth, they came to Him and asked what they should do to work the works of God. He had been telling them to labor not for the bread that perisheth, but for the meat that endureth unto everlasting life. Then they asked Him, "What shall we do that we may work the works of God?" What did Jesus tell them to do? Did He tell them to go and feed the hungry, to clothe the naked, to visit the widow and the fatherless in their affliction? Perhaps you may say that, according to Scripture, is "pure and undefiled religion." Granted; but something comes before that. That is all right and necessary in its place. But when these men wanted to know what they had to do to inherit eternal life, Jesus said: "This is the work of God, that ye believe on Him whom He hath sent."

YOU CAN BELIEVE.

A friend lately called my attention to the fact that God has put the offer of salvation in such a way that the whole world can lay hold of it. All men can believe. A lame man might not perhaps be able to visit the sick; but he can believe. A blind man by reason of his infirmity cannot do many things; but he can believe. A deaf man can believe. A dying man can believe. God has put salvation so simply that the young and the old, the wise and the foolish, the rich and the poor, can all believe if they will.

Do you think that Christ would have come down from heaven, would have gone to Gethsemane and to Golgotha, would have suffered as He did, if man could have worked his way up to heaven?—if he could have merited salvation by his own efforts? I think if you give five minutes' consideration to this question you will see, that if man could have saved himself Christ need not have suffered at all. Remember, too, what Christ says: "He that climbeth up some other way, the same is a thief and a robber." He has marked out the way to God. He has opened up a new and shining way, and He wants us to take His way. Certainly the attempt to work our way up to heaven is "climbing up some other way," is it not? If ever a man did succeed in working his way into heaven we should never hear the last of it! I have got so terribly sick of these so-called "self-made men." There are some men whom you cannot approach without hearing them blow their trumpet, saying, "I am a self-made man. I came here a poor man ten years ago; and now I am rich." It is all I—I—I! They go on boasting, and telling what wonderful beings they are! There is one thing that is excluded from the kingdom of heaven; and that is—boasting. If you and I ever get there it will be by the sovereign grace of God. There will be no credit due to ourselves.

"Saved by grace alone!
This is all my plea:
Jesus died for all mankind,
And Jesus died for me."

CHAPTER III
POSSESSING, AND "WORKING OUT"

I CAN imagine some one asking: What does that passage mean—"Work out your own salvation with fear and trembling?" Well, I want you to emphasize the word your: "Work out your salvation." That is most important. You hear people talk of working out salvation, when all the time they have not got it. How can you work out what you do not possess? Paul is here writing to the Christians at Philippi. They were already saved by the grace of God. Now that they had got this wonderful gift, he says: "Go, work it out." When you see a person working for salvation, you may know that he has got a false idea of the teaching of the Scripture. We have salvation as a gift; and of course we cannot get it by working for it. It is our appreciation of this gift that makes us work.

Many people are working and working, as Rowland Hill says, like children on a rocking horse—it is a beautiful motion, but there is no progress. Those who are working for salvation are like men on a treadmill, going round, and round, and round; toiling, and toiling, and toiling; but nothing comes of it all. There is no progress, and there cannot be until you have the motive power within, till the breath of life comes from God, which can alone give you power to work for others.

Suppose I say to my son: "You are going away from home; and I want you to be very careful how you spend that $500." "Well," he says, "if you will give me $500, I will be careful about it; but how can I be careful in spending what I have not got?" And so, unless you have salvation, you cannot work it out.

Take another illustration. One summer my boy asked me to give him a piece of ground that he might have a garden all to himself. I said I would give it to him; but that I expected he would keep it clear of weeds, and use it in some way that would make it pleasant and profitable to him. He was to work out the piece of land; but he could not do that until I had given it to him. Neither was it his working it out that secured him the garden. I gave it to him freely, apart from any merit of his own; but I did so on the understanding that he should employ it to the best advantage. I think that is a fair illustration of our working out the salvation that God has given us.

Of course these illustrations fail in some points. I could not impart to my son the willingness to work out the piece of land, though I could provide him with all the necessary implements. God not only gives us salvation freely, but he gives us the power to work it out.

A writer says on this point: "Paul does not command the Philippians to save themselves. There was no thought in his mind of any meritorious self-righteousness. Man can by no work of his own either procure salvation or merit salvation. God worketh the salvation within the soul—man only worketh that salvation out in the Christian life. To break off from known sin; to renounce all self-righteousness; to cast ourselves in loving faith on the merits of Christ crucified; to commence at once a life of self-denial, of prayer, of obedience; to turn from all that God forbids, resolutely and earnestly, unto all that God requires—this is what the text implies. But then this is not salvation. Salvation is of God—of grace—of free grace. From the germ to the fruit, from foundation to top-stone—it is of grace, free grace, altogether and only. But the 'working out of salvation'—is man's part in the work of salvation. God will not repent for the man; nor believe for the man; nor lead a holy life for the man. God worketh inwardly—man worketh outwardly. And this outward human work is as necessary as the inward Divine work."

God works in us; and then we work for Him. If He has done a work in us, we certainly ought to go and work for others. A man must have this salvation, and must know it, before he can work for the salvation of others.

Many of you have tried hard to save yourselves; but what has been the end of it all? I remember a lady in the North of England who became quite angry when I made this remark publicly: "No one in this congregation will be saved till they stop trying to save themselves." Down she came from the gallery, and said to me: "You have made me perfectly miserable." "Indeed," I said, "how is that?" "Why, I always thought that if I kept on trying, God would save me at some time; and now you tell me to stop trying: what, then, am I to do?" "Why, let the Lord save you." She went off in something like a rage. It is not always a bad sign when you see a man or a woman wake up cross, if it is the Word of God that wakes them up. A day or two afterwards she came and thanked me. She said she had been turning over in her mind what I had said; and at last the truth dawned upon her, that though she had worked long, though she had formed a good many resolutions, she had made no progress. So she gave up the struggle; and then it was that the Lord Jesus saved her.

I want to ask you this question: If sin needs forgiveness—and all sin is against God—how can you work out your own forgiveness? If I stole $100 from a friend, I could not forgive myself, could I? No act of mine would bring about forgiveness, unless my friend forgave me. And so, if I want forgiveness of sin, it must be the work of God. If we look at salvation as a new life, it must be the work of God. God is the author of life: you cannot give yourself life. If we consider it as a gift, it must come from some one outside of ourselves. That is what I read in the Bible—Salvation as a gift. While I am speaking, you can make up your mind that you will stop trying, and take this gift.

I wish I could get this whole audience to drop the word try, and put the word trust in its place. The forgiving grace of God is wonderful. He will save you this very minute, if you are willing to be saved. He delights in mercy. He wants to show that mercy to every soul. The religion of Christ is not man working his way up to God; it is God coming down to man. It is Christ coming down to the pit of sin and woe where we are, bringing us out of the pit, putting our feet upon a rock, and a new song in our mouth. He will do it this minute, while I am speaking, if you will let Him. Will you let Him? That is the question.

I do not believe much in dreams; but they sometimes illustrate a point. I heard about a woman who had been trying for a long time, just like many of you, to be better and better. She tried to save herself, but made no progress. One night she fell asleep in a very troubled state of mind, and she had a dream. She thought that she was in a pit striving to get out—climbing and slipping, climbing and slipping, climbing and slipping; at last she gave up the struggle, and laid herself down at the bottom of the pit to die. She happened to look up, and she saw through the mouth of the pit a beautiful star. She fixed her eye on it; and it seemed as if the star lifted her up till she was almost out. But the thought of herself came to her mind; she looked off at the sides of the pit: immediately she lost sight of the star, and down to the bottom of the pit she went. Again she fixed her eye on the star; and again it seemed to lift her almost out. But once again she took her eye off the star, and looked at herself; down into the pit she fell again! The third time she fixed her eye on the star and was lifted higher and higher, until all at once her feet struck the ground above, and she awoke from her sleep.

God taught her a lesson by the dream. She learned that if ever she was to be saved, she must give up the struggle, and let Jesus Christ save her. My friends, give up the struggle today! You have tried long and hard. It has been a hard battle, has it not? Give it up; and repose in the arms of Jesus Christ. Say "Lord, I come to thee as a poor sinner; wilt Thou not save me and help me?" "The gift of God is eternal life." It is offered to all: who will have it?

I see some children here: let me tell you a story. If you have not heard it before, please do not forget it. A Sunday school teacher wished to show his class how free the gift of God is. He took a silver watch from his pocket one day, and offered it to the eldest boy in the class. "It is yours, if you will take it." The little fellow sat and grinned at the teacher. He thought he was joking. The teacher offered it to the next boy, and said: "Take that watch: it is yours." The little fellow thought he would be laughed at if he held out his hand, and therefore he sat still. In the same way the teacher went nearly round the class: but not one of them would accept the proffered gift. At length he came to the smallest boy. When the watch was offered to the little fellow, he took it and put it into his pocket. All the class laughed at him. "I am thankful, my boy," said the teacher, "that you believe my word. The watch is yours. Take good care of it. Wind it up every night." The rest of the class looked on in amazement; and one of them said: "Teacher, you don't mean that the watch is his? You don't mean that he hasn't to give it back to you?" "No," said the teacher, "he hasn't to give it back to me. It is his own now." "Oh—h—h! if I had only known that, wouldn't I have taken it!"

I see you laugh; but my friends you are laughing at yourselves. You need not go far away to find these boys. Salvation is freely offered to all, but the trouble is that men do not believe God's Word, and do not accept the gift. Who will accept it now?

I found a few lines the other day on this point that I thought very good. I will close with them:

Sovereign Grace

"I would not work my soul to save,
For that my Lord hath done;
But I would work like any slave,
For love of God's dear Son."

CHAPTER IV
GRACE ABOUNDING TO THE CHIEF OF SINNERS

I WANT to lay emphasis on the fact that God desires to show mercy to all. Christ's last command to His disciples was, "Go ye into all the world and preach the Gospel to every creature." There may be some hearing me who have not received this grace, though it has often been pressed on their acceptance. One reason why many do not become partakers of this grace is that they think they can do better without it. The Jews said they were the seed of Abraham. They had Moses and the Law: therefore they had no need of the pardoning grace of God that Christ had come to bring. We read in the book of Revelation of a church that said it was "rich, and increased in goods, and had need of nothing." That was the trouble when Christ was down here. Instead of coming to Him to be blessed, the people too often went away thinking and saying they had no need of His favor and blessing.

THE TWO PRAYERS.

In the Gospel by Luke Christ brings two men before us. I do not know that we can get any two cases in Scripture that will give us more light on this subject than those of the Pharisee and the Publican, who went into the temple to pray. One went away as empty as he came. He was like the church described in Revelation, to which I have referred. He went into the temple desiring nothing; and he got nothing. The other man asked for something; he asked for pardon and mercy. And he went down to his house justified.

Take the prayer of the Pharisee. There is no confession in it, no adoration, no contrition, no petition. As I have said, he asked for nothing and he got nothing. Some one has said that he went into the temple not to pray but to boast. The sun and the moon were as far apart as these two men. One was altogether of a different spirit to the other. The one prayed with his head, and the other with his heart. The one told God what a wonderfully great and good man he was: "I am not as other men or even as this publican." His prayer was not a long one; it consisted of thirty-four words; yet there were five capital "I's" in it. It was self in the beginning, self in the middle, self in the end—self all through. "'I fast twice a week;' 'I give tithes of all I possess;' I am a wonderfully good man, am I not, Lord?" He struck a balance twice a week, and God was his debtor every time. He paraded his good deeds before God and man. Such a one was not in a condition to receive the favor of God.

You can divide the human family to-day into two classes—pharisees and publicans. There are those who are poor in spirit: the dew of God's grace will fall upon them. There are others who are drawing around them the rags of their self-righteousness: they will always go away without the blessing of God. There were but seven words in the prayer of the Publican: "God be merciful to me a sinner!" He came to God confessing his sins, and asking for mercy; and he received it.

If you were to run through Scripture, you would find that where men have gone to God in the spirit of the Publican, He has dealt with them in mercy and grace.

A young man came to one of our meetings in New York a few years ago. He was convicted of sin; and he made up his mind he would go home and pray. He lived a number of miles away, and he started for home. On the way, as he was meditating about his sins and wondering what he was going to do when he got home, the thought occurred to him: "Why should I not pray right here in the street?" But he found he did not know just how to begin. Then he remembered that when he was a child, his mother had taught him this prayer of the Publican: "God be merciful to me a sinner!" So he began just where he stood. He said afterwards, that before he got to the little word "me," God met him in grace, and blessed him. And so the moment we open our lips to ask God for pardon, if the request comes from the heart, God will meet us in mercy.

Let our cry be that of the Publican: "Be merciful to me!"—not to some one else. A mother was telling me some time ago that she had trouble with one of her sons, because he had not treated his brother rightly. She sent him upstairs; and after awhile she asked him what he had been doing. He replied that he had been praying for his brother! Although he had been the naughty one, he was acting as if the fault lay with his brother instead of himself. So many of us can see the failings of others readily enough but when we get a good look at ourselves, we will get down before God as the Publican did and cry for mercy: and that cry will bring an immediate answer. God delights to deal in grace with the poor in spirit. He wants to see in us a broken and contrite heart. If we take the place of a sinner, confessing our sins and asking for mercy, the grace of God will meet us right then and there; and we shall have the assurance of His forgiveness.

In Matthew we see how God deals in grace with those who come in the right spirit. "Then came she and worshipped Him, saying, Lord, help me!" But he answered and said, "It is not meet to take the children's bread, and to cast it to dogs." And she said, "Truth, Lord: yet the dogs eat of the crumbs which fall from their master's table." Then Jesus answered and said unto her, "O woman, great is thy faith: be it unto thee even as thou wilt. And her daughter was made whole from that very hour."

The disciples did not understand how full of grace was the heart of Christ. This poor woman belonged to the far-off coasts of Tyre and Sidon. She was a poor Gentile, and they wanted to send her away. They thought she was not one of the elect; she did not belong to the house of Israel. So they said to the Master, "Send her away, for she crieth after us." Can you conceive of the loving Saviour sending away a poor troubled one who comes to Him? I challenge you to find a single instance of His doing such a thing, from the beginning to the end of His ministry. Send her away! I believe He would rather send an angel away than a poor suppliant for His mercy; He delighted to have such as she come to Him. But He was going to test her, as well as to give an object-lesson to those who should come after. "It is not meet," He said, "to take the children's bread, and to cast it to dogs."

A HUMBLE SPIRIT.

I am afraid if some of us had been in her place we would have answered somewhat in this fashion: "You call me a Gentile dog, do you? I would not take anything from you now if you were to give it to me. Why, I know a Jewish woman who lives in my town. Though she is a daughter of Abraham she is the meanest woman in the whole street. I would not let my dogs associate with her." If this poor woman had replied to the Master in such a fashion, she would not have got anything. Yet you will find a good many men who respond to the Saviour in that way when He wants to deal in grace with them.

What does this Gentile woman say? "Truth Lord; yet the dogs eat of the crumbs which fall from their masters' table." She took her right place down at the feet of the blessed Master. There was humility for you! She was willing to take any place if the Lord would but meet her need; the Lord blessed her. See asked for a crumb, and He gave her a whole loaf!

I once heard Rev. William Arnot say that he was the guest of a friend who had a favorite dog. The animal would come into the room where the family were sitting at the dinner table and would stand looking at his master. If the master threw him a crumb, the dog would seize it before it got to the floor. But if he put the joint of meat down on the floor the dog would look at it and leave it alone, as if it were too good for him. "So," said Mr. Arnot, "there are many Christians who are satisfied to live on crumbs, when God wants to give them the whole joint."

A FULL BLESSING.

This poor woman got all she wanted; and if we will come in the right spirit—if we are humble and poor in spirit—and call upon God for what we want, He will not disappoint us. She went right to the Son of God, and appealed to His great loving heart with the cry, "Lord help me!" and he helped her. Let that cry go up to him today, and see how quickly the answer will come. I never knew a case where God did not answer right on the spot, where there was the spirit of meekness. If on the other hand we are conceited, and think we have a right to come, putting ourselves on an equality with God, we shall get nothing.

"WORTHINESS."

In the Gospel by Luke we read of the centurion who had a sick servant. He felt as though he were not worthy to go himself and ask Christ to come to his house; so he asked some of his friends to beseech the Master to come and heal his servant. They went and delivered the centurion's message, saying, "He is worthy for whom Thou shouldst do this: for he loveth our nation, and he hath built us a synagogue." The Jews could not understand grace; so they thought Christ would grant the request of this man, because he was worthy. "Why," they said, "he hath built us a synagogue!" It is the same old story that we hear to-day. Let a man give a few thousand dollars to build a church and he must have the best pew; "he is worthy." Perhaps he made his money by selling or making strong drink; but he has put the Church under an obligation by this gift of money, and he is considered "worthy." The same spirit was at work in the days of Christ.

The Master immediately started for the centurion's house; and it looked as though He were going because of his personal worthiness. But if He had done so, it would have upset the whole story as an illustration of grace. As the Saviour was on the way, out came the Roman officer himself and told Jesus that he was not worthy to receive Him under his roof. He had a very different opinion of himself to that of his Jewish friends. Suppose he had said, "Lord, you will be my guest; come and heal my servant because I am worthy: I have built a synagogue." Do you think Christ would have gone? I do not think he would. But he said, "I am not worthy that Thou shouldst enter under my roof. Neither thought I myself worthy to come unto Thee; but say in a word, and my servant shall be healed."

Jesus marveled at the man's faith. It pleased Him wonderfully to find such faith and humility. Like the Syro-Phenician woman, he had low thoughts of himself, and high thoughts of God: therefore he was in a condition to receive the grace of God. His servant, we are told, was healed that very hour. His petition was granted at once. Let us learn a lesson from this man, and take a humble position before God, crying to him for mercy; then help will come.

GREAT FORGIVENESS.

I never noticed till lately an interesting fact about the story of the poor sinful woman mentioned in Luke's Gospel, who went into Simon's house. If you have not observed it before, it will be quite interesting for you to know it. The incident occurred immediately after Christ had uttered those memorable words we read in Matthew: "Come unto Me, all ye that labor and are heavy-laden, and I will give you rest." Matthew closes the narrative there; but in the seventh chapter of Luke you will find what the result of that invitation was. A poor fallen woman came into the house where He was, and obtained the blessing of rest to her soul. I think that many ministers will bear me out in this statement, that when one has preached to a large congregation, and has given an invitation to those who would like to remain and talk about salvation, probably the only one to do so is a poor fallen one, who will thus become a partaker of the grace of God.

We find that the Saviour was invited to the house of Simon, a Pharisee. While he was there, this poor sinful woman crept into the house. Perhaps she watched for a chance when the servants were away from the door, and then slipped into the room where the Master was. She got down on her knees, and began to wash his feet with her tears, wiping them with the hairs of her head. While the feast was going on the Pharisee saw this; and he said to himself: "Jesus must be a bad man, if He knows who this poor woman is. Even if He did not know, He would be unclean according to the Mosaic law"—because he had allowed the woman to touch Him. But the Master knew what Simon was thinking about. He put some questions to him: "And Jesus answering said unto him, Simon, I have somewhat to say unto thee. And he saith, Master, say on. There was a certain creditor which had two debtors: the one owed five hundred pence, and the other fifty. And when they had nothing to pay, he frankly forgave them both. Tell me therefore, which of them will love him most? Simon answered and said, I suppose that he to whom he forgave most. And He said unto him, Thou hast rightly judged."

Then He makes the application, "I came to your house," He says, "and you gave me no water for my feet; you gave me no kiss; and no oil for my head. You refused me the common hospitalities of life." In those days when one went into a gentleman's house, a servant would be at the door with a basin of water; the guest would slip off his sandals, and the servant would wash his feet. Then the master of the house would salute him with a kiss instead of shaking hands as we do. There would also be oil for his head. Christ had been invited to Simon's house; but the Pharisee had got Him there in a patronizing spirit. "You gave me no water, no kiss, no oil; but this woman hath washed my feet with her tears, and wiped them with the hairs of her head: she hath not ceased to kiss my feet, and she hath anointed them with ointment. She was forgiven much: and so she loves much." To the poor woman herself Jesus said, "Thy sins are forgiven." They may have risen up like a dark mountain before her; but one word from the Saviour and they were all gone!

The spirit shown by Simon was altogether different from that of the poor woman. Christ said that the publicans and harlots would go into the kingdom of God before the self-righteous Pharisees!

Simon, the Pharisee, got nothing; and so there are many who go away from religious meetings without one drop of heaven's dew, because they do not seek for it. From the morning of the creation down to the present time no man or woman ever went to God with a broken heart without experiencing the forgiving love and grace of God, if they believed His Word. It was so with this poor woman. Notice, the Master did not extract any pledge or promise from her. He did not ask her to join some synagogue; all He said was, "Thy sins are forgiven thee." She found grace. So it was with the Syro-Phenician woman. Christ did not ask any pledge from her; He met her in grace, and blessed her according to her soul's desire.

You know what touched the heart of the father of the prodigal; it was the broken and contrite spirit of his returning son. Would not the same thing move the heart of any parent here? Suppose you had a son who had gone astray: the boy comes home; and when you meet him he begins to confess his sin. Would you not take him to your bosom and forgive him? Nothing in the wide world would you more readily do than forgive him. So if we come to God with this contrite spirit, He will deal in grace with us and receive us freely, When Saul left Jerusalem, there was nothing he wished for less than to receive the grace of God. Yet the moment he said, "Lord, what wilt Thou have me to do?" the forgiving grace of the Master flowed out towards him. We are told by Matthew and Mark that the thief on the cross, who was converted, railed on the Saviour at first like the other: but the moment his heart was broken down and he said, "Lord, remember me!" that very moment Christ heard and answered his prayer. God is waiting to cover all your sins today; He has a long and a strong arm that can reach down to the darkest, vilest, deepest depths of sin. He will lift you up on a rock, and put a new song into your mouth. Will you let him do it?

A man was telling me some time ago that he had prayed for over ten years that God would have mercy upon him. "Has not God answered your prayer?" "No." "Indeed! Let me ask you one question: suppose I offered you that Bible as a gift, and you were afterwards to come and ask me for it; what would I think of you?" "I do not know what you would think." "Well, but what do you suppose I would think?" "You would perhaps think I had gone a little wrong in my head." "What is the use of your asking that God would deal in grace with you, if you are not willing to receive it; or if you do not believe that He gives it to you?"

When I was on the Pacific coast some years ago, I stayed with a friend who had a large garden, with a great many orange trees. He said to me: "Make yourself perfectly at home; if you see anything you want just help yourself." When I wanted some oranges, I did not go into the garden and pray to the oranges to tumble into my mouth; I just put out my hand and took all I required. So it is with us. Why should we go on asking and beseeching God to have mercy upon us, when He has already given His Son, and given His Holy Spirit? What we need is to have a broken and a contrite heart, and to be willing to receive Him. The trouble with us is that we have locked the doors of our hearts against Him.

There is a story that Dr. Arnot was accustomed to tell of a poor woman who was in great distress because she could not pay her landlord his rent. The Doctor put some money in his pocket and went round to her house intending to help her. When he got there he knocked at the door. He thought he heard some movement inside; but no one came to open the door. He knocked louder and louder still; but yet no one came. Finally he kicked at the door, causing some of neighbors to look out and see what was going on. But he could get no entrance; and at last he went away thinking his ears must have deceived him, and that there was really no one there. A day or two afterwards he met the woman in the street, and told her what had happened. She held up her hands and exclaimed, "Was that you? I was in the house all the while; but I thought it was the landlord, and I had the door locked!"

Many people are keeping the door of their heart locked against the Saviour in just the same way. They say "I am afraid I shall have to give up so much." That is something like a ragged beggar being unwilling to give up his rags, in order to get a new suit of good clothes. I pity those people who are all the time looking to see what they will have to give up. God wants to bestow His marvelous grace on His people; and there is not a soul who has believed on Jesus, for whom God has not abundance of grace in store. What would you say of a man dying of thirst on the banks of a beautiful river, with the stream flowing past his feet? You would think he was mad! The river of God's grace flows on without ceasing; why should we not partake of it, and go on our way rejoicing?

Do you say you are sinners? It is just to such as you that God's grace is given. There was a sailor whose mother had long been praying for him. I do think mothers' prayers are sure to be answered some day. One night the memory of his mother came home to this man; he thought of the days of his childhood, and made up his mind he would try and lead a different life. When he got to New York he thought he would join the Odd-fellows; he imagined that would be a good way to begin. What miserable mistakes men make when they get trying to save themselves! This man applied to a lodge of Odd-fellows for admission; but the committee found that he was a drinking man, and so they black-balled him. Then he thought he would try the Freemasons; they discovered what sort of a man he was, and they black-balled him too. One day he was walking along Fulton Street, when he received an invitation to come to the daily prayer-meeting held there. He went in, and heard about the Saviour; he received Christ into his heart, and found the peace and power he wanted. Some days after he stood up in the meeting and told the story how the Odd-fellows had black-balled him; how the Freemasons had black-balled him; and how he came to the Lord Jesus Christ, who had not black-balled him, but took him right in. That is what Christ will do to every poor penitent sinner. "This Man receiveth sinners." Come to Him to-day, and He will receive you: His marvelous, sovereign grace will cover and put away all your sins.

I am so glad that we have a Saviour who can save unto the very uttermost. He can save the drunkard, the man who for years has been the slave of his passions. I was talking to a friend not long ago, who said that if a man had a father and a mother who were drunkards, he would inherit the taste for drink, and that there was not much chance of saving him. I want to say that there is a grand chance for such men, if they will call upon Jesus Christ to save them. He is able to destroy the very appetite for drink. He came to destroy the works of the devil; and if this appetite for gin and whiskey is not the work of the devil, I want to know what is. I do not know any more terrible agency that the devil has got than this intoxicating liquor.

An Englishman went out from England to Chicago, and became one of the greatest drunkards in that city. His father and his mother were drunkards before him. He said that when he was four years old, his father took him into a public-house, and put the liquor to his lips. By and by he got a taste for it; and for several years he was a confirmed drunkard. He became what in America we call a "tramp." He slept out of doors. One night, on the shore of a lake, he awoke from his slumber, and began to call upon God to save him. There, at the midnight hour, this poor, wretched, forlorn object got victory over his sin. The last time I met him he had been nine-and-a-half years a sober man. From that memorable midnight hour, he said, he had never had any desire to touch or taste strong drink. God had kept him all those years. I am so thankful we have a Gospel that we can carry into the home of the drunkard, and tell him that Christ will save him. That is the very thing He came to do.

Bunyan represents the power of grace, as shown by its first offer to the Jerusalem sinners, the murderers of Christ, thus: "Repent, every one of you: be baptized, every one of you, in His name, for the remission of sins; and you shall, every one of you, receive the Holy Ghost."

"But I was one of those who plotted to take away His life. May I be saved by Him?"

"Every one of you."

"But I was one of those who bore false witness against Him. Is there grace for me?"

"For every one of you."

"But I was one of those who cried out, Crucify Him! crucify Him! and who desired that Barrabas, the murderer, might live, rather than He. What will become of me, think you?"

"I am to preach repentance and remission of sins to every one of you."

"But I was one of those who did spit in His face when He stood before His accusers; I also was one that mocked Him when, in anguish, He hung bleeding on the tree. Is there room for me?"

"For every one of you."

"But I was one of those who, in His extremity, said, Give Him gall and vinegar to drink! Why may I not expect the same when pain and anguish are upon me?"

"Repent of these thy wickednesses; and here is remission of sins for every one of you."

"But I railed on Him; I reviled Him; I hated Him; I rejoiced to see Him mocked at by others. Can there be hope for me?"

"There is; for every one of you."

Oh, what a blessed "Every-one-of-you" is here! How willing was Peter and the Lord Jesus by the ministry of Peter—to catch these murderers with the word of the Gospel, that they might be monuments of the grace of God!

Now it is a solemn fact that every one who receives the offer of the Gospel can lock and bolt the door of his heart, and say to the Lord Jesus Christ he refuses to let Him in. But it is also a blessed truth that you can unlock that door and say to Him, "Welcome! thrice welcome, Son of God, into this heart of mine!" The question is: Will you let Christ come in and save you? It is not a question of whether He is able. Who will open their hearts, and let the Saviour come in?

"There's a stranger at the door:
Let Him in!
He has been there oft before:
Let Him in!
Let Him in, ere He is gone;
Let Him in, the Holy One,
Jesus Christ, the Father's Son:
Let Him in!
Open now to Him your heart:
Let Him in!
If you wait He will depart:
Let Him in!
Let Him in, He is your Friend;
He your soul will sure defend;
He will keep you to the end:
Let Him in!
Hear you now His loving voice?
Let Him in!
Now, oh now, make Him your choice:
Let Him in!
He is standing at the door;
Joy to you He will restore,
And His name you will adore:

Let Him in!
Now admit the heavenly Guest.
Let Him in!
He will make for you a feast:
Let Him in!
He will speak your sins forgiven,
And when earth-ties all are riven,
He will take you home to heaven,
Let Him in!"
Rev. J. B Atchinson

CHAPTER V

LAW AND GRACE

IN his Epistle to the Romans, Paul writes "For as by one man's disobedience many were made sinners, so by the obedience of One shall many be made righteous. Moreover, the law entered that the offense might abound. But where sin abounded, grace did much more abound: that as sin hath reigned unto death, even so might grace reign through righteousness unto eternal life by Jesus Christ our Lord."

Moses was the representative of the law. You remember that he led the children of Israel through the wilderness, and brought them to Jordan; but there he left them. He could take them up to the river, which is a type of death and judgment; but Joshua (which means Jesus—Saviour) led them right through death and judgment—through the Jordan into the Promised Land. Here we have the difference between Law and Grace; between the Law and the Gospel.

Take another illustration. John the Baptist was the last prophet of the old dispensation—the last prophet under the law. You remember that before Christ made His appearance at the Jordan, the cry of John, day by day was, "Repent: for the kingdom of God is at hand!" He thundered out the law. He took his hearers down to the Jordan and baptized them. He put them in the place of death; and that was as far as he could take them. But there was One coming after him who could take them into the Promised Land. As Joshua led the people through the Jordan into Canaan,—so Christ went down into the Jordan of death, through death and judgment, on to resurrection ground.

If you run all through Scripture you will find that the law brings to death. "Sin reigned unto death." A friend was telling me lately that an acquaintance of his, a minister, was once called upon to officiate at a funeral, in the place of a chaplain of one of Her Majesty's prisons, who was absent. He noticed that only one solitary man followed the body of the criminal to the grave. When the grave had been covered, this man told the minister that he was an officer of the law whose duty it was to watch the body of the culprit until it was buried out of sight; that was "the end" of the British law.

And that is what the law of God does to the sinner; it brings him right to death, and leaves him there. I pity deep down in my heart those who are trying to save themselves by the law. It never has; it never will; and it never can—save the soul. When people say they are going to try and do their best, and so save themselves by the law, I like to take them on their own ground. Have they, ever done their very best? granting that there might be a chance for them if they had, was there ever a time when they could not have done a little better? If a man wants to do his best, let him accept the grace of God; that is the best thing that any man or woman can possibly do.

But you will ask, What is the law given for? It may sound rather strange, but it is given that it may stop every man's mouth. "We know that what things soever the law saith, it saith to them who are under the law: that every mouth may be stopped, and all the world may become guilty before God. Therefore by the deeds of the law there shall no flesh be justified in His sight; for by the law is the knowledge of sin." The law shuts my mouth; grace opens it. The law locks up my heart; grace opens it—and then the fountain of love begins to flow out. When men get their eyes opened to see this glorious truth, they will cease their constant struggle. They will give up trying to work their way into the kingdom of God by the deeds of the law. They will give themselves up for lost, and take salvation as a free gift.

Life never came through the law. As some one has observed: When the law was given, three thousand men lost life; but when grace and truth came at Pentecost, three thousand obtained life. Under the law, if a man became a drunkard the magistrates would take him out and stone him to death. When the prodigal came home, grace met him and embraced him. Law says, Stone him!—grace says, Embrace him! Law says, Smite him!—grace says, Kiss him! Law went after him, and bound him; grace said, loose him and let him go! Law tells me how crooked I am; grace comes and makes me straight.

I pity those who are always hanging around Sinai, hoping to get life there. I have an old friend in Chicago who is always lingering at Sinai. He is a very good man; but I think he will have a different story to tell when he gets home to heaven. He thinks I preach free grace too much; and I must confess I do like to speak of the free grace of God. This friend of mine feels as though he has a kind of mission to follow me; and whenever he gets a chance he comes in with the thunders of Sinai. I never yet met him but he was thundering away from Horeb. The last time I was in Chicago, I said to him, "Are you still lingering around Sinai?" "Yes," said he, "I believe in the law." I have made inquiries, and I never heard of any one being converted under his preaching: the effects have always dwindled and died out. If the law is the door to heaven, there is no hope for any of us. A perfect God can only have a perfect standard. He that offends in one point is guilty of all: so "all have sinned and come short of the glory of God."

Paul says to the Galatians: "Is the law then against the promises of God? God forbid: for if there had been a law given which could have given life, verily righteousness should have been by the law. But the Scripture hath concluded all under sin that the promise by faith of Jesus Christ might be given to them that believe. But before faith came, we were kept under the law, shut up unto the faith which should afterwards be revealed. Wherefore the law was our schoolmaster to bring us unto Christ, that we might be justified by faith. But after that faith is come, we are no longer under a schoolmaster. For ye are all the children of God by faith in Jesus Christ."

THE SOFTENING POWER OF GRACE.

So we see that the law cannot give life; all it can do is to bring us to Him who is the life. The law is said to be "a schoolmaster." Perhaps some of you do not know what a schoolmaster is. If you had been under the same schoolmaster as I was when a boy you would have known. He had a good cane and it was frequently in use. In the little country district where I went to school, there were two parties: for the sake of illustration we may call the one the "law" party and the other the "grace" party. The law party said that boys could not possibly be controlled without the cane: and they kept a schoolmaster there who acted on their plan. The struggle went on, and at last, on one election day, the law party was put out, and the grace party ruled in their stead. I happened to be at the school at that time; and I remember we said to each other that we were going to have a grand time that winter. There would be no more corporal punishment, and we were going to be ruled by love.

I was one of the first to break the rules of the school. We had a lady teacher, and she asked me to stay behind. I thought the cane was coming out again; and I was going to protest against it. I was quite in a fighting mood. She took me alone. She sat down and began to talk to me kindly. I thought that was worse than the cane; I did not like it. I saw that she had not got any cane. She said: "I have made up my mind that if I cannot control the school by love, I will give it up. I will have no punishment; and if you love me, try and keep the rules of the school." I felt something right here in my throat. I was not one to shed many tears; but they would come—I could not keep them back. I said to her, "You will have no more trouble with me;" and she did not. I learned more that winter than in the other three put together.

That was the difference between law and grace. Christ says, "If you love Me, keep My commandments." He takes us out from under the law, and puts us under grace. Grace will break the hardest heart. It was the love of God that prompted Him to send His only-begotten Son into the world that He might save it. I suppose the thief had gone through his trial unsoftened. Probably the law had hardened his heart. But on the cross no doubt that touching prayer of the Saviour, "Father, forgive them!" broke his heart, so that he cried, "Lord, remember me!" He was brought to ask for mercy. I believe there is no man so far gone but the grace of God will melt his heart.

It is told of Isaac T. Hopper, the Quaker, that he once encountered a profane colored man, named Cain, in Philadelphia, and took him before a magistrate, who fined him for blasphemy. Twenty years after, Hopper met Cain, whose appearance was much changed for the worse. This touched the Friend's heart. He stepped up, spoke kindly, and shook hands with the forlorn being. "Dost thou remember me," said the Quaker, "how I had thee fined for swearing?"

"Yes, indeed, I do: I remember what I paid as well as if it was yesterday."

"Well, did it do thee any good?"

"No, never a bit: it made me mad to have my money taken from me."

Hopper invited Cain to reckon up the interest on the fine, and paid him principal and interest too. "I meant it for thy good, Cain; and I am sorry I did thee any harm."

Cain's countenance changed; the tears rolled down his cheeks. He took the money with many thanks, became a quiet man, and was not heard to swear again.

PEACE, GRACE AND GLORY.

So there is a great deal of difference between law and grace. "Being justified by faith we have peace with God through our Lord Jesus Christ; by whom also we have access by faith into this grace wherein we stand, and rejoice in hope of the glory of God." There are three precious things here: peace for the past; grace for the present; and glory for the future. There is no peace until we see the finished work of Jesus Christ—until we can look back and see the Cross of Christ between us and our sins. When we see that Jesus was "the end of the law for righteousness;" that He "tasted death for every man;" that He "suffered the Just for the unjust"—then comes peace. Then there is "the grace wherein we now stand." There is plenty of grace for us as we need it day by day, and hour by hour.

Then there is glory for the time to come. A great many people seem to forget that the best is before us. Dr. Bonar says that everything before the true believer is "glorious." This thought took hold of my soul; and I began to look the matter up, and see what I could find in Scripture that was glorious hereafter. I found that the kingdom we are going to inherit is glorious: our crown is to be a "crown of glory;" the city we are going to inhabit is the city of the glorified; the songs we are to sing are the songs of the glorified; we are to wear garments of "glory and beauty;" our society will be the society of the glorified; our rest is to be "glorious;" the country to which we are going is to be full of "the glory of God and of the Lamb." There are many who are always looking on the backward path, and mourning over the troubles through which they have passed; they keep lugging up the cares and anxieties they have been called on to bear, and are forever looking at them. Why should we go reeling and staggering under the burdens and cares of life when we have such prospects before us?

If there is nothing but glory beyond, our faces ought to shine brightly all the time. If a skeptic were to come up here and watch the countenances of the audience he would find many of you looking as though there was anything but glory before you. Many a time it seems to me as if I were at a funeral, people look so sad and downcast. They do not appear to know much of the joy of the Lord. Surely if we were looking right on to the glory that awaits us, our faces would be continually lit up with the light of the upper world. We can preach by our countenances if we will. The nearer we draw to that glory-land, where we shall be with Christ—the more peace, and joy, and rest we ought to have. If we will but come to the throne of grace, we shall have strength to bear all our troubles and trials. If you were to take all the afflictions that flesh is heir to and put them right on any one of us, God has grace enough to carry us right through without faltering.

Some one has compiled the following, which beautifully describes the contrast between law and grace:

The Law was given by Moses.

Grace and truth came by Jesus Christ.

The Law says—This do, and thou shalt live.

Grace says—Live, and then thou shalt do.

The Law says—Pay me that thou owest.

Grace says—I frankly forgive thee all.

The Law says—The wages of sin is death.

GRACE says—The gift of God is eternal life.

The Law says—The soul that sinneth, it shall die.

Grace says—Whosoever believeth in Jesus, though he were dead, yet shall he live; and whosoever liveth and believeth in Him shall never die.

The Law pronounces—Condemnation and death.

Grace proclaims—Justification and life.

The Law says—Make you a new heart and a new spirit.

Grace says—A new heart will I give you, and a new spirit will I put within you.

The Law says—Cursed is every one that continueth not in all things which are written in the book of the law to do them.

Grace says—Blessed is the man whose iniquities are forgiven, whose sin is covered; blessed is the man to whom the Lord will not impute iniquity.

The Law says—Thou shalt love the Lord thy God with all thy heart, and with all thy mind, and with all thy strength.

Grace says—Herein is love: not that we love God, but that He loved us, and sent His Son to be the propitiation for our sins.

The Law speaks of what man must do for God.

Grace tells of what Christ has done for man.

The Law addresses man as part of the old creation.

Grace makes a man a member of the new creation.

The Law bears on a nature prone to disobedience.

Grace creates a nature inclined to obedience.

The Law demands obedience by the terror of the Lord.

Grace beseeches men by the mercies of God.

The Law demands holiness.

Grace gives holiness.

The Law says—Condemn him.

Grace says—Embrace him.

The Law speaks of priestly sacrifices offered year by year continually, which could never make the comers thereunto perfect.

Grace says—But this Man, after he had offered one sacrifice for sins forever . . . by one offering hath perfected forever them that are sanctified.

The Law declares—That as many as have sinned in the Law, shall be judged by the Law.

Grace brings eternal peace to the troubled soul of every child of God, and proclaims God's salvation in defiance of the accusations of the adversary. "He that heareth My word, and believeth on Him that sent me, hath everlasting life, and shall not come into judgment (condemnation), but is passed from death unto life."

"Whence to me this tranquil spirit—

Me all sinful as I am?

Is it thus descends the merit

Of the sin-atoning Lamb?

Grace, all power to deliver,

Gift of a Creative Giver,

Sovereign Grace

Like a full, refreshing river,
Ever flowing.
Over all my course of sinning
Spread its waters without bound,
Cleansing, fertilizing, winning
For the Lord the barren ground.
Lavish from the heavenly treasure,
Fountains of a Father's pleasure,
All the marks of human measure
Overflowing.
Not my virtue or repenting
Earned the precious boon for me.
Thine, my Saviour, the relenting,
Thine the pangs which set me free—
Gift of grace beyond all knowing,
From the heart of Jesus flowing,
Ever flowing, overflowing,
Flowing freely."

CHAPTER VI
GRACE FOR LIVING

NOW we come to a very important part of our subject—Grace for living. One of the saddest things in the present day is the fact that so many professed Christians have no spiritual power. They bear no testimony for Christ. There are so few who can go to the homes of the sick and read the Bible to them, pray with them, and minister comfort to their souls. How few can go to the abode of the drunkard, and tell him of Christ's power to save! How few there are who are wise in winning souls to Christ!

It is the low spiritual state of so many in the Church of Christ that is the trouble. We are not living up to our privileges. As you go through the streets of London you will see here and there the words, "Limited Company." There are many Christians who practically limit the grace of God. It is like a river flowing by; and we can have all we need: but if we do not come and get a continual supply, we cannot give it out to others.

Mother! father! are you not longing to see your children won to Christ? What is the trouble? Is it the fault of the minister? I believe that though ministers were to preach like angels, if there is a low standard of Christian life in the home, there will be little accomplished. What we want, more than anything else, is more grace in our lives, in our business affairs, in our homes, in our daily walk and conversation. I cannot but believe that the reason of the standard of Christian life being so low, is that we are living on stale manna. You know what I mean by that. So many people are living on their past experience—thinking of the grand times they had twenty years ago, perhaps when they were converted. It is a sure sign that we are out of communion with God if we are talking more of the joy, and peace, and power, we had in the past, than of what we have to-day. We are told to "grow in grace;" but a great many are growing the wrong way.

You remember the Israelites used to gather the manna fresh every day: they were not allowed to store it up. There is a lesson here for us Christians. If we would be strong and vigorous, we must go to God daily and get grace. A man can no more take in a supply of grace for the future than he can eat enough to-day to last him for the next six months; or take sufficient air into his lungs at once to sustain life for a week to come. We must draw upon God's boundless stores of grace from day to day, as we need it.

I knew a man who lived on the banks of Lake Erie. He had pipes laid to his house from the lake; and when he wanted water, all he had to do was to turn the tap and the water flowed in. If the Government had presented him with the lake, he would not have known what to do with it. So we may say that if God were to give us grace enough for a lifetime, we should not know how to use it. He has given us the privilege of drawing on Him day by day—not "forty days after sight." There is plenty of grace in the bank of heaven; we need not be afraid of its becoming exhausted.

We are asked to come boldly to the throne of grace—as sons to a father—that we may find grace. You have noticed that a son is very much more bold in his father's house than if he were simply a servant. A good many Christians are like servants. If you go into a house, you can soon tell the difference between the family and the servants. A son comes home in the evening; he goes all over the house—perhaps talks about the letters that have come in, and wants to know all that has been going on in the family during his absence. It is very different with a servant, who perhaps does not leave the kitchen or the servants' hall all day except when duty requires it.

Suppose some one had paid a million dollars into the bank in your name, and had given you a check-book so that you could draw out just as you wanted: would you go to work and try to live on ten dollars a month? Yet that is exactly what many of us are doing as Christians. I believe this low standard of Christian life in the Church is doing more to manufacture infidels than all the skeptical books that were ever written.

Hear what the Apostle says: "My God shall supply all your need." Look at these words carefully. It does not say He will supply all your wants. There are many things we want that God has not promised to give. It is "your need" and "all your need." My children often want many things they do not get; but I supply all they need, if it is in my power to give it to them. I do not supply all their wants by any means. My boy would probably want to have me give him a horse; when I know that what he really needs, perhaps, is grace to control his temper. Our children might want many things that it would be injurious for them to have. And so, though God may withhold from us many things that we desire, He will supply all our need. There can come upon us no trouble or trial in this life, but God has grace enough to carry us right through it, if we will only go to Him and get it. But we must ask for it day by day. "As thy days, so shall thy strength be."

I met a man once in Scotland who taught me a lesson that I shall never forget. A Christian friend wanted me to go and have a talk with him. He had been bedridden for many years. This afflicted saint comforted me and told me some wonderful things. He had fallen and broken his back when he was about fifteen years of age, and had lain there on his bed for some forty years. He could not be moved without a good deal of pain, and probably not a day has passed all those years without suffering. If any one had told him he was going to lie there and suffer for forty years, probably he would have said he could not do it. But day after day the grace of God has been granted to him; and I declare to you it seemed to me as if I were in the presence of one of God's most highly-favored children. It seemed that when I was in that man's chamber, I was about as near heaven as I could get on this earth. Talk about a man's face shining with the glory of the upper world! I very seldom see a face that shines as did his. I can imagine that the very angels when they are passing over the city on some mission of mercy, come down into that man's chamber to get refreshed. There he has been lying all these years, not only without a murmur, but rejoicing all the while.

I said to him: "My friend, does the devil never tempt you to doubt God, and to think He is a hard master?" "Well now," he said, "that is just what he tries to do. Sometimes, as I look out of the window and see people walking along in health, Satan whispers: 'If God is so good, why does He keep you here all these weary years? Why, if He loved you, instead of lying here and being dependent on others, you might now have been a rich man, and riding in your own carriage.'" "What do you do when the devil tempts you?" "Oh, I just take him up to the Cross; and he had such a fright there eighteen hundred years ago, that he cannot stand it; and he leaves me." I do not think that bedridden saint has much trouble with doubts; he is so full of grace.

And so if we will only come boldly to God, we shall get all the help and strength we need. There is not a man or woman alive but may be kept from falling, if they will let God hold them up in His almighty arms.

There is a story in the history of Elisha the prophet that I am very fond of; most of you are familiar with it. Sometimes we meet with people who hesitate to accept Christ, because they are so afraid they will not hold out. You remember there was a young prophet who died and left a widow with two little boys. It has been said that misfortunes do not come singly, but in battalions. This woman had not only lost her husband, but a creditor was going to take her boys and sell them into slavery. That was a common thing in those days. The widow went and told Elisha all about it. He asked her what she had in the house. Nothing, she said, but a pot of oil. It was a very hard case.

Elisha told her to go home and borrow all the vessels she could. His command was: "Borrow not a few." I like that. She took him at his word, and borrowed all the vessels her neighbors would lend to her. I can imagine I see the woman and her two sons going from house to house asking the loan of their vessels. No doubt there were a good many of the neighbors who were stretching their necks, and wondering what it all meant; just as we sometimes find people coming into the inquiry-room to see what is going on. If this woman had been like some modern skeptics, she would have thought it very absurd for the prophet to bid her do such a thing; she would have asked what good could come of it. But faith asks no questions: so she went and did what the man of God told her to do. I can see her going up one side of the street knocking at every door and asking for empty vessels. "How many do you want?" "All you can spare." There are the two sons carrying the great vessels; some of them perhaps nearly as large as the boys themselves. It was hard work. When they had finished one side of the street, they went down the other. "Borrow not a few," she had been told; so she went on asking for as many as she could get. If there were as much gossip in those days as there is now, all the people in the street would have been talking about her. Why, this woman and her boys have been carrying vessels into the house all day; what can be the matter?

But now they have all the vessels the neighbors would lend. She locks the door; and she says to one of the boys, "James, you are the younger; bring me the empty vessels. John, you are the stronger; when, I have filled them you take them away." So she began to pour. Perhaps the first vessel was twice as big as the one she poured from; but it was soon filled: and she kept on pouring into vessel after vessel. At last her son says, "Mother, this is the last one;" and we are told that the oil was not stayed till the last vessel was full.

Dear friends, bring your empty vessels; and God will fill them. I venture to say that the eyes of those boys sparkled as they saw this beautiful oil, fresh from the hand of the Creator. The woman went and told the man of God what had happened; he said to her, "Go, sell the oil, and pay thy debt; and live thou and thy children off the rest." That is grace for the present, and for the future. "As thy days so shall thy strength be." You will have grace not only to cover all your sins, but to carry you right into glory. Let the grace of God into your heart; and He will bring you safely through.

Let me close by quoting the words of an old prayer: "God give us grace to see our need of grace; give us grace to ask for grace; give us grace to receive grace; give us grace to use the grace we have received."

"Grace taught my soul to pray,

And pardoning love to know;

'Twas grace that kept me to this day,

And will not let me go.

Grace all the work shall crown,

Through everlasting days;

It lays in heaven the topmost stone,

And well deserves the praise!"

CHAPTER VII
GRACE FOR SERVICE

"FOR the grace of God that bringeth salvation to all men hath appeared; teaching us that, denying ungodliness and worldly lusts, we should live soberly, righteously, and godly, in this present world; looking for that blessed hope, and the glorious appearing of the great God and our Saviour Jesus Christ, who gave Himself for us, that He might redeem us from all iniquity, and purify unto Himself a peculiar people, zealous of good works."

In this wonderful passage we see grace in a threefold aspect: grace that bringeth salvation; grace for holy living; and grace for service. I have had three red-letter days in my experience: the first was, when I was converted; the next was when I got my lips opened, and I began to confess Christ; the third was, when I began to work for the salvation of others.

I think there are a great many who have got to the first stage; some have got to the second; very few have got to the third. This is the reason, I believe, why the world is not reached.

Many say they are anxious to "grow in grace." I do not think they ever will, until they go out into the harvest field and begin to work for others. We are not going to have the grace we need to qualify us for work until we launch out into the deep, and begin to use the abilities and the opportunities we already possess. Many fold their arms, and wait for the grace of God to come to them; but we do not get it in that way. When we "go forward," then it is that God meets us with His Grace.

If Moses had stayed in Horeb until he got the grace he needed, he never would have started for Egypt at all. But when he had set out, God met him in the way and blessed him day by day as he needed. Many grow discouraged because there is a little opposition; but if we are going to work for God we must expect opposition. No real work was ever done for God without opposition. If you think that you are going to have the approval of a godless world, and of cold Christians, as you launch out into the deep with your net, you are greatly mistaken. A man said to me some time ago, that when he was converted he commenced to do some work in connection with the Church; he was greatly discouraged because some of the older Christians threw cold water on him, so he gave up the whole thing.

I pity a man who cannot take a little cold water without being any the worse for it. Why, many of the Christians in old times had to go through the fire, and did not shrink from it. A little cold water never hurts any one.

Others say they have so many cares and troubles, they have as much as they can carry. Well, a good way to forget your trouble is—to go and help some one else who is carrying a heavier burden than yourself. It was when Job began to pray for his friends that he forgot his own troubles. Paul gloried in his infirmity, and in the tribulations he had to undergo, so that the power of Christ might all the more rest upon him. He gloried in the Cross: and you must bear in mind that the Cross was not so easy to bear in his day as it is in ours. Every one was speaking against it. "I glory in the Cross of Christ," he said. When a man gets to that point, do you tell me that God cannot use him to build up His kingdom? In his second letter to the Corinthians, Paul speaks of "the thorn in the flesh;" he prayed the Lord to take it away. The Lord said He was not going to take it away: but He would give His servant grace to bear it. So the apostle learned to thank God for the thorn, because he got more grace. It is when the days are dark that people are brought nearer to God. I suppose that is what Paul meant.

If there is any child of God who has a "thorn in the flesh," God has grace enough to help you to bear it if you will but go to Him for it. The difficulty is that so many are looking at their troubles and sorrows, instead of looking toward the glorious reward, and pressing on their way by God's help.

In II Corinthians 9:8, we read: "God is able to make all grace abound towards you; that ye, always having all sufficiency in all things, may abound to every good work." There are three thoughts here—God makes all grace to abound, that we may have all sufficiency in all things. I think this is one of the most wonderful verses in the Bible.

There is plenty of grace. Many Christians, if they have grace enough to keep them from outward sin, seem to be perfectly satisfied; they do not press on to get fullness of grace, so as to be ready for God's work. Many are satisfied to go into the stream of grace ankle deep, when God wants them to swim in it.

If we always came to meetings desiring to get strength, then we should be able to go out to work and speak for Christ. There are a great many who would be used of God, if they would only come boldly to His throne of grace, and "find grace to help in time of need." Is it not a time of need now? God has said, "I will pour water on him that is thirsty." Do we thirst for a deeper work of grace in our hearts?—for the anointing of the Spirit? Here is the promise: "I will pour water on him that is thirsty." Let all who are hungering and thirsting for blessing come and receive it.

Another reason why many Christians do not get anything is—because they do not give out to others. They are satisfied with present attainments, instead of growing in grace. We are not the fountain; we are only a channel for the grace of God to flow through. There is not one of us but God wants to use in building up His kingdom. That little boy, that grey-haired man, these young men and maidens; all are needed: and there is a work for all. We want to believe that God has grace enough to qualify us to go out and work for Him.

If we have known Jesus Christ for twenty years or more, and if we have not been able to introduce an anxious soul to Him, there has been something wrong somewhere. If we were full of grace, we should be ready for any call that comes to us. Paul said, when he had that famous interview with Christ on the way to Damascus, "Lord, what wilt Thou have me to do?" Isaiah said, "Here am I, send me." Oh that God would fill all His people with grace, so that we may see more wonderful things than He has ever permitted us to see! No man can tell what he can do, until he moves forward. If we do that in the name of God, instead of there being a few scores or hundreds converted, there will be thousands flocking into the Kingdom of God. Remember, that we honor God when we ask for great things. It is a humiliating thing to think that we are satisfied with very small results.

It is said that Alexander the Great had a favorite General to whom he had given permission to draw upon the royal treasury for any amount. On one occasion this General had made a draft for such an enormous sum that the Treasurer refused to honor it until he consulted the Emperor. So he went into his presence and told him what the General had done. "Did you not honor the draft?" said the Emperor. "No; I refused till I had seen your Majesty; because the amount was so great." The Emperor was indignant. His Treasurer said that he was afraid of offending him if he had paid the amount. "Do you not know," replied the Emperor, "that he honors me and my kingdom by making a large draft?" Whether the story be authentic or not, it is true that we honor God when we ask for great things.

It is said that on one occasion when Cæsar gave a very valuable present, the receiver replied that it was too costly a gift. The Emperor answered that it was not too great for Cæsar to give. Our God is a great King; and He delights to use us: so let us delight to ask Him for great grace, that we may go out and work for him.

I find that many Christians are in trouble about the future; they think they will not have grace enough to die by. It is much more important that we should have grace enough to live by. It seems to me that death is of very little importance in the meantime. When the dying hour comes there will be dying grace; but you do not require dying grace to live by. If I am going to live perhaps for fifteen or twenty years, what do I want with dying grace? I am far more anxious about having grace enough for my present work.

I have sometimes been asked if I had grace enough to enable me to go to the stake and die as a martyr. No; what do I want with martyr's grace? I do not like suffering; but if God should call on me to die a martyr's death, He would give me martyr's grace. If I have to pass through some great affliction, I know God will give me grace when the time comes; but I do not want it till it comes.

There is a story of a martyr in the second century. He was brought before the king, and told that if he did not recant they would banish him. Said he, "O king, you cannot banish me from Christ; for He has said, I will never leave thee nor forsake thee!" The apostle John was banished to the island of Patmos; but it was the best thing that could have happened: for if John had not been sent there, probably we should never have had that grand Book of Revelation. John could not be separated from his Master.

So it was with this brave martyr, of whom I was speaking. The king said to him, "Then I will take away your property from you." "You cannot do that: for my treasure is laid up on high, where you cannot get at it?" "Then I will kill you." "You can not do that; for I have been dead these forty years: my life is hid with Christ in God." The king said, "What are you going to do with such a fanatic as that?"

Let us remember that if we have not grace enough for service, we have no one to blame but ourselves. We are not straitened in God: He has abundance of grace to qualify us to work for Him.

Sovereign Grace

MORE TO FOLLOW.

I heard a story about two members of a Church: one was a wealthy man, and the other was one of those who cannot take care of their finances—he was always in debt. The rich brother had compassion on his poor brother. He wanted to give him some money; but he would not give it to the man all at once: he knew he would not use it properly. So he sent the amount to the minister, and asked him to supply the needs of this poor brother. The minister used to send him a five-dollar bill, and put on the envelope "More to follow." I can imagine how welcome the gift would be; but the best of all was the promise—"More to follow." So it is with God: there is always "more to follow." It is such a pity that we are not ready to be used by God when He wants to use us.

Dear friends, let me put this question to you: Are you full of grace? You shake your head. Well, it is our privilege to be full. What is the best way to get full of grace? It is to be emptied of self. How can we be emptied? Suppose you wish to get the air out of this tumbler; how can you do it? I will tell you: by pouring water into the tumbler till it is full to overflowing. That is the way the Lord empties us of self. He fills us with His grace. "I will pour water on him that is thirsty." Are you hungering to get rid of your sinful selves? Then let the Spirit of God come in and fill you. God is able to do it.

See what He did for John Bunyan—how He made one of the mightiest instruments for good the world ever saw, out of that swearing Bedford tinker. If we had a telescope which would enable us to look into heaven as Stephen did, I can imagine we should see the thief, who believed in Jesus while on the cross, very near the throne. Ask him how he got there; and he would tell you it was through the grace of God. See how the grace of God could save a Mary Magdalene possessed of seven devils! Ask her what it was that melted her heart: and she would tell you that it was the grace of God. Look again at that woman whom Christ met at the well at Sychar. The Saviour offered her a cup of the living water: she drank, and now she walks the chrystal pavement of heaven. See how the grace of God could change Zaccheus, the hated publican of Jericho! Now he is in yonder world of light; he was brought there by the sovereign grace of God.

You will have noticed that many of those who were about the most unlikely, have, by the power of God's grace, become very eminent in His service. Look at the twelve apostles of Christ; they were all unlettered men. This ought to encourage all whose education is limited to give themselves to God's work. When our earthly work is ended, then, like our Master, we shall enter into glory. It has been well remarked: "Grace is glory militant; and glory is grace triumphant. Grace is glory begun; glory is grace made perfect. Grace is the first degree of glory: glory is the highest degree of grace."

"Oh, to grace how great a debtor
Daily I'm constrained to be!
Let Thy grace, Lord, like a fetter,
Bind my wandering heart to thee.
Prone to wander, Lord, I feel it—
Prone to leave the God I love—
Here's my heart, oh take and seal it,
Seal it for Thy courts above."

CHAPTER VIII
A CHIME OF GOSPEL BELLS

IN Baltimore, a few years ago, we held a number of meetings for men. I am very fond of this hymn; and we used to let the choir sing the chorus over and over again, till all could sing it.

"Oh, word of words the sweetest,
Oh, word in which there lie
All promise, all fulfillment,
And end of mystery!
Lamenting or rejoicing,
With doubt or terror nigh,
I hear the 'Come!' of Jesus,
And to His cross I fly.
Come! oh, come to me!
Come! oh, come to me!
Weary heavy-laden,
Come! oh, come to Me!
O soul! why shouldst thou wander
From such a loving Friend?
Cling closer, closer to Him,
Stay with Him to the end
Alas! I am so helpless,
So very full of sin;
For I am ever wandering,
And coming back again.
Oh, each time draw me nearer,
That soon the 'Come!' may be

Nought but a gentle whisper
To one close, close to Thee;
Then, over sea and mountain,
Far from, or near, my home,
I'll take Thy hand and follow,
At that sweet whisper, 'Come!'"

There was a man in one of the meetings who had been brought there against his will; he had come through some personal influence brought to bear upon him. When he got to the meeting, they were singing the chorus of this hymn—

"Come! come! come!"

He said afterwards he thought he never saw so many fools together in his life before. The idea of a number of men standing there singing, "Come! come! come!" When he started home he could not get this little word out of his head; it kept coming back all the time. He went into a saloon, and ordered some whiskey, thinking to drown it. But he could not; it still kept coming back. He went into another saloon, and drank some more whiskey; but the words kept ringing in his ears: "Come! come! come!" He said to himself, "What a fool I am for allowing myself to be troubled in this way!" He went to a third saloon; had another glass, and finally got home.

He went off to bed, but could not sleep; it seemed as if the very pillow kept whispering the word, "Come! Come!" He began to be angry with himself: "What a fool I was for ever going to that meeting at all!" When he got up he took the little hymn book, found the hymn, and read it over. "What nonsense!" he said to himself; "the idea of a rational man being disturbed by that hymn." He set fire to the hymn book; but he could not burn up the little word "Come!" "Heaven and earth shall pass away: but My word shall not pass away."

He declared he would never go to another of the meetings; but the next night he came again. When he got there, strange to say, they were singing the same hymn. "There is that miserable old hymn again," he said; "what a fool I am for coming!" I tell you, when the Spirit of God lays hold of a man, he does a good many things he did not intend to do. To make a long story short, that man rose in a meeting of young converts, and told the story that I have now told you. Pulling out the little hymn book for he had bought another copy and opening it at this hymn, he said: "I think this hymn is the sweetest and the best in the English language. God blessed it to the saving of my soul." And yet this was the very hymn he had despised.

I want to take up this little word "Come!" Sometimes people forget the text of a sermon; but this text will be short enough for any one to remember. Let me ring out a chime of Gospel bells, every one of which says, "Come!" The first bell I will ring is,

COME AND HEAR!

"Incline your ear, and come unto me; hear, and your soul shall live; and I will make an everlasting covenant with you, even the sure mercies of David." "Incline your ear," God says. You have sometimes seen a man who is a little deaf, and cannot catch every word, put his hand up to his ear and lean forward. I have seen a man sometimes put up both hands to his ears, as if he were determined to catch every word. I like to see that. This is the figure that the prophet uses when he says on God's behalf, "Incline your ear."

Man lost spiritual life and communion with his Maker by listening to the voice of the tempter, instead of the voice of God. We get life again by listening to the voice of God. The Word of God gives life. "The words that I speak unto you," says Christ, "they are spirit, and they are life." So, what people need is—to incline their ear, and hear. It is a great thing when the Gospel preacher gets the ear of a congregation—I mean the inner ear. For a man has not only two ears in his head; he has also what we may call the outer ear, and the inner ear—the ear of the soul. You may speak to the outward ear, and not reach the ear of the soul at all. Many in these days are like the "foolish people" to whom the prophet Jeremiah spoke: "Which have eyes, and see not; which have ears, and hear not." There are many in every congregation whose attention I am not able to secure for five minutes together. Almost any little thing will divert their minds. We need to give heed to the words of the Lord: "He that hath ears to hear, let him hear."

You remember when Peter was sent to Cornelius, he was to speak to him words whereby he and his house were to be saved.

If you are to be saved, it must be by listening to the Word of God. Here is the promise: "Hear; and your soul shall live."

There was an architect in Chicago who was converted. In giving his testimony, he said he had been in the habit of attending church for a great many years, but he could not say that he had really heard a sermon all the time. He said that when the minister gave out the text and began to preach, he used to settle himself in the corner of the pew and work out the plans of some building. He could not tell how many plans he had prepared while the minister was preaching. He was the architect for one or two companies; and he used to do all his planning in that way. You see, Satan came in between him and the preacher, and caught away the good seed of the Word. I have often preached to people, and have been perfectly amazed to find they could hardly tell one solitary word of the sermon; even the text had completely gone from them.

A colored man once said that a good many of his congregation would be lost because they were too generous. He saw that the people looked rather surprised; so he said, "Perhaps you think I have made a mistake; and that I ought to have said you will be lost because you are not generous enough. That is not so; I meant just what I said. You give away too many sermons. You hear them, as it were, for other people." So there are a good many now hearing me who are listening for those behind them: they say the message is a very good one for neighbor So-and-so; and they pass it over their shoulders, till it gets clear out at the door. You laugh; but you know it is so. Listen! "Verily, verily, I say unto you, he that heareth My word, and believeth on Him that sent Me, hath everlasting life, and shall not come into condemnation; but is passed from death unto life."

The next note in this peal of bells I wish to ring out is—

COME AND SEE!

Scripture not only uses the ear, but the eye, in illustrating the way of salvation. When a man both hears and sees a thing, he remembers it twice as long as if he only heard it. You remember what Philip said to Nathanael: "Philip findeth Nathanael, and saith unto him, we have found Him of whom Moses in the Law, and the Prophets, did write—Jesus of Nazareth, the son of Joseph. And Nathanael said unto him, Can there any good thing come out of Nazareth? Philip saith unto him, Come and see." Philip was a wise winner of souls. He brought his friend to Christ. Nathanael had one interview with the son of God; he became His disciple and never left Him. If Philip had gone on discussing the matter with him, and had tried to prove that some good thing could come out of Nazareth, he might have never been a disciple at all.

After all, we do not gain much by discussion. Let objectors or inquirers only get one personal interview with the Son of God; that will scatter all their darkness, all their prejudice, and all their unbelief. The moment that Philip succeeded in getting Nathanael to Christ, the work was done.

So we say to you, "Come and see!" I thought, when I was converted, that my friends had been very unfaithful to me, because they had not told me about Christ. I thought I would have all my friends converted inside of twenty-four hours; and I was quite disappointed when they did not at once see Christ to be the Lily of the Valley, and the Rose of Sharon, and the Bright and Morning Star. I wondered why it was. No doubt many of those who hear me now have had that experience; you thought when you saw Christ in all His beauty that you could soon make your friends see Him in the same light.

But we need to learn that God alone can do it. If there is a skeptic now hearing me, I want to say that one personal interview with the Son of God will scatter all your infidelity and atheism. One night, in the inquiry-room, I met the wife of an atheist, who had been brought to God at one of our meetings. She was converted at the same time. She had brought two of her daughters to the meeting, desiring that they too should know Christ. I said to the mother: "How is it with your skepticism now?" "Oh," said she, "it is all gone." When Christ gets into the heart, atheism must go out; if a man will only come and take one trustful, loving look at the Saviour, there will be no desire to leave Him again.

A gentleman was walking down the street in Baltimore, a few years ago. It was near Christmas-time, and many of the shop-windows were filled with Christmas presents, toys, etc. As this gentleman passed along, he saw three little girls standing before a shop window, and he heard two of them trying to describe to the third the things that were in the window. It aroused his attention, and he wondered what it could mean. He went back, and found that the middle one was blind—she had never been able to see—and her two sisters were endeavoring to tell her how the things looked.

The gentleman stood beside them for some time, and listened; he said it was most interesting to hear them trying to describe the different articles to the blind child—they found it a difficult task. As he told me, I said to myself, "That is just my position in trying to tell other men about Christ: I may talk about Him; and yet they see no beauty in Him that they should desire Him. But if they will only come to Him, He will open their eyes and reveal Himself to them in all His loveliness and grace."

Looking at it from the outside, there was not much beauty in the Tabernacle that Moses erected in the desert. It was covered on the outside with badgers' skins—and there was not much beauty in them. If you were to pass into the inside, then you would find out the beauty of the coverings. So the sinner sees no beauty in Christ till he comes to Him—then he can see it.

You have looked at the windows of a grand church erected at the cost of many thousands of dollars. From the outside they did not seem very beautiful; but get inside, when the rays of the sun are striking upon the stained glass, and you begin to understand what others have told you of their magnificence. So it is when you have come into personal contact with Christ; you find Him to be the very Friend you need. Therefore we extend to all the sweet Gospel invitation "Come and see!"

Let me now ring out the third bell—

COME AND DRINK!

"Ho, every one that thirsteth, come ye to the waters: and he that hath no money; come ye, buy, and eat: yea, come, buy wine and milk without money and without price." If you will come and drink at this fountain, Christ says you shall never thirst again. He has promised to quench your thirst. "If any man thirst," He says, "let him come unto Me and drink."

I thank God for those words: "If any man." That does not mean merely a select few respectable people; it takes in all—every drunkard, every harlot, every thief, every self-righteous Pharisee.

"If any man thirst." How this world is thirsting for something that will satisfy! What fills the places of amusement—the dance houses, the music halls, and the theaters, night after night? Men and women are thirsting for something they have not got. The moment a man turns his back upon God, he begins to thirst; and that thirst will never be quenched until he returns to "the fountain of living waters." As the prophet Jeremiah tells us, we have forsaken the fountain of living waters, and hewn out for ourselves cisterns, broken cisterns, that can hold no water. There is a thirst this world can never quench: the more we drink of its pleasures, the thirstier we become. We cry out for more and more; and we are all the while being dragged down lower and lower. But there is "a fountain opened to the House of David . . . for sin and for uncleanness." Let us press up to it, and drink and live.

I remember after one of the great battles in the War we were coming down the Tennessee River with a company of wounded men. It was in the spring of the year, and the water was not clear. You know that the cry of a wounded man is: "Water! water!" especially in a hot country. I remember taking a glass of the muddy water to one of these men. Although he was very thirsty, he only drank a little of it. He handed the glass back to me, and as he did so, he said, "Oh for a draught of water from my father's well!" Are there any thirsty ones here? Come and drink of the fountain opened in Christ; your longing will be satisfied, and you will never thirst again. It will be in you "a well of water springing up into everlasting life." Water rises to its own level; and as this water has come down from the throne of God, it will carry us back to the presence of God. Come, O ye thirsty ones, stoop down and drink, and live! You are all invited: come along! When Moses took his rod and struck the flinty rock in the wilderness, out of it there came a pure crystal stream of water, which flowed or through that dry and barren land. All that the poor thirsty Israelites had to do was to stoop and drink. It was free to all. So the grace of God is free to all. God invites you to come and take it: will you come?

I remember being in a large city where I noticed that the people resorted to a favorite well in one of the parks. I said to a man one day, "Does the well never run dry?" The man was drinking of the water out of the well; and as he stopped drinking, he smacked his lips, and said: "They have never been able to pump it dry yet. They tried it a few years ago. They put the fire engines to work, and tried all they could to pump the well dry; but they found there was a river flowing right under the city." Thank God, the well of salvation never gets dry, though the saints of God have been drinking from it for six thousand years! Abel, Enoch Noah, Abraham. Moses, Elijah, the Apostles all have drunk from it; and they are now up yonder, where they are drinking of the stream that flows from the throne of God. "They shall hunger no more, neither thirst any more; neither shall the sun light on them, nor any heat. For the Lamb which is in the midst of the throne shall feed them, and shall lead them unto living fountains of waters: and God shall wipe away all tears from their eyes."

Let me ring another Gospel bell:

COME AND DINE!

My brother, my sister—are you hungry? Then come along and dine. Some people are afraid of being converted, because they think they will not hold out. Mr. Rainsford once said, "If the Lord gives us eternal life, He will surely give us all that is needful to preserve it." He not only gives life; but He gives us our daily bread to feed that life.

After the Saviour had risen from the dead, He had not appeared to His disciples for some days. Peter said to the others, "I go a fishing." Seven of them started off in their boats. They toiled all night but caught nothing. In the grey of the morning, they saw a Stranger on the shore. He addressed them and said "Children, have ye any meat?" They told Him they had not. "Cast the net on the right side of the ship; and ye shall find." I can imagine they said to each other, "What good is that going to do? We have been fishing here all night, and have got nothing? The idea that there should be fish on one side of the boat, and not on the other!" However, they obeyed the command; and they had such a haul that there was no room for the fish in the boat. Then one of them said, "It is the Lord." When he heard that, Peter sprang right into the sea, and swam to the shore; and the others pulled the boat to land.

When they reached the shore the Master said, "Come and dine." What a meal that must have been. There was the Lord of Glory feeding His disciples. If He could set a table for His people in the wilderness, and feed three millions of Israelites for forty years, can He not give us our daily bread? I do not mean only the bread that perisheth; but the Bread that cometh from above. If He feeds the birds of the air, surely He will feed His children made in His own image! If He numbers the very hairs of our head, He will take care to supply all our temporal wants.

Not only so: He will give us the Bread of Life for the nourishment of the soul—the life that the world knows nothing of—if we will but go to Him. "I am the Bread of Life," He says. As we feed on Him by faith, we get strength. Let our thoughts rest upon Him; and He will lift us above ourselves, and above the world, and satisfy our utmost desires.

Another Gospel bell is—

COME AND REST!

Dear friend, do you not need rest? There is a restlessness all over the world to-day. Men are sighing and struggling after rest. The cry of the world is, "Where can rest be found?" The rich man that we read of in the parable pulled down his barns, that he might build greater; and said to his soul, "Take thine ease." He thought he was going to find rest in wealth; but he was disappointed. That night his soul was summoned away. No; there is no rest in wealth or pleasure.

Others think they will succeed in drowning their sorrows and troubles by indulging in drink; but that will only increase them. "There is no peace, saith my God, to the wicked:" they are like the troubled sea that cannot rest. We sometimes talk of the ocean as being as calm as a sea of glass; but it is never at rest: and here we have a faithful picture of the wicked man and woman.

O weary soul, hear the sweet voice that comes ringing down through the ages: "Come unto me, all ye that labor, and are heavy-laden; and I will give you rest." Thank God, He does not sell it! If He did, some of us are so poor we could not buy; but we can all take a gift. That little boy there knows how to take a gift; that old man, living on borrowed time, and almost on the verge of another world, knows how to take a gift. The gift Jesus wants to bestow is rest: Rest for time, and rest for eternity. Every weary soul may have this rest if he will. But you must come to Christ and get it. Nowhere else can this rest be found. If you go to the world with your cares, your troubles, and your anxieties, all it can do is to put a few more on the top of them. The world is a poor place to go to for sympathy. As some one has said: "If you roll your burdens anywhere but on Christ, they will roll back on you with more weight than ever. Cast them on Christ; and He will carry them for you."

Here is another bell—

COME AND REASON!

Perhaps there are some infidels reading this. They are fond of saying to us, "Come and reason." But I want to draw their attention to the verses that go before this one in the first chapter of Isaiah. The trouble with a good many skeptics is this—they take a sentence here and there from Scripture without reference to the context. Let us see what this passage says: "When ye spread forth your hands, I will hide mine eyes from you: yea, when ye make many prayers I will not hear: your hands are full of blood. Wash you, make you clean; put away the evil of your doings from before Mine eyes; cease to do evil; learn to do well; seek judgment, relieve the oppressed, judge the fatherless, plead for the widow."

Then we have the gracious invitation, "Come now, and let us reason together." Do you think God is going to reason with a man whose hands are dripping with blood, and before he asks forgiveness and mercy? Will God reason with a man living in rebellion against Him? Nay. But if we turn from and confess our sin, then He will reason with us, and pardon us. "Though your sins be as scarlet, they shall be as white as snow: though they be red like crimson, they shall be as wool."

But if a man persists in his rebellion against God, there is no invitation to him to come and reason, and receive pardon. If I have been justly condemned to death by the law of the State, and am waiting the execution of my sentence, I am not in a position to reason with the governor. If he chooses to send me a free pardon, the first thing I have to do is to accept it; then he may allow me to come into his presence. But we must bear in mind that God is above our reason. When man fell, his reason became perverted; and he was not in a position to reason with God. "If any man willeth to do His will he shall know of the teaching." We must be willing to forsake our sins. "Let the wicked forsake his way, and the unrighteous man his thoughts: and let him return unto the Lord, and He will have mercy upon him; and to our God, for He will abundantly pardon," The moment a man is willing to part with his sins, God meets him in grace and offers him peace and pardon.

The next bell I would like to sound out is—

COME TO THE MARRIAGE!

"Behold, I have prepared my dinner: . . . all things are ready; come unto the marriage." Who would not feel highly honored if they were invited to some fine residence, to the wedding of one of the members of the President's family? I can imagine you would feel rather proud of having received such an invitation. You would want all your friends to know it.

Probably you may never get such an invitation. But I have a far grander invitation for you here than that. I cannot speak for others; but if I know my own heart, I would rather be torn to pieces tonight, limb from limb, and die in the glorious hope of being at the marriage-supper of the Lamb, than live in this world a thousand years and miss that appointment at the last. "Blessed is he that is called to the marriage-supper of the Lamb." It will be a fearful thing for any of us to see Abraham, Isaac, and Jacob taking their place in the kingdom of God, and be ourselves thrust out.

This is no myth, my friends; it is a real invitation. Every man and woman is invited. All things are now ready. The feast has been prepared at great expense. You may spurn the grace, and the gift of God; but you must bear in mind that it cost God a good deal before He could provide this feast. When He gave Christ He gave the richest jewel that heaven had. And now He sends out the invitation. He commands His servants to go into the highways, and hedges, and lanes, and compel them to come in, that His house may be full. Who will come? You say you are not fit to come? If the President invited you to the White House, and the invitation said you were to come just as you were; and if the sentinel at the gate stopped you because you did not wear a dress suit, what would you do? Would you not show him the document signed in the name of the President? Then he would stand aside and let you pass. So, my friend, if you can prove to me that you are a sinner, I can prove to you that you are invited to this Gospel feast—to this marriage supper of the Lamb.

Let me ring out another bell in this Gospel chime—

"COME, INHERIT THE KINGDOM!"

"Then shall the King say unto them on His right hand, Come, ye blessed of My Father, inherit the kingdom prepared for you from the foundation of the world." A kingdom!—think of that! Think of a poor man in this world, struggling with poverty and want, invited to become possessor of a kingdom! It is no fiction; it is described as "an inheritance incorruptible and undefiled, and that fadeth not away, reserved in heaven for you, who are kept by the power of God through faith unto salvation, ready to be revealed in the last time." We are called to be kings and priests: that is a high calling.

Surely no one who hears me intends to miss that kingdom! Christ said, "Seek ye first the Kingdom of God." Those who inherit it shall go no more out.

Yet another bell—
"COME UP HITHER!"

In the Revelation we find that the two witnesses were called up to heaven when their testimony was ended. So if we are faithful in the service of our King, we shall by and by hear a voice saying, "Come up hither!" There is going to be a separation one day. The man who has been persecuting his godly wife will some day find her missing. That drunkard who beats his children because they have been taught the way into the Kingdom of God, will miss them some day. They will be taken up out of the darkness, and away from the persecution, up into the presence of God. When the voice of God saying, "Come up hither" is heard, calling His children home, there will be a grand jubilee. That glorious day will soon dawn. "Lift up your heads, for the time of your redemption draweth nigh."

One more bell to complete the chime—
"WHOSOEVER WILL, LET HIM COME!"

It is the last time that the word "Come" appears in the Bible; and it occurs there over one thousand nine hundred times. We find it away back in Genesis, "Come, thou and all thy house, into the ark"; and it goes right along through Scripture. Prophets, apostles, and preachers, have been ringing it out all through the ages. Now the record is about to be closed, and Christ tells John to put in one more invitation. After the Lord had been in glory for about sixty years, perhaps He saw some poor man stumbling over one of the apostles' letters about the doctrine of election. So He came to John in Patmos, and John was in the Spirit on the Lord's Day. Christ said to His disciple, "Write these things to the Churches." I can imagine John's pen moved very easily and very swiftly that day; for the hand of his Lord was upon him. The Master said to him, "Before you close up the Book, put in one more invitation; and make it so broad that the whole world shall know they are included, and not a single one may feel that he is left out." John began to write "The Spirit and the Bride say, Come," that is, the Spirit and the

Church; "and let him that heareth say, Come!" If you have heard and received the message yourself, pass it on to those near you; your religion is not a very real thing if it does not affect some one else. We have to get rid of this idea that the world is going to be reached by ministers alone. All those who have drunk of the cup of salvation must pass it around.

"Let him that is athirst, come." But there are some so deaf that they cannot hear; others are not thirsty enough or they think they are not. I have seen men in our after-meetings with two streams of tears running down their cheeks; and yet they said the trouble with them was that they were not anxious enough. They were anxious to be anxious. Probably Christ saw that men would say they did not feel thirsty; so He told the apostle to make the invitation still broader. So the last invitation let down into a thirsty world is this: "Whosoever will, let him take the water of life freely."

Thank God for those words "Whosoever will!" Who will come and take it? That is the question. You have the power to accept or to reject the invitation. A man in one meeting once was honest enough to say "I won't." If I had it in my power I would bring this whole audience to a decision now, either for or against. I hope many now reading these words will say, "I will!" If God says we can, all the devils in hell cannot stop us. All the infidels in the world cannot prevent us. That little boy, that little girl, can say, "I will!" If it were necessary, God would send down a legion of angels to help you; but He has given you the power, and you can accept Christ this very minute if you are really in earnest.

Let me say that it is the easiest thing in the world to become a Christian, and it is also the most difficult. You will say: "That is a contradiction, a paradox." I will illustrate what I mean. A little nephew of mine in Chicago, a few years ago, took my Bible and threw it down on the floor. His mother said, "Charlie, pick up Uncle's Bible." The little fellow said he would not, "Charlie, do you know what that word means?" She soon found out that he did, and that he was not going to pick up the Book. His will had come right up against his mother's will. I began to be quite interested in the struggle; I knew if she did not break his will, he would some day break her heart. She repeated, "Charlie, go and pick up Uncle's Bible, and put it on the table." The little fellow said he could not do it. "I will punish you if you do not." He saw a strange look in her eye, and the matter began to get serious. He did not want to be punished, and he knew his mother would punish him if he did not lift the Bible. So he straightened every bone and muscle in him, and he said he could not do it. I really believe the little fellow had reasoned himself into the belief that he could not do it.

His mother knew he was only deceiving himself; so she kept him right to the point. At last he went down, put both his arms around the Book, and tugged away at it; but he still said he could not do it. The truth was he did not want to. He got up again without lifting it. The mother said, "Charlie, I am not going to talk to you any more. This matter has to be settled; pick up that Book, or I will punish you." At last she broke his will, and then he found it as easy as it is for me to turn my hand. He picked up the Bible, and laid it on the table. So it is with the sinner; if you are really willing to take the Water of Life, you can do it.

"I heard the voice of Jesus say,
'Come unto Me, and rest;
Lay down, thou weary one, lay down,
Thy head upon My breast.'
I came to Jesus as I was—
Weary, and worn, and sad,
I found in Him a resting-place,
And He has made me glad.
I heard the voice of Jesus say,
'Behold, I freely give
The living water—thirsty one,
Stoop down, and drink, and live.'
I came to Jesus, and I drank
Of that life-giving stream;
My thirst was quenched, my soul revived,
And now I live in Him.
I heard the voice of Jesus say,
'I am this dark world's Light:
Look unto Me, thy morn shall rise,
And all thy day be bright.'

Sovereign Grace

I looked to Jesus, and I found
In Him my Star, my Sun;
And in that Light of life I'll walk
Till traveling days are done."
Dr. H. Bonar

GOSPEL DIALOGUES

I

MR. MOODY AND REV. MARCUS RAINSFORD
WHAT IT IS TO BE A CHILD OF GOD

MR. MOODY—What is it to be a child of God? What is the first step?

Rev. M. Rainsford—Well, sir, I am a child of God when I become united to the Son of God. The Son of God prayed that all who believed upon Him should be one with Him, as He was one with the Father. Believing on Jesus, I receive Him, and become united to Him; I become, as it were, a member of his Body. I am an heir of God, a joint-heir with Christ.

Mr. M.—What is the best definition of Faith?

Mr. R.—Trust in the Son of God, as the Saviour He has given to us. Simple trust, not only in a creed, but in a Person. I trust my soul to Him. I trust the keeping of my soul to Him. God has promised that whosoever trusts Him, mercy shall compass him on every side.

Mr. M.—Does not the Scripture say that the devils believe?

Mr. R.—They believe the truth, do they not? They believe that Jesus was manifested to destroy them; and they "tremble." I wish we believed as truly and as fully that God sent His Son into the world to save us.

Mr. M.—What is it to "trust?"

Mr. R.—I take it to mean four things:

(1) Believing on Christ: that is, taking Him at His Word.

(2) Hoping in Christ: that is, expecting help from Him, according to His Word.

(3) Relying on Christ: That is, resting on Him for the times, and ways, and circumstances in which He may be pleased to fulfill His promises according to His Word.

(4) Waiting on Christ: that is, continuing to do so, notwithstanding delay, darkness, barrenness, perplexing experiences, and the sentence of death in myself. He may keep me waiting awhile (I have kept Him a long time waiting); but He will not keep me waiting always. Believing in Him, hoping in Him, relying upon Him, and waiting for Him—I understand to be trusting in Him.

Mr. M.—Can all these friends here believe the promises?

Mr. R.—The promises are true, whether we believe them or not. We do not make them true by believing them. God could not charge me with being an unbeliever, or condemn me for unbelief, if the promises were not true for me. I could in that case turn round and say: "Great God, why did you expect me to believe a promise that was not true for me?" And yet the Scriptures set forth unbelief as the greatest sin I can continue to commit.

Mr. M.—How are we "cleansed by the Blood?"

Mr. R.—"The blood is the life." The sentence upon sinners for their sin was, "The soul that sinneth it shall die." That we might not die, the Son of God died. The blood is the poured-out life of the Son of God, given as the price, the atonement, the substitute, for the forfeited life of the believer in Jesus Christ. Any poor sinner who receives Christ as God's gift is cleansed from all sin by His Blood.

Mr. M.—Was the blood shed for us all?

Mr. R.—

"There is a fountain filled with blood,

Drawn from Immanuel's veins;

And sinners plunged beneath that flood,

Lose all their guilty stains.

The dying thief rejoiced to see

That fountain in his day;

And there may we, though vile as he,

Wash all our sins away."

Mr. M.—Some may think that this is only a hymn, and that it is not Scripture. Did the Lord ever say anything similar to what the hymn says?

Mr. R.—He said: "I have given you the blood upon the altar to make an atonement for your souls." That was said of the picture of the blood of Christ. And at the Last Supper our Lord said His blood was "the blood of the new testament which is shed for you and for many for the remission of sins."

Mr. M.—What is "the gift of God?"

Mr. R.—There are three great gifts that God has given to us—

(1) His blessed Son.

(2) The Holy Ghost, "the promise of the Father," that we might understand the unspeakable gift bestowed on us when He gave His Son.

(3) He has given us His Holy Word.

The Holy Ghost has inspired the writers of it that we may read, and hear, and know the love that God has to us, "in that while we were yet sinners Christ died for us." We could not have the Son for our Saviour, unless God gave Him. We could not understand the gift of God, unless the Holy Ghost had come to quicken us and teach us; and this He does through the Word.

Mr. M.—How much is there in Christ for us who believe?

Mr. R.—In Him dwelt "all the fullness of the Godhead bodily"—fullness of life, of righteousness, of sanctification, of redemption, title to heaven, and meetness for it; all that God wants from us, and all that we want from God, He gave in the person of Christ.

Mr. M.—How long does it take God to justify a sinner?

Mr. R.—How long? The moment we receive Him we receive authority to enroll ourselves among the children of God, and are then and there justified from all things. The sentence of complete justification does not take long to pronounce. Some persons profess to see a difficulty in the variety of ways in which a sinner is said to be justified before God: (1) Justified by God; (2) Justified by Christ; (3) Justified by His Blood; (4) Justified by grace; (5) Justified by faith; (6) Justified by works.

Justification has reference to a court of justice. Suppose a sinner standing at the bar of God, the bar of conscience, and the bar of his fellow-men, charged with a thousand crimes.

(1) There is the Judge: that is God, who alone can condemn or justify: "It is God that justifieth." That is justification by God.

(2) There is the Advocate, who appears at court for the sinner;

the counselor, the intercessor: that is Christ. "Justified by Christ."

(3) There is next to be considered the ground and reason on account of which the Advocate pleads before the Judge. That is the merit of His own precious Blood. That is justification by His Blood.

(4) Next we must remember the law which the Judge is dispensing. The law of works? Nay, but the law of grace and faith. That is justification by His grace.

(5) And now the judge himself pronounces the result. "Be it known unto you that through this Man is preached unto you the forgiveness of sins; and by Him all that believe are justified from all things." Now, for the first time, the sinner at the bar knows the fact. This is justification by faith.

(6) But now the justified man leaves the criminal's dock. He does not return to his prison, or to his chains. He walks forth from the court-house a justified man; and all men, friends or foes, are made aware that he is free. That is "justification by works."

Mr. M.—A man says: "I have not found peace." How would you deal with him?

Mr. R.—He is really looking for the wrong thing. I do not look for peace. I look for Christ; and I get peace with Him. Some people put peace in the place of Christ. Others put their repentance or prayers in the place of Christ. Anything put in the place of Christ, or between the sinner and Christ, is in the wrong place. When I get Christ, I possess in Him everything that belongs to Him, as my Saviour.

Mr. M.—Some think they cannot be Christians until they are sanctified.

Mr. R.—Christ is my Sanctification, as much as my Justification. I cannot be sanctified but by His blood. There is a wonderful passage in Exodus. The high priest there represented in picture the Lord Jesus Christ. There was to be placed on the forefront of the miter of the high priest, when he stood before God, a plate of pure gold, and graven upon it as with a signet, the words: "Holiness to the Lord." My faith sees it on the forefront of the miter on the brow of my High Priest in heaven. "And it shall be upon Aaron's forehead, that Aaron may bear the iniquity of the holy things, which the children of Israel shall hallow in all their holy gifts; and it shall be always upon his forehead, that they may be accepted before the Lord." That was for Israel of old! That on the brow of

Jesus Christ is for me. Yes—for me, "that I may be accepted before the Lord." As I believe this truth it purifies my heart, it operates on my affections and my desires; and I seek to walk with Him, because He is my Sanctification before God, just as I trust in Him as my Justification—because He shed His blood for me.

Mr. M.—What is it to believe on His name?

Mr. R.—His name is His revealed self. We are informed what it is in Exodus. Moses was in the mount with God, and He had shown him wonderful things of kindness and of love. And Moses said, "O God, show me thy glory!" And He said, "I will make all my goodness pass before thee." So He put Moses in the cleft of the rock, and proclaimed the name of the Lord: "The Lord, the Lord God, merciful and gracious, longsuffering, and abundant in goodness and truth; keeping mercy for thousands, forgiving iniquity, transgression, and sin"—there it is, root and branch "and that will by no means clear the guilty." That is His name; and His glory He will not give unto another: and to believe in the name of the Lord is just to shelter under His promises.

Mr. M.—What is it to "receive the Kingdom of God like a little child?"

Mr. R.—Well, I do not believe in a little child being an innocent thing. I think it means that we are to receive it in all our need and helplessness. A little child is the most dependent thing on earth. All its resources are in its parents' love: all it can do is to cry; and its necessities explain the meaning to the mother's heart. If we interpret its language, it means: "Mother, wash me; I cannot wash myself. Mother, clothe me; I am naked, and cannot clothe myself. Mother, feed me; I cannot feed myself. Mother, carry me; I cannot walk." It is written, "A mother may forget her sucking child; yet will not I forget thee." This it is to receive the Kingdom of God as a little child—to come to Jesus in our helplessness and say: "Lord Jesus, wash me!" "Clothe me!" "Feed me!" "Carry me!" "Save me, Lord, or I perish."

Mr. M.—A good many say they are going to try. What would you say to such?

Mr. R.—God wants no man to "try." Jesus has already tried. He has not only tried, but He has succeeded. "It is finished." Believe in Him who has "made an end of sins, making reconciliation for iniquity, finishing transgression, and bringing in everlasting righteousness."

Mr. M.—If people say they are "going to try," what would you say to them?

Mr. R.—I should say, Put trusting in the place of trying; believing in the place of doubting; and I should urge them to come to Christ as they are, instead of waiting to be better. There is nothing now between God the Father and the poor sinner, but the Lord Jesus Christ; and Christ has put away sin that I may be joined to the Lord. "And he that is joined unto the Lord is one spirit;" "And where the spirit of the Lord is, there is liberty."

Mr. M.—About the last thing an anxious inquirer has to contend with is his feelings. There are hundreds here very anxious to know they are safe in the Kingdom; but they think they have not the right kind of feeling. What kind of feeling should they have?

Mr. R.—I think there are several of those present who can say that they found a blessing in the after-meetings through one verse of Scripture. I will quote it as an answer to Mr. Moody's question. "Who is among you that feareth the Lord, that obeyeth the voice of His servant, that walketh in darkness, and hath no light? Let him trust in the name of the Lord, and stay upon his God." Some of you may be walking in darkness; that is how you feel. What is God's command? "Let him trust in the name of the Lord, and stay upon his God." If I am to trust God in the darkness, I am to trust Him anywhere.

Mr. M.—You would advise them, then, to trust in the Lord, whether they have the right kind of feeling or not?

Mr. R.—If I were to think of my feelings for a moment, I should be one of the most miserable men in this hall to-night. My feelings are those of a sinful corrupt nature. I am just to believe what God tells me in spite of my feelings. Faith is "the evidence of things not seen:" I might add, "the evidence of things not felt."

Mr. M.—Some may say that faith is the gift of God: and that they must wait till God imparts it to them.

Mr. R.—"Faith cometh by hearing." The word of God is the medium through which faith comes to us. God has given us Christ; and He has given us His Spirit, and His Word: what need is there to wait? God will give faith to the man who reads His Word and seeks for His Spirit.

Mr. M.—What, then, should they wait for?

Mr. R.—I do not know of anything they have to wait for. God

says: "Come now; Believe now." No, no; there is nothing to wait for. He has given us all He has to give: and the sooner we take it the better.

Mr. M.—Perhaps some of them think they have too many sins to allow their coming.

Mr. R.—The Lord Jesus has put away sin by the sacrifice of Himself. "As far as the east is from the west, so far hath He removed our transgressions from us." Why do we not believe him? He says He has "made an end of sins." Why do we not believe Him? Is He a liar?

Mr. M.—Is unbelief a sin?

Mr. R.—It is the root of all sin.

Mr. M.—Has a man the power to believe these things, if he will?

Mr. R.—When God gives a command, it means that we are able by His grace to do it.

Mr. M.—What do you mean by "coming" to Christ?

Mr. R.—Believing in Him. If I were to prepare a great feast in this hall to-morrow night, and say that any man that comes to it would have a grand feast and a five-pound note besides, there would not be any question as to what "coming" meant. God has prepared a great feast. He has sent His messengers to invite all to come; and there is nothing to pay.

Mr. M.—What is the first step.

Mr. R.—To believe.

Mr. M.—Believe what?

Mr. R.—God's invitation; God's promise; God's provision. Let us believe the faithfulness of Him who calls us. Does God intend to mock us, and make game of us? If He did so to one man, it would hush all the harps in heaven.

Mr. M.—Suppose the people do "come," and that they fall into sin tomorrow?

Mr. R.—Let them come back again. God says we are to forgive till seventy times seven. Do you think the great God will do less than He commands us to do?

Mr. M.—If they truly come, will they have the desire to do the things they used to do before?

Mr. R.—When a man really receives Christ into his heart, he experiences "the expulsive power of a new affection." The devil may tempt him to sin; but sin has lost its attraction. A man finds out that it does not pay to grieve God's Holy Spirit.

Mr. M.—What would you advise your converts to do?

Mr. R.—When you were little babes, if you had had no milk, no clothing, and no rest, you would not have lived very long. You are now the result of your fathers' and mothers' care. When a man is born in the family of God he has life; but he needs food. "Man doth not live by bread alone." If you do not feed upon God's promises you will be of no use in God's service: it will be well for you if your life does not die out altogether before long. Then you need exercise. If you only take food, and do no work, you will soon suffer from what I may call spiritual apoplexy. When you get hold of a promise, go and tell it to others. The best way for me to get help for myself is by trying to help others. There is one great promise that young disciples should never forget: "He that watereth shall be watered also himself."

Mr. M.—How are they to begin?

Mr. R.—I believe there are some rich ladies and rich gentlemen on the platform. When such persons are brought to the Lord, they are apt to be ashamed to speak about salvation to their old companions. If our Christian ladies would go amongst other ladies; Christian gentlemen amongst gentlemen of their own class; and so on we should see a grand work for Christ. Each of you have some friends or relations whom you can influence better than anybody else can. Begin with them; and God will give you such a taste for work that you will not be content to stay at home: you will go and work outside as well.

Mr. M.—A good place to start in would be the kitchen, would it not? Begin with some little kitchen meetings. Let some of you get fifteen or twenty mothers together; and ask them to bring their young children with them. Sing some of these sweet hymns; read a few verses of Scripture; get your lips opened; and you will find that streams of salvation will be breaking out all around. I always think that every convert ought to be good for a dozen others right away.

Mr. R.—Let me tell a little incident in my own experience. I was once asked to go and see a great man and tell him about Christ. He did not expect me; and if I had known that, perhaps I should not have had the faith to go at all. When I went he was very angry and very nearly turned me out of the house. He was an old man, and had one little daughter. A few weeks afterwards he went to the Continent, and his daughter went with him. One day when he was very ill he saw his daughter looking at him, while the tears rolled down her cheeks. "My child," he said, "what are you crying about?" "Oh, papa, you do not love the Lord Jesus Christ; I am afraid you are going to hell!" "Why do you say that?" "Do you not remember when Mr. Rainsford called to see you, you were very rude to him? I never saw you so angry. And he only wished to speak to you about Jesus." "Well, my child, you shall read to me about Jesus." If that man has gone to heaven—I do not say whether he has or not—the only light he had he got from his little daughter. You set to work; and you cannot tell what may be the result, by the blessing of God.

"Sons of God, beloved in Jesus

Oh, the wondrous word of grace!

In His Son the Father sees us,

And as sons He gives us place.

Blessed power now brightly beaming—

On our God we soon shall gaze;

And in light celestial gleaming

We shall see our Saviour's face.

By the power of grace transforming

We shall then His image bear;

Christ His promised word performing,

We shall then His glory share."

El Nathan

II

MR. MOODY AND REV. MARCUS RAINSFORD
HOW TO BECOME A CHRISTIAN

MR. MOODY.—Mr. Rainsford, how can one make room in their heart for Christ?

Rev. M. Rainsford.—First, do we really want Christ to be in our hearts? If we do, the best thing will be to ask Him to come and make room for Himself. He will surely come and do so. "I can do all things through Christ which strengtheneth me." "Without Me ye can do nothing."

Mr. M.—Will Christ crowd out the world if He comes in?

Mr. R.—He spake a parable to that effect. "When a strong man armed keepeth his palace [the poor sinner's heart], his goods are in peace. But when a stronger than he shall come upon him and overcome him, he taketh from him all his armour wherein he trusted [unbelief, false views of God, worldliness, and love of sin], and divideth his spoils." The devil keeps the heart, because Christ desires it for His throne—until Christ drives Him out.

Mr. M.—What is the meaning of the promise?—"Him that cometh unto Me I will in no wise cast out."

Mr. R.—I think we often put the emphasis upon the wrong word. People are troubled about how they are going to come, when they should put the emphasis on Him to whom they are coming. "Him that cometh unto Me I will in no wise cast out:" no matter how he may come. I remember hearing this incident at an after-meeting. A gentleman was speaking to an anxious inquirer, telling him to come to Christ, to trust in Christ; but the man seemed to get no comfort. He said that was just where he found his difficulty. By and by, another friend came and spoke to the anxious one. All he said was: "Come to CHRIST; trust in CHRIST." The man saw it in a minute. He went and told the other gentleman, "I see the way of salvation now." "Tell me," said he, "what did that man say to you?" "Well, he told me to trust in Christ." "That is what I told you." "Nay, you bade me trust in Christ, and come to Christ; he bade me trust in Christ, and come to Christ." That made all the difference.

Mr. M.—What does Christ mean by the words "in no wise?"

Mr. R.—It means that if the sins of all sinners on earth and all the devils in hell were upon your soul, He will not refuse you. Not even in the range of God's omniscience is there a reason why Christ will refuse any poor sinner who comes to Him for pardon.

Mr. M.—What is the salvation He comes to proclaim and to bestow?

Mr. R.—To deliver us from the power of darkness and the bottomless pit, and set us upon the throne of glory. It is salvation from death and hell, and curse and ruin. But that is only the half of it. It is salvation to God, and light, and glory, and honor, and immortality; and from earth to heaven.

Mr. M.—If the friends here do not come and get this salvation, what will be the true reason?

Mr. R.—Either they are fond of some sin which they do not intend to give up, or they do not believe they are in a lost condition, and under the curse of God, and therefore do not feel their need of Him who "came to seek and to save that which was lost." Or they do not believe God's promises. I have sometimes asked a man, "Good friend, are you saved!" "Well, no, I am not saved." "Are you lost?" "Oh, God forbid! I am not lost." "Where are you, then, if you are neither saved nor lost?" May God wake us up to the fact that we are all in one state or the other!

Mr. M.—What if any of them should fall into sin after they have come to Christ?

Mr. R.—God has provided for the sins of His people, committed after they come to Christ, as surely as for their sins committed before they came to Him. Christ "ever liveth to make intercession for all that come unto God by Him." "If we say that we have no sin we deceive ourselves, and the truth is not in us. If we confess our sins, He is faithful and just to forgive us our sins, and to cleanse us from all unrighteousness." . . . . For, "if any man sin, we have an Advocate with the Father, Jesus Christ the righteous. And He is the propitiation for our sins." He will take care of our sinful, tried and tempted selves, if we trust ourselves to Him.

Mr. M.—Is it not said that if we sin willfully after we have received the knowledge of the truth, "there remaineth no more sacrifice for sins?"

Mr. R.—Yes. Paul wrote it in his Epistle to the Hebrews. Some of them were trifling with the blood of Christ, reverting to the types and shadows of the Levitical Law, and trusting to a fulfilled ritual for salvation. He is not referring to ordinary acts of sin. By sinning willfully he means, as he explains it, a "treading under foot the Son of God," and a total and final apostatizing from Christ. Those who reject or neglect Him will find no other sacrifice for sin remaining. Before Christ came the Jewish ceremonies were shadows of the good things to come; but Christ was the substance of them. But now that he has come to put away sin by the sacrifice of Himself, there is no other sacrifice for sin remaining for those who reject Him. God will send no other Saviour, and no further atonement; no second "fountain shall be opened for sin and uncleanness." There remains, therefore, nothing for the rejector of salvation by Christ, but "a fearful looking-for of judgment."

Mr. M.—There are some who say they do not know that they have the right kind of faith.

Mr. R.—God does not ask us if we have the right kind of faith. He tells us the right thing to believe, and the right faith is to believe the right thing, even what God has told us and promised us. If I told you, Mr. Moody, that I had found a hymn-book last night you would believe me, would you not? (Mr. Moody: Yes.) Suppose I said it was the valuable one you lost the other night, you would believe me also just the same. There is no difference in the kind of faith; the difference is in the thing believed. When the Son of God tells me that He died for sinners, that is a fact for my faith to lay hold of: the faith itself is not some thing to be considered. I do not look at my hand, when I take a gift, and wonder what sort of a hand it is. I look at the gift.

Mr. M.—What about those people who say their hearts are so hard, and they have no love to Christ?

Mr. R.—Of course they are hard and cold. No man loves Christ till he believes that Christ loves him. "We love Him, because He first loved us." It is the love of God shed abroad in our hearts by the Holy Ghost that makes the change.

Mr. M.—Paul said he was "crucified with Christ." what did he mean?

Mr. R.—Oh, that is a grand text! Thank God I have been "crucified with Christ." The Cross of Christ represents the death due to the sinner who had broken God's laws. When Christ was crucified every member of His body was crucified: but every believer that was, or is, or shall be, is a member of Christ's body, of His flesh, and of His bones. Again, we read: "Whether one member suffer, all the members suffer with it; or one member be honored, all the members rejoice with it: now ye are the body of Christ, and members in particular." So when Christ was crucified for sin, I was also crucified in Him; and now I am dead and gone as far as my old self is concerned. I have already suffered for sin in Him. Yes; I am dead and buried with Christ. That is the grand truth that Paul laid hold upon. I am stone dead as a sinner in the sight of God. As it is written, I am "become dead to the law by the body of Christ, that I might be married to another, even to Him who is raised from the dead, that I should bring forth fruit unto God." "I am crucified with Christ; nevertheless I live; yet not I, but Christ liveth in me;" and God Himself commands me so to regard my standing before Him as His believing child. "In that Christ died, He died, unto sin once: but in that He liveth, He liveth unto God. Likewise reckon ye also yourselves to be dead indeed unto sin, but alive unto God through Jesus Christ our Lord."

Mr. M.—Should not a man repent a good deal before he comes to Christ?

Mr. R.—"Repent a good deal!" I do not think any man repents in the true sense of the word till he loves Christ and hates sin. There are many false repentances in the Bible. We are told that Pharaoh repented when the judgment of God came upon him, and he said, "I have sinned;" but as soon as the judgment passed away, he went back to his sin. We read that Balaam said: "I have sinned." Yet "he loved the wages of unrighteousness." When Saul lost his kingdom he repented; "I have sinned," he said. When Judas Iscariot found that he had made a great mistake, he said: "I have sinned, in that I have betrayed innocent blood;" yet he went "to his own place." I would not give much for these repentances; I would rather have Peter's repentance: when Christ looked upon His fallen saint it broke His heart, and he went out and wept bitterly. Or the repentance of the Prodigal, when his father's arms were around his neck, and his kisses on his cheek, and he said, "Father, I have sinned against heaven and before thee, and am no more worthy to be called thy son."

Mr. M.—What is your title to heaven?

Mr. R.—The Person, the Life, Death, and Righteousness, of the

God-man, the Son of God, my Substitute, and my Saviour.

Mr. M.—How do you obtain that?

Mr. R.—By receiving Him. "As many as received Him, to them gave He authority to become the sons of God, even to them that believed on His name."

Mr. M.—What is your meetness for heaven?

Mr. R.—The Holy Ghost dwelling in my heart is my fitness for heaven. I have only to get there; and I have, by this great gift, all tastes, desires, and faculties, for it: I have the eyes to contemplate it: I have the ears for heaven's music: and I can speak the language of the country. The Holy Ghost in me is my fitness and qualification for the splendid inheritance for which the Son of God has redeemed me.

Mr. M.—Would you make a distinction between Christ's work for us and the Spirit's work in us?

Mr. R.—Christ's work for me is the payment of my debt; the giving me a place in my Father's home, the place of sonship in my Father's family. The Holy Spirit's work in me is to make me fit for His company.

Mr. M.—You distinguish, then, between the work of the Father, the work of the Son, and the work of the Holy Ghost.

Mr. R.—Thanks be to God, I have them all, and I want them all—Father, Son, and Holy Ghost. I read that my Heavenly Father took my sins and laid them on Christ; "The Lord hath laid on Him the iniquity of us all." No one else had a right to touch them. Then I want the Son, who "His own self bare my sins in His own body on a tree." And I want the Holy Ghost. I should know nothing about this great salvation, and care nothing for it, if the Holy Ghost had not come and told me the story, and given me grace to believe it.

Mr. M.—What is meant when we are told that Christ saves "to the uttermost?"

Mr. R.—That is another grand truth. Some people are troubled by the thought that they will not be able to hold out if they come to Christ. There are so many crooked ways, and pitfalls, and snares in the world; there is the power of the flesh, and the snare of the devil. So they fear they will never get home. The idea of the passage is this. Suppose you are on the top of some splendid mountain, very high up. You look away to where the sun sets, and you see many a river, and many a country, and many a barren waste between. Christ is able to save you through and over them all, out and out, and beyond to the uttermost.

Mr. M.—Suppose a man came in here just out of prison: all his life he has been falling, falling, till he has become discouraged. Can Christ save him all at once?

Mr. R.—It is just as easy for Christ to save a man with the weight of ten thousand sins upon him and all his chains around him, as to save a man with one sin. If a man has offended in one point, the Scripture says he is guilty of all.

Mr. M.—If a man is forgiven, will he go out and do the same thing to-morrow?

Mr. R.—Well, I hope not. All I can say is that if we do, we shall smart for it. I have done many a thing since the Lord revealed Himself to my soul that I should not have done—I have gone backward and downward; but I have always found that it does not pay when I do anything that grieves my Heavenly Father. I think He sometimes allows us to taste the bitterness of what it is to depart from Him. And this is one of the many ways by which He keeps us from falling.

Mr. M.—What do you consider to be the great sin of sins?

Mr. R.—The Word of God tells us that there is only one sin of which God alone can convince us. If I cut a man's throat or if I steal, it does not need God to convince me that that is a sin. But it takes the power of the Holy Ghost to convince me that not to receive Christ, not to love Christ, not to believe in Christ, is the sin of sins, the root of sins. Christ says, "When the Spirit is come, He will convince the world of sin, because they believe not on Me."

Mr. M.—What do you mean by the Word of God?

Mr. R.—The Son of God is the Word of God incarnate: the Bible is the Word of God written. The one is the Word of God in my nature: the other is the Word of God in my language.

Mr. M.—If a man receives the word of God into his heart, what benefit is it to him, right here to-night?

Mr. R.—The Father and the Son will make their abode with him; and he will be the temple of the Holy Ghost. Where He goes the whole Trinity goes; and all the promises are his. "Man doth not live by bread alone; but by every word that proceedeth out of the mouth of God."

Mr. M.—Who is it that judges a man to be unworthy of eternal life?

Mr. R.—Himself!! There is a verse in Acts xiii that is worth remembering: "Seeing ye put it [the Word of God] from you, and judge yourselves unworthy of everlasting life, lo, we turn to the Gentiles." God does not judge us unworthy. He has given His Son for our salvation. When a man puts away the Word of God from him and refuses to receive Christ into his heart, he judges himself unworthy of salvation.

Mr. M.—I understand, then, that if a man rejects Christ to-night, he passes judgment on himself as unworthy of eternal life?

Mr. R.—He is judging himself unworthy, while God does not so consider him. God says you are welcome to eternal life.

Mr. M.—If any one here wants to please God to-night, how can he do it?

Mr. R.—God delights in mercy. Come to God and claim His mercy in Christ; and you will delight His heart.

Mr. M.—Suppose a man say he is not "elected?"

Mr. R.—Do you remember the story of the woman of Canaan? Poor soul; she had come a long journey. She asked the Lord to have mercy on her afflicted child. He wanted to try her faith, and He said: "I am not sent but to the lost sheep of the house of Israel." That looked as if He Himself told her that she was not one of the elect. But she came and worshipped Him, saying, "Lord, help me!" and He helped her there and then. No; there is no election separating between the sinner and Christ.

Mr. M.—Say that again.

Mr. R.—There is no election separating between the sinner and Christ.

Mr. M.—What is there between the sinner and Christ?

Mr. R.—Mercy!! Mercy!!

Mr. M.—That brings me near to Christ.

Mr. R.—So near that we cannot be nearer. But we must claim it. In John we get God's teaching about election. "This is the Father's will which hath sent Me, that of all which He hath given Me I should lose nothing; but should raise it up again at the last day."

He will do his work, you may depend upon it. Then in the next verse we read: "And this is the will of Him that sent Me, that every one which seeth the Son, and believeth on Him, may have everlasting life: and I will raise him up at the last day." That is the part I am to take: and when I have done so I shall know the Father's will concerning me.

Mr. M.—What do you mean by the New Birth?

Mr. R.—I judge it by what I know of the Old Birth. I was born of human parents into the human family; so I belong to Adam's race by nature and by generation, and I inherit Adam's sin and curse accordingly. The new birth is from my union by faith with the second Adam; but this is by grace, not nature: and when I receive the Lord Jesus Christ I am born of God—not by generation, but by regeneration. As I am united to the first Adam by nature and generation, so I am united by faith through grace and regeneration to the second Adam, and inherit all His fullness accordingly.

Mr. M.—What is the meaning of being "saved by the Blood?"

Mr. R.—A gentleman asked me that in the inquiry-room; "What do you mean by the shed Blood?" It is the poured-out life of the Son of God forfeited as the atonement for sinners' sins.

Mr. M.—Is it available now?

Mr. R.—Yes; as much as ever it was.

Mr. M.—You mean it is just as powerful to-day as it was eighteen hundred years ago when He shed it?

Mr. R.—If the blood of Abel cried out for vengeance against his slayer, how much more does the blood of Christ cry out for pardon for all who plead it! "It cleanseth (present tense) from all sin."

Mr. M.—How do you get faith?

Mr. R.—By hearing God's Word. "Faith cometh by hearing; and hearing by the Word of God."

Mr. M.—How do you get the Holy Ghost?

Mr. R.—In the same way as you get faith. The Holy Ghost uses the Word as the chariot by which He enters the believer's soul. The Gospel is called "the ministration of the Spirit."

Mr. M.—Is the Word of God addressed to all here?

Mr. R.—"He that hath an ear, let him hear what the Spirit saith to the Churches" (Rev. iii 22).

Mr. M.—What is the Gospel?

Mr. R.—"Good tidings of great joy, which shall be to all people." If our Gospel, proclaiming life, pardon, and peace, is not as applicable for salvation to the vilest harlot here as to the greatest saint in London, it is not Christ's Gospel we preach.

Mr. M.—What reason does the Scripture give tor the Gospel being hid to some?

Mr. R.—It is "hid to them that are lost; in whom the God of this world hath blinded the minds of them which believe not, lest the light of the glorious Gospel of Christ, who is the image of God, should shine into them." May God open all our eyes, and take away the veil of unbelief with which the devil may be blinding any of us!

Mr. M.—Are there not many who give an intellectual assent to all these things; and who yet have no power, and no divine life?

Mr. R.—An intellectual assent is not faith. I have never found anyone who really believed God's Word who did not get power in believing it. People may assent to it; but I do not admit that that is believing it. I do not think there is any man or woman here who really believes the Gospel of the grace of God, who has not been taught it by the Holy Ghost. I could easily cross-examine any one of those "intellectual believers" who imagines he believes God, but really does not; and he would break down in a few minutes.

Mr. M.—For whom, then, did Christ die?

Mr. R.—For "the ungodly."

Mr. M.—Why is salvation obtained by faith?

Mr. R.—That it might be by grace. "For this cause it is of faith, that it may be according to grace?"

Mr. M.—How may a man know if he has eternal life?

Mr. R.—By not treating God as if He were a liar, when He tells us He has given us eternal life in His Son.

Mr. M.—What is the means by which the New Birth we were speaking of is effected?

Mr. R.—"Of His own will begat He us with the word of truth." "Being born again, not of corruptible seed, but of incorruptible, by the Word of God . . . . and this is the Word, which by the Gospel is preached unto you."

"Oh, the wondrous love of Jesus
To redeem us with His blood!
Through His all-atoning merit,
He has brought us near to God:
For the boundless grace that saves us
We His name will magnify;
He is coming in His glory,
We shall see Him by and by!
Oh, the wondrous love of Jesus
To redeem our souls from death!
We will thank Him, we will praise Him,
While His mercy lends us breath:
We are waiting—only waiting—
Till He comes our souls to bear
To the Home beyond the shadows,
In His Kingdom over there!"
F. J. Crosby

III

MR. MOODY AND MR. RADSTOCK
WHAT IT IS TO BE CONVERTED

MR. MOODY: Christ says, "Except ye be converted, and become as little children, ye shall not enter into the kingdom of heaven." What is it to be converted?

Mr. Radstock: To be "converted" is to turn to God, who is the only one that can save. We cannot save ourselves even by our religion. Therefore, in order to salvation we must turn to God, who alone has the grace, the wisdom, and the power to save.

Mr. M.—What is it to be born of the Spirit?

Mr. R.—Man, by nature, cannot enter into the thoughts of God. He cannot hold communion with God until he has a new nature. The natural man receiveth not the things of the Spirit of God: he has no capacity until he has the new life which God will give him by the power of the Holy Ghost.

Mr. M.—Can he get that to-day if he repents?

Mr. R.—Yes. Repentance means a change of mind—a turning away from his own thoughts to hear the voice and the message of God. If we listen to the voice of God and confess our sins, God is "faithful and just to forgive us our sins."

Mr. M.—To whom are we to confess our sins?

Mr. R.—When the light of God comes in, we see that we are guilty before him; then we are constrained to go and lay our case before Him. If we confess our sins, He is faithful and just to forgive us.

Mr. M.—There is a passage that says the Lord Jesus Christ bear our sins. In what sense did He bear our sins.

Mr. R.—The Lord Jesus Christ had really laid to His charge sins which He had never committed. He was punished as if He had been the sinner. Therefore on the cross He cried out, "My God, my God, why hast Thou forsaken me?" God was dealing with Jesus as if He had really been the guilty one.

Mr. M.—Do we get any help by believing that?

Mr. R.—When I believe God's testimony, God's witness about Jesus, I then can trust myself to God, Giving myself to God, God becomes my Saviour.

Mr. M.—Have these friends the power to believe?

Mr. R.—They are commanded to believe. They can believe it just as well as they can believe any other fact, if they only listen to God's voice. But they must get rid of their own thoughts, and listen to God: Hearing His voice they will believe. "Faith cometh by hearing: and hearing by the Word of God."

Mr. M.—All the sinner has to do is to repose in the promises of God?

Mr. R.—Simply to trust Himself to God.

Mr. M.—What would you say to a man who says he has tried a good many times and failed; and who has become discouraged?

Mr. R.—That man has probably made a good many resolutions, hoping that he would gradually make himself a Christian by going through this or that process, or by doing this or that thing. Of course he failed, because he tried to make himself a Christian. Instead of trying to save himself, let him trust in God, who has pledged His word that every one who believes on the Lord Jesus Christ has at that moment everlasting life.

Mr. M.—Should a man not break off from some of his sins before he comes to God? Suppose he swears or has a bad temper, should he not get a little control over his temper, or stop swearing, before he comes to Christ?

Mr. R.—God knows that a man's nature is wrong: therefore He has promised to give a man a new nature. We must therefore go to God, just as a man goes to a physician, because he needs to be cured of some disease.

Mr. M.—Can a drunkard or a blasphemer be saved all at once?

Mr. R.—Paul says: "To him that worketh not, but believeth on Him that justifieth the ungodly" bad people, lost people, ruined people—"his faith is counted for righteousness." When he believes God, God becomes his Saviour. God is the friend of sinners.

Mr. M.—What is it to believe God?

Mr. R.—To take Him at His word.

Mr. M.—Do you not think there are a good many here who believe that Jesus Christ is the Saviour of the world; and yet they are not saved?

Mr. R.—No doubt; because they have not believed for themselves. A man at the time of the Deluge, for instance, might have said, "Yes, I believe it is a very good ark indeed; and that it will save those who get into it." But it does not follow that he got into it himself. The ark only saved those who went into it. So, when a man trusts in Jesus Christ for himself, Jesus becomes his personal and eternal Saviour.

Mr. M.—What if he should fall into sin after he has believed in Christ?

Mr. R.—"These things write I unto you that ye sin not," says John; "and if any man sin, we have an Advocate with the Father." The Good Physician will not give up His case because of the disease; He will deal with it. The Good Shepherd will not turn His poor wandering sheep away; He will go after it, and bring it back. He has promised that He will save His people from their sins.

Mr. M.—Is salvation within the reach of every man here tonight?

Mr. R.—Jesus said, "God so loved the world that He gave his only begotten Son, that whosoever believeth in Him should not perish, but have everlasting life."

Mr. M.—But some say they do not feel that; they do not realize it.

Mr. R.—When they take God at His word, and cast themselves upon Him, whether they feel it or not—when they confess Jesus Christ as their Lord—the Holy Ghost will come as a power to make them realize it. For instance, a man at the time of the Deluge might have stood outside the ark, and said, "I cannot realize how this ark will lift me up above the waters." But if he were inside when the flood came he would realize it. The sinner must believe first, and have his experience afterwards. A man is told that a certain train will take him to Edinburgh. He has never been there: he does not understand about this particular train; and he cannot realize that it will take him there. But he knows that he may trust the friend who told him; so he gets into the train. Then he realizes that he is in the train; by and by he will be able to realize that he is in Edinburgh.

Mr. M.—Would you advise people to come to God as they are, with their unfeeling, treacherous, hard hearts—with any kind of heart?

Mr. R.—God has provided this salvation for lost sinners—those who are thoroughly bad and corrupt. It is for such that God has shown His salvation, His love, His grace.

Mr. M.—What would you say to any one who thinks he has no power to believe?

Mr. R.—He has the power to believe. Probably he is trying to believe something about himself; to feel something about himself instead of giving credit to God—He is not asked to realize this or that about himself, but to believe the faithful God.

Mr. M.—Some say they have no power to overcome a besetting sin?

Mr. R.—Jesus came proclaiming liberty to the captives. As we read in the beautiful words of the Church of England Prayer-book: "Though we be tied and bound by the chains of our sin, let the pitifulness of Thy mercy save us." Jesus Christ takes the prisoners of sin and breaks off their chains.

Mr. M.—There is something said about confessing Christ. Would you advise any one who wants to become a Christian to start right here by confessing Christ with the mouth?

Mr. R.—God is already on your side, whoever you are. Christ is Immanuel—God with us and for us. He is already on your side, whether you believe it or not. Now it is for you to decide whether He shall be your Saviour. He says that if you own Him as Lord—who is now the one rejected by the world—He is responsible to be your Saviour from that moment.

SOWING AND REAPING

By

D. L. Moody

'Whatsoever a man soweth, that shall he also reap.'
Gal. vi: 7.

CONTENTS

Chapter 1. Sowing and Reaping   107

Chapter 2. Be Not Deceived: God Is Not Mocked   116

Chapter 3. When a Man Sows, He Expects to Reap   124

Chapter 4. A Man Reaps the Same Kind as He Sows   135

Chapter 5. A Man Reaps More than He Sows   144

Chapter 6. Ignorance of the Seed Makes No Difference   149

Chapter 7. Forgiveness and Retribution   157

Chapter 8. Warning   167

CHAPTER I
SOWING AND REAPING

"Be not deceived; God is not mocked: for whatsoever a man soweth, that shall he also reap. For he that soweth to his flesh shall of the flesh reap corruption; but he that soweth to the Spirit shall of the Spirit reap life everlasting." Galatians vi: 7, 8.

I think this passage contains truths that no infidel or sceptic will dare to deny. There are some passages in the Word of God that need no other proof than that which we can easily find in our daily experience. This is one of them. If the Bible were to be blotted out of existence, the words I have quoted would be abundantly verified by what is constantly happening around us. We have only to take up the daily papers to see them being fulfilled before our eyes.

I remember giving out this text once when a man stood right up in the audience and said:

"I don't believe it."

I said, "My friend, that doesn't change the fact. Truth is truth whether you believe it or not, and a lie is a lie whether you believe it or not."

He didn't want to believe it. When the meeting broke up, an officer was at the door to arrest him. He was tried and sent to the penitentiary for twelve months for stealing. I really believe that when he got into his cell, he believed that he had to reap what he sowed.

We might as well try to blot the sun out of the heavens as to blot this truth out of the Word of God. It is heaven's eternal decree. The law has been enforced for six thousand years. Did not God make Adam reap even before he left Eden? Had not Cain to reap outside of Eden? A king on the throne, like David, or a priest behind the altar, like Eli; priest and prophet, preacher and hearer, every man must reap what he sows. I believed it ten years ago, but I believe it a hundred times more to-day.

My text applies to the individual, whether he be saint or sinner or hypocrite who thinks he is a saint; it applies to the family; it applies to society; it applies to nations. I say the law that the result of actions must be reaped is as true for nations as for individuals; indeed, some one has said that as nations have no future existence, the present world is the only place to punish them as nations. See how God has dealt with them. See if they have not reaped what they sowed. Take Amalek: "Remember what Amalek did unto thee by the way, when ye were come forth out of Egypt; how he met thee, by the way, and smote the hindmost of thee, even all that were feeble behind thee, when thou wast faint and weary; and he feared not God." What was to be the result of this attack? Was it to go unpunished? God ordained that Amalek should reap as they sowed, and the nation was all but wiped out of existence under King Saul.

What has become of the monarchies and empires of the world? What brought ruin on Babylon? Her king and people would not obey God, and ruin came upon them. What has become of Greece and all her power? She once ruled the world. What has become of Rome and all her greatness? When their cup of iniquity was full, it was dashed to the ground. What has become of the Jews? They rejected salvation, persecuted God's messengers, and crucified their Redeemer; and we find that eleven hundred thousand of them perished at one time. Look at the history of this country. With an open Bible, our forefathers planted slavery; but judgment came at last. There was not a family North or South that had not to mourn over some one taken from them. Take the case of France. It is said that a century ago men were spending millions every year in France in the publication and distribution of infidel literature. What has been the harvest? Has France not reaped? Mark the result: "The Bible was suppressed. God was denied. Hell broke loose. Half the children born in Paris were bastards. More than a million of persons were beheaded, shot, drowned, outraged, and done to death between September, 1792, and December, 1795. Since that time France has had thirteen revolutions in eighty years; and in the republic there has been an overturn on an average once in nine months. One-third of the births in Paris are illegitimate; ten thousand new-born infants have been fished out at the outlet of the city sewers in a single year; the native population of France is decreasing; the percentage of suicides is greater in Paris than in any city in Christendom; and since the French Revolution there have been enough French men and women slaughtered in the streets of Paris in the various insurrections, to average more than two thousand five hundred each year!"

The principle was not new in Scripture or in history when Paul enunciated it in his letter to the Galatians. Paul clothes it in language derived from the farm, but in other dress the Law of Sowing and Reaping may be seen in the Law of Cause and Effect, the Law of Retribution or Retaliation, the Law of Compensation. It is not to my purpose to enter now into a philosophical discussion of the law as it appears under any of these names. We see that it exists. It is beyond reasonable dispute. Whatever else sceptics may carp at and criticise in the Bible, they must acknowledge the truth of this. It does not depend upon revelation for its support; philosophers are agreed upon it as much as they are agreed upon any thing.

The Supremacy of Law

The objection may be made, however, that while its application may be admitted in the physical world, it is not so certain in the spiritual sphere. It is just here that modern research steps in. The laws of the spiritual world have been largely identified as the same laws that exist in the natural world. Indeed, it is claimed that the spiritual existed first, that the natural came after, and that when God proceeded to frame the universe, He went upon lines already laid down.

In short, that God projected the higher laws downward, so that the natural world became "an incarnation, a visible representation, a working model of the supernatural." "In the spiritual world the same wheels work—without the iron."

Our whole life is thus bounded and governed by laws ordained and established by God, and that a man reaps what he sows is a law that can be easily observed and verified, whether we regard sowing to the flesh or sowing to the Spirit. The evil harvest of sin and the good harvest of righteousness are as sure to follow the sowing as the harvest of wheat and barley. "Life is not casual, but causal."

We shall see, as we proceed, that the working of the law is evident in the earliest periods of Bible history. Job's three friends reasoned that he must be a great sinner, because they took it for granted that the calamities that overtook him must be the results of his wickedness. "Remember, I pray thee," said one of them, "who ever perished, being innocent? or where were the righteous cut off? Even as I have seen, they that plough iniquity, and sow wickedness, reap the same."

In the book of Proverbs we find it written: "The wicked worketh a deceitful work: but to him that soweth righteousness shall be a sure reward." And again: "He that soweth iniquity shall reap vanity."

In Isaiah we find these words: "Say ye to the righteous that it shall be well with him; for they shall eat the fruit of their doings. Woe unto the wicked! it shall be ill with him: for the reward of his hands shall be given him."

Hosea prophesied regarding Israel: "They have sown the wind, and they shall reap the whirlwind." "Sow to yourselves in righteousness," he advised them, "reap in mercy."

Teaching from Analogy

The Bible is full of analogies drawn from nature. When Christ was on earth, it was His favorite mode of teaching to convey heavenly truths in earthly dress. "Truths came forth from His lips," wrote one, "not stated simply on authority, but based on the analogy of the universe. His human mind, in perfect harmony with the Divine mind with which it was united, discerned the connection of things, and read the eternal will in the simplest laws of nature. For instance, if it were a question whether God would give His Spirit to them that asked, it was not replied to by a truth revealed on His authority: the answer was derived from facts lying open to all men's observation. 'Behold the fowls of the air'; 'behold the lilies of the field'—learn from them the answer to your question. A principle was there. God supplies the wants He has created. He feeds the ravens—He clothes the lilies—He will feed with His Spirit the craving spirits of His children."

This is the style of teaching that Paul adopts in the text. He takes the simple process of sowing and reaping, a process familiar to all, and reads in it a deeply spiritual and moral meaning. It is as if he said that every man as he journeys through life is scattering seed at every step. The seed consists of his thoughts, his words, his actions. They pass from him, and by and by (it may be sooner or later), they spring up and bear fruit, and the reaping time comes.

Life a Seed-Time

The analogy contains some solemn lessons. Life is to be regarded as a seed-time. Every one has his field to sow, to cultivate, and finally, to reap. By our habits, by our intercourse with friends and companions, by exposing ourselves to good or bad influences, we are cultivating the seed for the coming harvest. We cannot see the seed as it grows and develops, but time will reveal it.

Just as the full-grown harvest is potentially contained in the seed, so the full results of sin or holiness are potentially contained in the sinful or holy deed. "When lust hath conceived, it bringeth forth sin, and sin, when it is finished, bringeth forth death."

Just as we cannot reap a good harvest unless we have sown good seed, so we cannot reap eternal life unless we have sown to the Spirit. Weeds are easy to grow. They grow without the planting. And sin springs up naturally in the human heart. Ever since our first parents broke away from God, the human heart has of itself been thoroughly vile, and all its fruits have been evil. "The heart of the sons of men is fully set in them to do evil." Do you doubt it? If you do, ask yourself what would become of a child if it was left to itself—no training, no guidance, no education. In spite of all that is done for children, the evil too often gets the upper hand. The good seed must be planted and cared for, often with toil and trouble: but the harvest will be sure.

Do we desire the love of our fellows in our seasons of trial? Then we must love them when they need its cheering influence most. Do we long for sympathy in our sorrow and pain? Then we shall have it if we have also wept with those who weep. Are we hoping to reap eternal life? Then we must not sow to the flesh, or we shall reap corruption, but to the Spirit, then the promise is that we shall reap its immortal fruits.

Dr. Chalmers has drawn attention to the difference between the act of sowing and the act of reaping. "Let it be observed," he says, "that the act of indulging in the desires of the flesh is one thing and the act of providing for the indulgence of them is another. When a man, on the impulse of sudden provocation, wreaks his resentful feelings upon the neighbor who has offended him, he is not at that time preparing for the indulgence of a carnal feeling, but actually indulging it. He is not at that time sowing, but reaping (such as it is) a harvest of gratification. This distinction may serve to assist our judgment in estimating the ungodliness of certain characters. The rambling voluptuary who is carried along by every impulse, and all whose powers of mental discipline are so enfeebled that he has become the slave of every propensity, lives in the perpetual harvest of criminal gratification. A daughter whose sole delight is in her rapid transitions from one scene of expensive brilliancy to another, who dissipates every care and fills every hour among the frivolities and fascinations of her volatile society,—she leads a life than which nothing can be imagined more opposite to a life of preparation for the coming judgment or the coming eternity. Yet she reaps rather than sows. It lies with another to gather the money which purchaseth all things, and with her to taste the fruits of the purchase. It is the father who sows. It is he who sits in busy and brooding anxiety over his speculations, wrinkled, perhaps, by care, and sobered by years into an utter distaste for the splendors and insignificancies of fashionable life." The father sows, and he reaps in his daughter's life.

"Painting for Eternity"

A famous painter was well known for the careful manner in which he went about his work. When some one asked him why he took such pains, he replied:

"Because I am painting for eternity."

It is a solemn thing to think that the future will be the harvest of the present—that my condition in my dying hour may depend upon my actions to-day! Belief in a future life and in a coming judgment magnifies the importance of the present. Eternal issues depend upon it. The opportunity for sowing will not last forever; it is slipping through our fingers moment by moment; and the future can only reveal the harvest of the seed sown now.

A sculptor once showed a visitor his studio. It was full of statues of gods. One was very curious. The face was concealed by being covered with hair, and there were wings on each foot.

"What is his name?" said the visitor.

"Opportunity," was the reply.

"Why is his face hidden?"

"Because men seldom know him when he comes to them."

"Why has he wings on his feet?"

"Because he is soon gone, and once gone can never be overtaken."

It becomes us, then, to make the most of the opportunities God has given us. It depends a good deal on ourselves what our future shall be. We can sow for a good harvest, or we can do like the Sioux Indians, who once, when the United States Commissioner of Indian Affairs sent them a supply of grain for sowing, ate it up. Men are constantly sacrificing their eternal future to the passing enjoyment of the present moment; they fail or neglect to recognize the dependence of the future upon the present.

Nothing Trifling

From this we may learn that there is no such thing as a trifle on earth. When we realize that every thought and word and act has an eternal influence, and will come back to us in the same way as the seed returns in the harvest, we must perceive their responsibility, however trifling they may seem. We are apt to overlook the results that hinge on small things. The law of gravitation was suggested by the fall of an apple. It is said that some years ago a Harvard professor brought some gypsy-moths to this country in the hope that they could with advantage be crossed with silkworms. The moths accidentally got away, and multiplied so enormously that the Commonwealth of Massachusetts has had to spend hundreds of thousands of dollars trying to exterminate them.

When H. M. Stanley was pressing his way through the forests of Darkest Africa, the most formidable foes that he encountered, those that caused most loss of life to his caravan and came the nearest to entirely defeating his expedition, were the little Wambutti dwarfs. So annoying were they that very slow progress could be made through their dwelling places.

These little men had only little bows and little arrows that looked like children's playthings, but upon these tiny arrows there was a small drop of poison which would kill an elephant or a man as quickly and as surely as a Winchester rifle. Their defense was by means of poison and traps. They would steal through the darkness of the forest and, waiting in ambush, let fly their deadly arrows before they could be discovered. They dug ditches and carefully covered them over with leaves. They fixed spikes in the ground and tipped them with the most deadly poison, and then covered them. Into these ditches and on these spikes man and beast would fall or step to their death.

A lady once writing to a young man in the navy who was almost a stranger, thought "Shall I close this as anybody would, or shall I say a word for my Master?" and, lifting up her heart for a moment, she wrote, telling him that his constant change of scene and place was an apt illustration of the word, "Here we have no continuing city," and asked if he could say: "I seek one to come." Tremblingly she folded it and sent it off.

Back came the answer. "Thank you so much for those kind words! I am an orphan, and no one has spoken to me like that since my mother died, long years ago." The arrow shot at venture hit home, and the young man shortly after rejoiced in the fulness of the blessing of the gospel of peace.

An obscure man preached one Sunday to a few persons in a Methodist chapel in the South of England. A boy of fifteen years of age was in the audience, driven into the chapel by a snowstorm. The man took as his text the words, "Look unto me and be ye saved," and as he stumbled along as best he could, the light of heaven flashed into that boy's heart. He went out of the chapel saved, and soon became known as C. H. Spurgeon, the boy-preacher.

The parsonage at Epworth, England, caught fire one night, and all the inmates were rescued except one son. The boy came to a window, and was brought safely to the ground by two farm-hands, one standing on the shoulder of the other. The boy was John Wesley. If you would realize the responsibility of that incident, if you would measure the consequences of that rescue, ask the millions of Methodists who look back to John Wesley as the founder of their denomination.

CHAPTER II
BE NOT DECEIVED; GOD IS NOT MOCKED

"Let no man deceive you."—Eph. v: 6.

"As one man mocketh another, do ye so mock Him?"—Job xiii: 9.

We have all lived long enough to know what it is to be deceived. We have been deceived by our friends, by our enemies, our neighbors, our relatives. Ungodly companions have deceived us. At every turn of life we have been imposed upon in one way or another.

False teachers have crossed our path, and under pretence of doing us good, have poisoned our mind with error. They have held out hopes to us that have proved false; apples of Sodom, fair without, but full of ashes within. They have told us that there is no God, no future life, no judgment to come; or they have said that all men will be saved, that there is ample time to repent, that we may be saved by doing the best we can.

Sin has deceived us. Every sinner is under a delusion. Sin meets him smilingly, and holds out to him pleasures and delights that are not pure and lasting.

During our meetings in Boston a young man came into the Tabernacle. He looked around, and he thought to himself the people that came there were great fools—those who had business, and comfortable homes, and good clothes. He had nothing in the world—he was a tramp, and went in there to keep himself warm. But to think that people who had homes would come and spend their time in listening to such stuff as I preached was more than he could understand.

One night after he had been coming there for two weeks, I happened to point right down where he was sitting, and I said, "Young man, be not deceived!" God used that as an arrow. He began to think about himself. His mind went back to the time when he had a good situation in Boston; when he was a young man getting a good salary; when he was in good society, and had a great many friends.

Then he looked at his present condition. His friends were all gone, his clothes were gone, his money was gone; and there he was, an outcast in that city. He said to himself, "I have been deceived," and that very hour God waked him. He wanted to get friends to pray for him; but as he was not able to buy a piece of paper, or pay for a postage stamp, he got an old piece of soiled paper, stood up in the street, and wrote a request to be read in the Tabernacle, that if God would save a poor, lost man like him, he wanted to be saved. That prayer was answered. As in the case of Nebuchadnezzar, his friends gathered around him again, and the Lord restored him to position and to society. His eyes were opened to see how he had been deceived.

Satan

How many men all over the world are being deceived by the god of this world! It has been asserted that during the late Franco-German war, German drummers and trumpeters used to give the French beats and calls in order to deceive their enemies. The command to "halt," or "cease firing," was often given by the Germans, it has been said, and the French soldiers were thus placed in positions where they could be shot down like cattle.

Satan is the arch-enemy of our souls, and he has often blinded our reason and deceived our conscience by his falsehoods. He has often come as an angel of light, concealing his hideousness under a borrowed cloak. He says to a young man: "Sow your wild oats. Time enough to be religious when you grow old." The young man yields himself to a life of extravagance and excess, under the false hope that he will obtain solid satisfaction; and it is well if he awakens to the deception before his appetites become tyrants, dragging him down into depths of want and woe. Satan promises great things to his victims in the indulgence of their lusts, but they never realize the promises. The promised pleasure turns out to be pain, the promised heaven a hell.

Beware lest Satan deceive you as he deceived Eve in the beginning. "There is no truth in him. When he speaketh a lie, he speaketh of his own, for he is a liar, and the father of it."

Our Heart

But we have been deceived by our own heart most of all. Who has not proved the truth of the Scripture: "The heart is deceitful above all things and desperately wicked; who can know it?" "How many times we have said that we never would do a certain thing again, and then have done it within twenty-four hours! A man may think he has fathomed its depths, but he finds there are further depths he has not reached. What gross self-deception is due to it! "He that trusteth in his own heart is a fool," said Solomon. Luther once said he feared his own heart more than the Pope and all the cardinals.

Many a weeping wife has come to me about her husband, saying: "He is good at heart." The truth is—that is the worst spot in him. If the heart was good, all else would be right. Out of the heart are the issues of life. Christ said: "From within, out of the heart of men, proceed evil thoughts, adulteries, fornications, murders, thefts, covetousness, wickedness, deceit, lasciviousness, an evil eye, blasphemy, pride, foolishness." That is Christ's own statement regarding the unregenerate heart.

Some years ago a remarkable picture was exhibited in London. As you looked at it from a distance, you seemed to see a monk engaged in prayer, his hands clasped, his head bowed. As you came nearer, however, and examined the painting more closely, you saw that in reality he was squeezing a lemon into a punch bowl!

What a picture that is of the human heart! Superficially examined, it is thought to be the seat of all that is good and noble and pleasing in a man; whereas in reality, until regenerated by the Holy Ghost, it is the seat of all corruption. "This is the condemnation, that light is come into the world, and men loved darkness rather than light."

A Jewish rabbi once asked his scholars what was the best thing a man could have in order to keep him in the straight path. One said a good disposition; another, a good companion; another said wisdom was the best thing he could desire. At last a scholar replied that he thought a good heart was best of all.

"True," said the rabbi, "you have comprehended all that the others have said. For he that hath a good heart will be of a good disposition, and a good companion, and a wise man. Let every one, therefore, cultivate a sincerity and uprightness of heart at all times, and it will save him an abundance of sorrow." We need to make the prayer of David—"Create in me a clean heart, O God, and renew a right spirit within me!"

God Is Not Mocked

Bear in mind, the God of the Bible has never deceived anyone, and never can, and never will; that is the difference between the God of the Bible and the god of this world. He beholds the ways of men; He looks into their hearts; He knows their secret ways; they need not tell Him or try to conceal anything from Him.

However successfully we may deceive or be deceived by ourselves or others, we cannot deceive Him. Adam and Eve tried it in Eden when they hid themselves from the presence of Jehovah amongst the trees of the garden. Saul tried it when he spared the best of the sheep and oxen of the Amalekites under the pretence of sacrificing them to God. Ananias and Sapphira tried it when they kept back part of the price of the land they sold. "Why hath Satan filled thine heart to lie unto (deceive) the Holy Ghost? * * * Thou hast not lied unto men, but unto God."

Men try it every day. They have got it into their heads that God can be mocked. Because they can deceive their pastor, and their employer, and their friends, they think they can deceive God. They put on false appearances, they use empty words, they perform unreal service, they make idle excuses, they indulge in all kinds of hypocrisy. But it is of no avail. God cannot be imposed upon. He sees the corruption inside the whited sepulchre.

Warning to Christians

It is worth noticing that this warning was given by Paul to Christian men—converts in the Galatian church. After all, a man is not all the time deceived about the grosser sins. The drunkard realizes in his sober moments what must be the end of a course of intemperance. Loss of self-respect and of the esteem of friends, the marks he soon begins to bear in his body—unsteady hands and discolored features—these things are the quick harvest of drunkenness, and may easily be detected as they ripen. The licentious man, also, reaps the early fruit of his sin in diseases of the body, which are often effective warnings against continuing in such a dangerous path. But with "respectable" sins it is different. A man may be sowing for years, and not even realize it himself.

You remember that in the parable of the sower some seeds fell among thorns, and the thorns sprung up and choked them. Our Master, expounding this parable, said: "He that received seed among the thorns is he that heareth the word: but the care of this world and the deceitfulness of riches choke the word, and he becometh unfruitful." Who would have expected this result of the world or of riches? But it has been said that Christ never spoke of riches except in words of warning. We are not apt to regard them in that light to-day. Men are trampling each other down in the pursuit of wealth. "Be not deceived." He who sets his heart upon money is sowing to the flesh, and shall of the flesh reap corruption.

"Adversity hath slain her thousands, but prosperity her tens of thousands."

"What is the value of this estate?" said a gentleman to another, as they passed a fine mansion surrounded by fair and fertile fields.

"I don't know what it is valued at; I know what it cost its late possessor."

"How much?"

"His soul."

An English clergyman was called to the death-bed of a wealthy parishioner. Kneeling beside the dying man the pastor asked him to take his hand as he prayed for his upholding in that solemn hour, but he declined to give it. After the end had come, and they turned down the coverlet, the rigid hands were found holding the safe-key in their death-grip. Heart and hand, to the last, clinging to his possessions, but he could not take them with him.

A man may be proud, and his very sin reckoned a virtue. Hear what the Word of God says: "Haughtiness of eyes and a proud heart is sin"; "every one that is proud in heart is an abomination to the Lord."

These are the mistakes men make. They are leading respectable lives, and they think that all is well. They do not recognize the taint of corruption upon many of the most cherished objects of their hearts. Christian professors, most of all, need to beware lest they are being deceived.

Neglect

How watchful men should be of their thoughts, their practices, their feelings! The reason of deception is, for the most part, neglect. Men do not stop to examine themselves, to lay their hearts and minds bare as in the sight of God, and judge themselves by His most holy will. A man need not shoot himself in order to commit suicide: he need only neglect the proper means of sustenance, and he will soon die. Where an enemy is strong and aggressive, an army is doomed to sure defeat and capture unless a sharp look-out is kept, every man wide awake at his post of duty.

It has been noticed that there are more accidents in Switzerland in fine seasons than in stormy ones. People are apt to undertake expeditions that they would not take under less favorable conditions, and they are less careful in their conduct. And so it is that moral and spiritual disaster usually overtakes men when they are off their guard, careless against temptation. They become proud and self-reliant in seasons of prosperity, whereas adversity drives them to the living God for guidance and comfort.

Dr. Johnson once said that it is more from carelessness regarding the truth than from intentional lying that there is so much falsehood in the world.

Hence the necessity of continual watchfulness. The Persians had an annual festival when they slew all the serpents and venomous creatures they could find; but they allowed them to swarm as fast and freely as ever until the festival came round once more. It was poor policy. Sins, like serpents, breed quickly, and need to be constantly watched.

And we ought to watch on every side. Many a man has fallen at the very point where he thought he was safest. The meekness of Moses has passed into a proverb. Yet he lost the Promised Land, because he allowed the children of Israel to provoke him, and "he spake unadvisedly with his lips." Peter was the most zealous and defiant of the disciples, bold and outspoken; yet he degenerated for a short time into a lying, swearing, sneaking coward, afraid of a maid.

There is an old fable that a doe that had but one eye used to graze near the sea; and in order to be safe, she kept her blind eye toward the water, from which side she expected no danger, while with the good eye she watched the country. Some men, perceiving this, took a boat and came upon her from the sea and shot her. With her dying breath, she said:

"Oh! hard fate! that I should receive my death-wound from

that side whence I expected no harm, and be safe in the part where I looked for most danger."

Let danger and need drive you closer to God. He never slumbers or sleeps, and in His keeping you will be safe. Seize hold of Him in prayer. "Watch and pray."

Christianity Not Responsible

Christianity is not responsible for the deception that exists among its professing disciples. The illustration has been used before that you might just as reasonably hold the Cunard company responsible for the suicide of a passenger who jumps overboard one of their vessels at sea. Had the person remained on the vessel, he would have been safe; and had the disciple remained true to his principles, he would never have turned out a hypocrite. Was anybody ever more severe in denouncing hypocrisy than Christ? Do you want to know the reason why, every now and then, the church is scandalized by the exposure of some leading church member or Sabbath school superintendent? It is not his Christianity, but his lack of it. Some secret sin has been eating at the heart of the tree, and in a critical moment it is blown down and its rottenness revealed.

The Deception Can Not Last Forever

It is impossible for the deception to last forever. Lincoln had a saying that you may be able to deceive all the people some of the time, and some of the people all of the time, but you will not be able to deceive all the people all of the time. Death will uncover the deception, if it has not been detected sooner; and the unfortunate victim will stand, undeceived, in the presence of a God who cannot be mocked.

CHAPTER III

WHEN A MAN SOWS, HE EXPECTS TO REAP

"Behold, the husbandman waiteth for the precious fruit of the earth, and hath long patience for it, until he receive the early and latter rain."—James v: 7.

Notice these four things about sowing and reaping: A man expects to reap when he sows; he expects to reap the same kind of seed that he sows; he expects to reap more; and ignorance of the kind of seed makes no difference.

First: When a man sows, he expects to reap.

If a farmer went on sowing, spring after spring, and never reaping in the autumn, you would say he was a fit subject for the lunatic asylum. No; he is always looking forward to the time when he will reap the reward of his toil. He never expects that the seed he has sown will be lost.

A young man serves a long apprenticeship to some trade or profession; but he expects by and by to reap the fruit of all those years of patient industry. Ask an engineer why he works so hard for five, six, or seven years in the endeavor to learn his profession. He replies that he is looking forward to the reaping time, when his fortune and reputation will be made. The lawyer studies long and hard; but he, too, anticipates the time when his clients will be numerous, and he will be repaid for his toil. A great many medical students have a hard time trying to support themselves while they are at college. As soon as they get their diploma and become doctors they expect that the reaping time is coming; that is what they have been working for.

Some harvests ripen almost immediately, but as a rule we

find it true in the natural world that there is delay before the seed comes to maturity. It is growing all the time, however; first the little green shoot breaking through the soil, then the blade, then the ear, then the full corn in the ear. The farmer is not disappointed because all his crops do not spring up in a night like mushrooms. He looks forward with patience, knowing that the reaping time will come in due season.

So with the harvest of our actions. Few men, if any, would indulge in sin unless they expected pleasure out of it. A drunkard does not drink for the mere sake of drinking, but in the hope of present enjoyment. A thief does not steal for the mere sake of stealing, but for the sake of gain. And similarly with the good man. He does not make sacrifices merely for the sake of sacrifice, but because thereby he hopes and expects to do good, and help others. All these things are means to ends: there is always expectation of a harvest.

The Certainty of the Reaping

The text bids us look forward to the certainty of the reaping: "Whatsoever a man soweth, that shall he also reap."

We know what it is to have a failure of the crops, but in the spiritual world no such failure is possible. Wet soil may rot the seed, or frost may nip the early buds, or the weather may prove too wet or too dry to bring the crops to maturity, but none of these things occur to prevent the harvest of one's actions. The Bible tells us that God will render to every man according to his deeds. "To them who by patient continuance in well-doing seek for glory and honor and immortality, eternal life: but unto them that are contentious, and do not obey the truth, but obey unrighteousness, indignation and wrath, tribulation and anguish upon every soul of man that doeth evil." How careful we should be of our actions in all departments of our being, physical, moral, intellectual! The deeds we do, the words we speak, the thoughts we harbor, are all recorded, and shall meet their just reward, for God is no respecter of persons.

And it must not be overlooked that the harvest comes as a

necessary consequence of the sowing. It has been said that God is not a sort of a moral despot, as He is so frequently regarded. He does not sit on a throne, attaching penalties to particular actions as they come up for judgment. He has laid down certain laws, of which the law of sowing and reaping is one, and punishment is the natural outcome of sin. There is no escape. It must be borne; and though others may have to reap with you, no one can reap for you.

The text teaches, further, that the harvest is one or other of two kinds. There are two, and only two, directions in which the law leads: Sowing to the flesh, and a harvest of corruption—sowing to the Spirit, and a harvest of everlasting life.

Sowing to the Flesh

"Sowing to the flesh" does not mean simply taking due care of the body. The body was made in the image of God, and the body of a believer is a temple of the Holy Ghost, and we may be sure that due care for the image is well-pleasing to God. The expression refers rather to pandering to the lusts of the body, pampering it, providing gratification for its unlawful desires at the expense of the higher part of a man, indulging the animal propensities which in their excess are sinful. "Sowing to the flesh" is scattering the seeds of selfishness, which always must yield a harvest of corruption.

"When we were in the flesh, the motions of sins did work in our members to bring forth fruit unto death." And what does Paul say are the works of the flesh? "Adultery, fornication, uncleanness, lasciviousness, idolatry, witchcraft, hatred, variance, emulations, wrath, strife, seditions, heresies, envyings, murders, drunkenness, revellings, and such like."

I was at the Paris exhibition in 1867, and I noticed there a little oil painting, only about a foot square, and the face was the most hideous I have ever seen. On the paper attached to the painting were the words "Sowing the tares," and the face looked more like a demon's than a man's. As he sowed these tares, up came serpents and reptiles, and they were crawling up on his body, and all around were woods with wolves and animals prowling in them. I have seen that picture many times since. Ah! the reaping time is coming. If you sow to the flesh you must reap the flesh. If you sow to the wind you must reap the whirlwind.

And yet it must not be thought that indulgence in the grosser vices is the only way of sowing to the flesh. Every desire, every action that has not God for its end and object is seed sown to the flesh. If a man is sowing for a harvest of money or ambition, he is sowing to the flesh, and will reap corruption, just as surely as the liar and adulterer. No matter how "polite" and "refined" and "respectable" the seed may be, no matter how closely it resembles the good seed, its true nature will out, the blight of corruption will be upon it.

How foolish are the strivings of men in view of this judgment! Many a man will sacrifice time, health—even his character—for money. What does he gain? Corruption; something that is not eternal, that has not the qualities of "everlasting life." John said, "The world passeth away, and the lust thereof." Peter said, "All flesh is as grass, and all the glory of man as the flower of grass. The grass withereth, and the flower thereof falleth away." None of these fleshly things have their roots in the eternal. You may even outlive them in your own short life.

No Bridge Between

Now, men make this mistake—they sow to the flesh, and they think they will reap the harvest of the spirit; and on the other hand, they sow to the spirit and are disappointed when they do not reap a temporal harvest.

A teacher had been relating to his class the parable of the rich man and Lazarus, and he asked:

"Now, which would you rather be, boys, the rich man or Lazarus?"

One boy answered, "I would rather be the rich man while I live, and Lazarus when I die."

That cannot be: it is flesh and corruption, or, Spirit and

everlasting life. There is no bridge from one to the other.

"Seed which is sown for a spiritual harvest has no tendency whatever to procure temporal well-being. Christ declared, 'Blessed are the pure in heart; for they shall see God; blessed are they that hunger and thirst after righteousness, for they shall be filled' (with righteousness); 'blessed are they that mourn, for they shall be comforted.' You observe the beatific vision of the Almighty—fulness of righteousness—divine comfort. There is nothing earthly here, it is spiritual results for spiritual labor. It is not said that the pure in heart shall be made rich; or that they who hunger and thirst after righteousness shall be filled with bread, or that they who mourn shall rise in life, and obtain distinction. Each department has its own appropriate harvest, reserved exclusively to its own method of sowing.

"Everything reaps its own harvest, every act has its own reward. And before you covet the enjoyment which another possesses, you must first calculate the cost at which it was procured.

"For instance, the religious tradesman complains that his honesty is a hindrance to his success; that the tide of custom pours into the doors of his less scrupulous neighbor in the same street, while he himself waits for hours idle. My brother, do you think that God is going to reward honor, integrity, high-mindedness, with this world's coin? Do you fancy that He will pay spiritual excellence with plenty of custom? Now consider the price that man has paid for his success. Perhaps mental degradation and inward dishonor. His advertisements are all deceptive, his treatment of his workmen tyrannical, his cheap prices made possible by inferior articles. Sow that man's seed, and you will reap that man's harvest. Cheat, lie, be unscrupulous in your assertions, and custom will come to you. But if the price be too high, let him have his harvest, and you take yours—a clear conscience, a pure mind, rectitude within and without. Will you part with that for his harvest?"

Sowing to the Spirit

"Sowing to the Spirit" implies self-denial, resistance of evil, obedience to the Spirit, walking in the Spirit, living in the Spirit, guidance by the Spirit. We sow to the Spirit when we use our abilities and means to advance Spiritual things; when we support and encourage those who are extending the influence of the Spirit. We sow to the Spirit when we crucify the flesh and all its lusts, when we yield ourselves to Him as we once yielded ourselves to the flesh. A Jewish rabbi once said: "There are in every man two impulses, good and evil. He who offers God his evil impulses offers the best sacrifice."

The fruit of such sowing is "love, joy, peace, longsuffering, gentleness, goodness, faith, meekness, temperance."

In this world the harvest is growth of character, deeper respect, increasing usefulness to others; in the next world, acceptance with God, everlasting life.

Among the last recorded words of Henry Lloyd Garrison in his public speeches in England were these "I began my advocacy of the anti-slavery cause in the Northern States of America, in the midst of brickbats and rotten eggs; and I ended it on the soil of South Carolina almost literally buried beneath the wreaths of flowers which were heaped upon me by her liberated bondmen."

A young man was employed by a large commission firm in New York City during the late civil war, to negotiate with a certain party for a lot of damaged beans. The beans were purchased, delivered, and spread out upon the upper floor of the building occupied by the firm.

Men were employed to turn them over and over, and to sprinkle them with a solution of soda, so as to improve their appearance and render them more salable. A large lot of the first quality of beans was then purchased; some of the good beans were first put into barrels, then the barrels were nearly filled with the poor ones; after this the good ones were again put on the top and the barrels headed up for sale.

The employer marked the barrels, "Beans—A 1." The clerk

seeing this, said: "Do you think, sir, that it is right to mark those beans A 1?"

The employer retorted sharply: "Are you head of the firm?"

The clerk said no more. The barreling and heading went on. When all was ready, the beans (many hundreds of barrels) were put on the market for sale. Specimens of the best quality were shown in the office to buyers.

At length a shrewd purchaser came in (no man is so sharp in business but he will often meet his equal), examined the samples in the office, inquired the price, and then wished to see the stock in bulk. The clerk was ordered to go with the buyer to the upper loft and show him the stock. An open barrel was shown apparently of the same quality of the sample. The buyer then said to the clerk:

"Young man, the samples of beans shown me are of the first quality, and it is impossible to purchase beans anywhere in the market for the price at which you offer them; there is something wrong here. Tell me, are these beans the same quality throughout the entire barrel as they appear on the top?"

The clerk now found himself in a strange position. He thought, "Shall I lie for my employer, as he undoubtedly means I shall; or shall I tell the truth, come what will?" He decided for the truth, and said:

"No, sir, they are not."

"Then," said the customer. "I do not want them"; and he left.

The clerk enterers the office. The employer said to him: "Did you sell that man those beans?"

He said, "No, sir."

"Why not?"

"Well, sir, the man asked me if those beans were of the same quality through the entire barrel as they appeared on the top. I told him they were not. He then said: 'I do not want them,' and left."

"Go to the cashier," said the employer, "and get your wages; we want you no longer."

He received his pay and left the office, rejoicing that he had not lied for the purposes of abetting a sordid avariciousness, and benefiting an unprincipled employer.

Three weeks after this the firm sent after the young clerk, entreated him to come back again into their employ, and offered him three hundred dollars salary more per year than they had ever before given him.

And thus was his honesty and truthfulness rewarded. The firm knew and felt that the man was right, although apparently they had lost largely by his honesty. They wished to have him again in their employ, because they knew that they could trust him, and never suffer through fraud and deception. They knew that their financial interests would be safe in his custody. They respected and honored that young man.

The Lesson of Patience

Let us learn the lesson of patience. "Behold the husbandman waiteth for the precious fruit of the earth, and hath long patience for it, until he receive the early and latter rain." Delay does not mean denial. Too often one generation sows and another has to reap. God is a jealous God, "visiting the iniquity of the fathers upon the children unto the third and fourth generation of them that hate Him."

In the early years of Israel's existence as a separate people, God commanded them to give the land of Canaan rest every seventh year.

"Six years thou shalt sow thy land, and shalt gather in the fruits thereof: but the seventh year thou shalt let it rest and lie still; that the poor of thy people may eat, and what they leave the beasts of the field shall eat. In like manner thou shalt deal with thy vineyard, and with thy olive yard." From the anointing of Saul to be king this law was not observed. After four hundred and ninety years God gave the nation into captivity for seventy years. During this period the land had rest; seventy sabbath years to compensate for the sabbath years of which it had been deprived. Those Israelites sowed the bitter seed of disobedience, and their descendants had to reap the harvest in exile and captivity.

A leading surgeon performed a critical operation before his class one day. The operation was successful, as far as his part was concerned. But he turned to the class and said: "Six years ago a wise way of living might have prevented this disease. Two years ago a safe and simple operation might have cured it. We have done our best to-day as the case now stands, but Nature will have her word to say. She does not always repeal her capital sentences." Next day the patient died, reaping the fruit of his excesses.

Paul says: "Let us not be weary in well-doing; in due season we shall reap if we faint not."

In a recent chat with an interviewer, Mr. Edison quite unconsciously preached a most powerful sermon on perseverance and patience.

He described his repeated efforts to make the phonograph reproduce the aspirated sound, and added: "From eighteen to twenty hours a day for the last seven months I have worked on this single word 'specia.' I said into the phonograph, 'specia, specia, specia,' but the instrument responded, 'pecia, pecia, pecia.' It was enough to drive one mad! But I held firm, and I have succeeded."

An insurance case was brought to Daniel Webster when he was a young lawyer in Portsmouth. Only a small amount was involved, and a twenty-dollar fee was all that was promised. He saw that to do his client full justice, a journey to Boston would be desirable, in order to consult the law library. He would be out of pocket by the expedition, and for the time he would receive no adequate compensation. But he determined to do his best, cost what it might. He accordingly went to Boston and looked up the authorities, and gained the case.

Years after, Webster, who had meanwhile become famous, was passing through New York. An important insurance case was to be tried that day, and one of the counsel had suddenly been taken ill. Money was no object, and Webster was begged to name his terms and conduct the case.

"I told them," said Mr. Webster, "that it was preposterous to expect me to prepare a legal argument at a few hours notice. They insisted, however, that I should look at the papers; and this I finally consented to do. It was my old twenty-dollar case over again; and as I never forget anything, I had all the authorities at my fingers' ends. The court knew that I had no time to prepare, and were astonished at the range of my acquirements. So you see, I was handsomely repaid both in fame and money for that journey to Boston; and the moral is that good work is rewarded in the end."

Two men were digging in California for gold. They worked a good deal and got nothing. At last one of them threw down his tools and said:

"I will leave here before we starve"; and he left.

The next day his comrade's patience was rewarded by finding a nugget that supported him until he made a fortune.

"Because sentence against an evil work is not executed speedily, therefore the heart of the sons of men is fully set in them to do evil. Though a sinner do evil an hundred times, and his days be prolonged, yet surely I know that it shall be well with them that fear God, which fear before Him; but it shall not be well with the wicked, neither shall he prolong his days, which are as a shadow; because he feareth not before God."

The idea that because a person does a thing in the dark it will never be brought to light, is fatal—God says it shall be brought to light. It is folly for a man who has covered his sins to think there shall be no resurrection of them and no final adjudication. Look at the sons of Jacob. They sold Joseph and deceived their father. Twenty long years rolled away, and away down to Egypt their sin followed them; for they said: "We are guilty of the blood of our brother." The reaping time had come at last, for those ten boys who sold their brother.

I was once preaching in Chicago, and a woman who was nearly out of her mind came to me. You know there are some people who mock at religions meetings, and say that religion drives people mad. It is sin that drives people mad. It is the want of Christ that sinks people into despair. This was the woman's story: She had a family of children. One of her neighbors had died, and her husband had brought home a little child. She said, "I don't want the child," but her husband said, "You must take it and look after it." She said she had enough to do with her own, and she told her husband to take that child away. But he would not. She confessed that she tried to starve the child; but it lingered on. One night it cried all night; I suppose it wanted food. At last she took the clothes and threw them over the child, and smothered it. No one saw her; no one knew anything about it. The child was buried. Years had passed away; and she said, "I hear the voice of that child day and night. It has driven me nearly mad." No one saw the act; but God had seen it, and this retribution followed it. History is full of these things. You need not go to the Bible to find it out.

CHAPTER IV
A MAN EXPECTS TO REAP THE SAME KIND AS HE SOWS

"Herb yielding seed after his kind, and the tree yielding fruit . . . after his kind."—Gen. i: 12.

"Do men gather grapes of thorns, or figs of thistles?"—Matt. vii: 16.

"For if ye live after the flesh, ye shall die: but if ye through the Spirit do mortify the deeds of the body, ye shall live."—Romans viii: 13.

A Man Expects to Reap the Same Kind as He Sows

If I should tell you that I sowed ten acres of wheat last year and that watermelons came up, or that I sowed cucumbers and gathered turnips, you wouldn't believe it. It is a fixed law that you reap the same kind of seed you sow. Plant wheat and you reap wheat, plant an acorn and there comes up an oak, plant a little elm and in time you have a big elm.

One day, the master of Lukman, an Eastern fabulist, said to him, "Go into such a field, and sow barley." Lukman sowed oats instead. At the time of harvest his master went to the place, and, seeing the green oats springing up, asked him:

"Did I not tell you to sow barley here? Why, then, have you sown oats?"

He answered, "I sowed oats in the hope that barley would grow up."

His master said, "What foolish idea is this? Have you ever

heard of the like?"

Lukman replied, "You yourself are constantly sowing in the field of the world the seeds of evil, and yet expect to reap in the resurrection day the fruits of virtue. Therefore I thought, also, I might get barley by sowing oats."

The master was abashed at the reply and set Lukman free.

Like produces like in vegetation, and like produces like in labor. If a man has learnt the trade of a carpenter, he does not expect to excel as a watchmaker. If he has toiled hard to acquire a knowledge of the law, he does not expect to practice medicine for a livelihood. Men expect to reap in the same line as they have learned.

This law is just as true in God's kingdom as in man's kingdom; just as true in the spiritual world as in the natural world. If I sow tares, I am going to reap tares; if I sow a lie, I am going to reap lies; if I sow adultery. I am going to reap adulterers; if I sow whisky, I am going to reap drunkards. You cannot blot this law out, it is in force. No other truth in the Bible is more solemn.

Suppose that a neighbor, whom I don't want to see, comes to my house and I tell my son to tell him, if he asks for me, that I am out of town. He goes to the door and lies to my neighbor; it will not be six months before that boy will lie to me; I will reap that lie.

A man said to me some time ago, "Why is it that we can not get honest clerks now?"

I replied, "I don't know, but perhaps I can imagine a reason. When merchants teach clerks to say that goods are all wool when they are half cotton, and to adulterate groceries and say they are pure, when they grind up white marble and put it into pulverized sugar, and the clerk knows it, you will not have honest clerks."

As long as merchants teach their clerks to lie and to misrepresent, to put a French or an English tag on domestic goods and sell them for imported goods, so long they will have dishonest clerks. Dishonest merchants make dishonest clerks. I am not talking fiction, I am talking truth. It is not poetry, but solemn prose that a man must reap the same kind of seed that he sows.

This is a tremendous argument against selling liquor. Leaving out the temperance and religious aspects of the question, no man on earth can afford to sell strong drink. If I sell liquor to your son and make a drunkard of him, some man will sell liquor to my son and make a drunkard of him. Every man who sells liquor has a drunken son or a drunken brother or some drunken relative. Where are the sons of liquor dealers? To whom are their daughters married? Look around and see if you can find a man who has been in that business twenty years who has not a skeleton in his own family.

I threw that challenge down once, and a man said to me the next day, "I wasn't at your meeting last night, but I understand you made the astounding statement that no man had been in the liquor business twenty years who hadn't the curse in his own family."

"Yes," I said, "I did."

"It isn't true," he said, "and I want you to take it back. My father was a rumseller, and I am a rumseller, and the curse has never come into my father's family or into mine."

I said, "What! two generations selling that infernal stuff, and the curse has never come into the family! I will investigate it, and if I find I am wrong I will make the retraction just as publicly as I did the statement."

There were two prominent citizens of the town in the room, on whose faces I noticed a peculiar expression as the man was talking. After he left, one of them said:

"Do you know, Mr. Moody, that man's own brother was a drunkard and committed suicide a few weeks ago and left a widow with seven children; they are under his roof now! He was a terrible drunkard himself until the shock of his brother's suicide cured him."

I don't know how you can account for it unless he thought his brother wasn't a relative. Perhaps he was a sort of a

Cainite, saying, "Am I my brother's keeper?"

When I was a pastor of a church in Chicago we were trying to get hold of the working-men. They used to say:

"Come down to the factory at dinner-time and we will give you a chance to speak."

I would ask them, "Why won't you come to the church?"

"Oh," they would say, "you have it all your own way there, and we can't answer back; but come to the factory and we will put a few questions to you."

So I went down, and they made it pretty hot for me sometimes. One of the favorite characters that they brought up was Jacob. Many a time I have had men say, "You think Jacob was a saint, don't you? He was a big rascal." Many have said they thought Jacob wasn't as good as Esau. Notice this fact. You read in the Bible, "I will punish Jacob according to his doings." This law of retribution runs through his Life; although he was a friend of God, a kinsman of Abraham, and was third in the line of the covenant, yet God made Jacob reap the same kind of seed he sowed. Some one has said that "Jacob's misfortunes were uniformly calculated to bring back to his recollection the picture as well as the punishment of his faults."

When Isaac in his old age wanted some venison, and sent Esau out to get it, Jacob slipped out and took a kid from his father's flock, and Rebekah, his mother, cooked it; he brought it to his old blind father and said he was Esau. The old man recognized his voice, but he had very cunningly put the skin of the kid on his hands and neck; so that the old man felt him and said;

"The voice is Jacob's voice, but the hands are the hands of Esau."

By this lie he got his brother's birthright blessing, but he paid ten thousand times more for it than it was worth. "Who steals my purse steals trash." A man who steals my pocketbook is the chief sufferer, not I. When Jacob had grown to be an old man, he lived in continual suspicion that his sons were deceiving him. The sin of deceiving his own father bore fruit.

Jacob was the great loser in this transaction. When Esau returned he had to flee for his life. Then God met him at Bethel. "And behold, the Lord stood above it and said, I am the Lord God of Abraham thy father, and the God of Isaac: the land whereon thou liest, to thee will I give it, and to thy seed: and thy seed shall be as the dust of the earth: and thou shalt spread abroad to the west and to the east and to the north and to the south, and in thee and in thy seed shall all the families of the earth be blessed.

"And, behold, I am with thee, and will keep thee in all places whither thou goest, and will bring thee again unto this land, for I will not leave thee, until I have done that which I have spoken to thee of."

Men will read that far in the life of Jacob and say, "I don't want anything more to do with a God who will deal in grace with a man who had done so mean a thing." My friend, hold on. Follow him to Padanaram. He was there twenty years, and during that time his wages were changed ten times. He worked seven years for the lovely Rachel, and then had another woman put upon him. Jacob had by deception obtained the blessing of the first-born son, but Laban sarcastically reminded him, "It must not be so done in my country to give the younger before the first-born." He found that Laban could drive as sharp a bargain as he. Wherever you find a sharp, shrewd man, you will always find that he draws just such men around him, and that he who cheats will himself be cheated. "Birds of a feather flock together"; blasphemers get together, and sharp, shrewd men get together. Jacob found in Laban just such a man as himself. It was "diamond cut diamond."

Look a little further. Jacob had twelve sons, but he loved Joseph and Benjamin more than the others because they were the sons of his beloved Rachel. He was partial to Joseph, and had a coat made of many colors for him. Partiality will raise the old Adam in any family.

One morning Joseph, in the innocence of his heart, tells a dream in which his father and all his brothers had bowed down to him. Then his brothers began to plan to get him out of the way, and when his father sent him to find them when they were tending the flocks, they said:

"Now we have him; let us slay him and cast him into a pit, and say that some beast has devoured him."

Later they sold him, and took his coat of many colors and dipped it in the blood of a kid, and, taking it to their father, said: "This have we found; know now whether it be thy son's coat or no." And he knew it and said, "It is my son's coat; an evil beast hath devoured him."

Now notice: Jacob deceived his father with the skin of a kid, and his sons deceived him with the blood of a kid. Jacob lied to his father, and his sons lied to him. The lie came home. Every lie is bound to come back to you. You cannot dig a grave so deep but that it will have a resurrection. Tramp, tramp, your sins will all come back.

"Be sure your sin will find you out." You may think you are very shrewd and far-sighted, and can plan and cover up, but it is the decree of high heaven that no sin shall be covered; God will uncover it. You cannot deceive the Almighty. Jacob found that out. He had to reap what he sowed.

Again, look at David. A man said to me some years ago:

"Don't you think David fell as low as Saul?"

Yes, he fell lower, because God had lifted him higher. The difference is that when Saul fell there was no sign of repentance, but when David fell, a wail went up from his broken heart; there was true repentance. No man in all the Scripture record rose so high and fell so low as David. God took him from the sheepfold and placed him on the throne. He gave him riches and lands in abundance. He was on a pinnacle of glory, and was loved and honored among men. But one day, you remember, David was walking upon the roof of the king's house, and he saw Bathsheba, and lusted after her, and committed the awful sin of adultery; and then, to cover up that sin, he made Bathsheba's husband drunk, and had him murdered. The decree came: "I will raise up evil in thy family and the sword shall never leave thy house." Amnon, David's son, commits adultery with David's own daughter. Absalom makes a feast for Amnon and has him murdered. Not long after he comes with an army to drive David, his father, from the throne, and publicly commits adultery with David's concubines on the roof of the king's house; if God had not been overruling, he would have killed his father.

David sowed adultery and reaped it in his own family. He sowed murder and reaped it in his own family. I believe that what brought the bitter wail from that father's heart when he said, "Oh, my son Absalom, my son, my son Absalom! Would God I had died for thee," was the fact that these were the wages of his own sin. From the time he fell into that sin with Uriah's wife until he went down to his grave, it was one billow after another rolling over him.

If God did not spare David, do you think He will spare us if we fall into sin and do not confess and turn from our sins? If ever a man had an opportunity to cover his sins, David had. No judge or jury dared to pronounce judgment against him. The thing was done in the dark, but his sin found him out. Nathan was sent across his path, and, young man, Nathan will appear to you some day. Some messenger will smite you in the way if you do not repent and turn from your sins. My friend, why not call on God now as David did when he came to himself? make the same prayer—how thankful we should be that we have the prayer! why not make it on your knees now?

David's Prayer for Forgiveness

"Have mercy upon me, O God, according to thy loving kindness: according unto the multitude of thy tender mercies blot out my transgressions.

Wash me thoroughly from mine iniquity, and cleanse me from my sin. For I acknowledge my transgressions; and my sin is ever before me.

Against thee, thee only, have I sinned, and done this evil in thy sight; that thou mightest be justified when thou speakest, and be clear when thou judgest.

Behold, I was shapen in iniquity; and in sin did my mother conceive me.

Behold, thou desirest truth in the inward parts; and in the hidden part thou shalt make me to know wisdom.

Purge me with hyssop, and I shall be clean; wash me, and I shall be whiter than snow.

Make me to hear joy and gladness; that the bones which thou hast broken may rejoice.

Hide thy face from my sins, and blot out all mine iniquities.

Create in me a clean heart, O God, and renew a right spirit within me.

Cast me not away from thy presence; and take not thy Holy Spirit from me.

Restore unto me the joy of thy salvation; and uphold me with thy free Spirit.

Then will I teach transgressors thy ways; and sinners shall be converted unto thee.

Deliver me from bloodguiltiness, O God, thou God of my salvation; and my tongue shall sing aloud of thy righteousness.

O Lord, open thou my lips; and my mouth shall shew forth thy praise.

For thou desirest not sacrifice; else would I give it; thou delightest not in burnt offering. The sacrifices of God are a broken spirit: a broken and a contrite heart, O God, thou wilt not despise."

Examples From History

But you say you don't believe in the Bible. Then look at his-

Sowing and Reaping

tory, and see if this law is not true. Maxentine built a false bridge to drown Constantine, but was drowned himself. Bajazet was carried about by Tamerlane in an iron cage which he intended for Tamerlane. Maximinus put out the eyes of thousands of Christians; soon after a fearful disease of the eyes broke out among his people, of which he himself died in great agony. Valens caused about eighty Christians to be sent to sea in a ship and burnt alive: he was defeated by the Goths and fled to a cottage, where he was burnt alive.

Alexander VI. was poisoned by wine he had prepared for another. Henry III. of France was stabbed in the same chamber where he had helped to contrive the cruel massacre of French Protestants. Marie Antoinette, riding to Notre Dame Cathedral for her bridal, bade the soldiers command all beggars, cripples, and ragged people to leave the line of the procession. She could not endure the sight of these miserable ones. Soon after, bound in the executioner's cart, she was riding toward the place of execution amidst crowds who gazed on her with hearts as cold as ice and hard as granite. When Foulon was asked how the starving populace was to live, he said: "Let them eat grass." Afterward, the mob, maddened with rage, caught him in the streets of Paris, hung him, stuck his head upon a pike and filled his mouth with grass.

CHAPTER V
A MAN REAPS MORE THAN HE SOWS

"But other fell into good ground, and brought forth fruit, some a hundredfold, some sixtyfold, some thirtyfold."—Matt. xiii: 8.

A Man Reaps More Than He Sows

If I sow a bushel, I expect to reap ten or twenty bushels. I can sow in one day what will take ten men to reap. The Spaniards have this proverb: "Sow a thought and reap an act. Sow an act, and reap a habit. Sow a habit, and reap a character. Sow a character and reap a destiny." And it takes a longer time to reap than to sow. I have heard of a certain kind of bean that reproduces itself a thousand fold. One thistle-down which blew from the deck of a vessel is said to have covered with thistles the entire surface of a South Sea island. The oak springs from an acorn, the mighty Mississippi from a little spring.

One glass of whisky may lead to a drunkard's death. One lie may ruin a man's career. One error in youth may follow a man all through life. Some one has said that many a Christian spends half his time trying to keep down the sprouts of seed sown in his young days. Unless it is held in check, the desire to "have a drink" will become a consuming thirst; the desire to "play a game of cards" an irresistible gambler's passion.

Abraham gave up his only son at God's bidding, and as the fruit of that act of obedience God gave him seed as numerous as the stars of the heaven and as the sands upon the seashore.

Jacob told one lie, and his ten sons came back with his

Sowing and Reaping

lie multiplied tenfold. For twenty years Jacob mourned for Joseph, supposing that he was dead. I have no doubt that night after night he wept for Joseph, and in his dreams saw the boy torn to pieces, and heard his cries for help. It took him a long time to reap the harvest.

Israel murmured against God because of the report of the land of Canaan brought back by the spies. Had they not to reap a multiplied harvest? Listen: "After the number of the days in which ye searched the land, even forty days, each day for a year, shall ye bear your iniquities, even forty years, and ye shall know my breach of promise."

When I made the remark in a meeting once that a man had to reap more than he sowed, a man in front of me dropped his head and sobbed aloud. After the meeting, a friend stepped up to him and said:

"What is your trouble?"

Pointing to me he said, "Every word that man has been saying is true. Four years ago I was the confidential clerk of a firm in this city. I have reason to believe that if I had continued as I began, I should have been in the firm now. But one night in a saloon under the influence of drink I committed a crime, and I was sent to the penitentiary, where I repented in sackcloth and ashes. To-day I came back for the first time, and went to the old house, and they ordered me out. I went to other business-houses I was acquainted with, and received the same treatment. I met men on the street whom I once knew, who had held inferior places to me, and I lifted my hat, but no one returned the bow."

The man wrung his hands in agony and said, "It is all true, it takes a longer time to reap than to sow."

Do you not believe it? Ask your neighbor who has drank up his character and reputation and home, and has brought a blight on his family. It takes a long time to build up a character, but you can blast it in a single hour.

A man died in the Columbus penitentiary some years ago who had spent over thirty years in his cell. He was one of the millionaires of Ohio. Fifty years ago when they were trying to get a trunk road from Chicago to New York, they wanted to lay the line through his farm near Cleveland. He did not want his farm divided by the railroad, so the case went into court, where commissioners were appointed to pay the damages and to allow the road to be built. One dark night after the tracks were laid, a train was thrown off the track, and several were killed. This man was suspected, was tried and found guilty, and was sent to the penitentiary for life. The farm was soon cut up into city lots, and the man became a millionaire, but he got no benefit from it. Before he died, the chaplain told me that he became a child of God. It may not have taken him more than an hour to lay the obstruction on the railroad, but he was over thirty years reaping the result of that one act!

In the history of France we read that a certain king wanted some new instrument to torture his prisoners with. One of his favorites suggested that he should build a cage, not long enough to lie down in, and not high enough to stand up in. The king accepted the suggestion; but the first one put into the cage was the very man who suggested it, and he was kept in it for fourteen years. It did not take him more than a few minutes, perhaps, to suggest that cruel device; but he was fourteen long years reaping the fruit of what he had sown.

If a man could do his reaping alone, it would not be so hard; but it is terrible when he has to make that godly father, and that mother who loves him, or that wife and family, reap along with him. Does not the drunkard make his wife and children reap a bitter harvest? Does not the gambler make his relatives reap? Does not the harlot make her parents reap agony and shame? What a bitter enemy is sin! May God help each one of us to turn from it at once!

Whenever I hear a young man talking in a flippant way about sowing his wild oats, I don't laugh. I feel more like crying, because I know he is going to make his gray-haired mother reap in tears; he is going to make his wife reap in shame; he is going to make his old father and his innocent children reap with him. Only ten or fifteen or twenty years will pass before he will have to reap his wild oats; no man has ever sowed them without having to reap them. Sow the wind and you reap the whirlwind.

We cannot control our influence. If I plant thistles in my field, the wind will take the thistle-down when it is ready, and blow it away beyond the fence; and my neighbors will have to reap with me. So my example may be copied by my children or my neighbors, and my actions reproduced indefinitely through them, whether for good or evil. How many have gone to ruin because of the sins of such men as Jacob and David and Lot!

Nothing But Leaves

Nothing but leaves! The Spirit grieves
O'er years of wasted life!
O'er sins indulged while conscience slept,
O'er vows and promises unkept,
And reap from years of strife—
Nothing but leaves! Nothing but leaves!

Nothing but leaves! No gathered sheaves
Of life's fair ripening grain;
We sow our seeds; lo! tares and weeds—
Words, idle words, for earnest deeds—
Then reap, with toil and pain,
Nothing but leaves! Nothing but leaves!

Nothing but leaves! Sad memory weaves
No veil to hide the past;
And as we trace our weary way,
And count each lost and misspent day,
We sadly find at last—
Nothing but leaves! Nothing but leaves!

Ah, who shall thus the Master meet,
And bring but withered leaves?
Ah, who shall, at the Saviour's feet,
Before the awful judgment-seat,
Lay down, for golden sheaves,
Nothing but leaves! Nothing but leaves?
—L. E. Ackerman.

CHAPTER VI
IGNORANCE OF THE SEED MAKES NO DIFFERENCE

"Marvel not at this: for the hour is coming, in the which all that are in the graves shall hear his voice, and shall come forth, they that have done good; unto the resurrection of life; and they that have done evil, unto the resurrection of damnation."—John v: 28, 29.

Ignorance of the Seed Makes no Difference

Now, notice again: Ignorance of the kind of seed makes no difference. If I think I am sowing good seed and it happens to be bad, I shall have a bad harvest; therefore, it becomes me to see what kind of seed I am sowing.

Suppose I meet a man who is sowing seed, and say: "Hello, stranger, what are you sowing?"

"Seed."

"What kind of seed?"

"I don't know."

"Don't you know whether it is good or bad?"

"No, I can't tell; but it is seed, that is all I want to know, and I am sowing it."

You would say that he was a first-class lunatic, wouldn't you? But he wouldn't be half so mad as the man who goes on sowing for time and eternity, and never asks himself what he is sowing or what the harvest will be.

Father, what seed are you sowing in your family? Are you setting your children a good or a bad example? Do you spend your time at the saloon or the club, until you have become almost a stranger to them? or are you training them for God and righteousness?

The story is told that a man once said he would not talk to his son about religion; the boy should make his own choice when he grew up, unprejudiced by him. The boy broke his arm, and when the doctor was setting it, he cursed and swore the whole time.

"Ah," said the doctor, "you were afraid to prejudice the boy in the right way, but the devil had no such prejudice. He has led your son the other way." The idea that a father is to let his children run wild! Nature alone never brings forth anything but weeds.

One of Coleridge's friends once objected to prejudicing the minds of the young by selecting the things they should be taught. The philosopher-poet invited him to take a look at his garden, and took him to where a luxuriant growth of ugly and infragrant weeds spread themselves over beds and walks alike.

"You don't call that a garden!" said his friend.

"What!" said Coleridge, "would you have me prejudice the ground in favor of roses and lilies?"

Have you never noticed the same thing about the mind and the heart? Let a child be idle, and Satan will soon lead him into mischief. He must be looked after. Those things that will help to develop character must be selected for him, and hurtful things must be kept out, just as industriously as the farmer cultivates the useful products of the soil, but wages continual war on weeds and all unwholesome growths.

A murderer was to suffer the penalty of his crime. Speaking of his reckless career, he said:

"How could it be otherwise, when I had such bad training? I was taught these things from my youth. When only four years old my mother poured whisky down my throat to see how I would act."

On the morning of his execution, the wretched mother bade

good-bye to the son whom her influence had helped to that shameful end.

A father started for his office early one morning, after a light fall of snow. Turning, he saw his two year-old boy endeavoring to put his tiny feet in his own great footprints. The little fellow shouted: "Go on, I'se comin', papa, I'se comin' right in ure tracks."

He caught the boy in his arms and carried him to his mother, and started again for his office.

His habit had been to stop on the way at a saloon for a glass of liquor. As he stood upon the threshold that morning he seemed to hear a sweet voice say: "Go on, I'se comin', papa, I'se comin' right in ure tracks."

He stopped, he hesitated, he looked the future squarely in the face.

"I cannot afford to make any tracks I would be ashamed or sorry to have my boy walk in," he said decidedly, and turned away.

Father, mother, neighbor, are your tracks true? Are they straight? Can you turn to any walking behind you and say: "Follow me as I follow Christ?" Are you leading the little ones safe to the Great Shepherd?

The best time to sow the good seed is before Satan has scattered the tares. God has given numerous warnings and instructions to do it. "Seek ye first the Kingdom of God and his righteousness." "Train up a child in the way he should go." "Provoke not your children to wrath, but bring them up in the nurture and admonition of the Lord." If a farmer neglects to plant in the spring-time, he can never recover the lost opportunity: no more can you, if you neglect yours. Youth is a seed-time, and if it is allowed to pass without good seed being sowed, weeds will spring up and choke the soil. It will take bitter toil to uproot them.

An old divine said that when a good farmer sees a weed in his field he has it pulled up. If it is taken early enough, the blank is soon filled in, and the crop waves over the whole field. But if allowed to run too late, the bald patch remains. It would have been better if the weed had never been allowed to get root.

Young man, are you letting some secret sin get the mastery over you, binding you hand and foot? It is growing. Every sin grows. When I was speaking to five thousand children in Glasgow some years ago, I took a spool of thread and said to one of the largest boys:

"Do you believe I can bind you with that thread?"

He laughed at the idea. I wound the thread around him a few times, and he broke it with a single jerk. Then I wound the thread around and around, and by and by I said:

"Now get free if you can."

He couldn't move hand or foot. If you are slave to some vile habit, you must either slay that habit or it will slay you.

My friend, what kind of seed are you sowing? Let your mind sweep over your record for the past year. Have you been living a double life? Have you been making a profession without possessing what you profess? If there is anything you detest it is hypocrisy. Do you tell me God doesn't detest it also? If it is a right eye that offends, make up your mind that you will pluck it out; or if it is a right hand or a right foot, cut it off. Whatever the sin is, make up your mind that you will gain the victory over it without further delay.

What kind of seed are you sowing, my friend, good seed or bad seed? There will be a harvest, and you are bound to reap, whether you want to or not. Tell me, how do you spend your spare time? Telling vile stories, polluting the minds of others, while your own mind is also polluted? Do you read any literature that makes your thoughts impure? How do you spend the Sabbath? Boating, fishing, hunting, or on excursions? Do you think ministers are old fogies—that the Bible belongs to the dark ages? Tell me bow you treat your parents, and I will tell you how your children will treat you. A man was making preparations to send his old father to the poorhouse, when his little child came up and said:

"Papa, when you are old shall I have to take you to the poorhouse?"

Do you never write home to your parents? They clothed you and educated you, and now do you spend your nights in gambling? You say to your godless companions that your father crammed religion down your throat when you were a boy. I have a great contempt for a man who says that of his father or mother. They may have made a mistake; but it was of the head, not of the heart. If a telegram was sent to them that you were down with smallpox, they would take the first train to come to you. They would willingly take the disease into their own bodies and die for you. If you scoff and sneer at your father and mother you will have a hard harvest; you will reap in agony. It is only a question of time. There is a saying—

"The mills of God grind slowly,

But they grind exceeding small."

The Lord Jesus said, "With what measure ye mete, it shall be measured to you again."

A man told me when I was last in London that England had the advantage of America in one respect. I asked how. He said:

"We have more respect for our laws in England than you do in America. You don't hang half your murderers, but all our murderers are hanged if they can be proved guilty."

I said: "Neither country hangs its worst murderers. If my son wants to murder me, I would rather have him kill me outright than to take five years to do it. A young man who goes home late night after night, and when his mother remonstrates, curses her gray hairs, and kills her by inches, is the worst sort of a murderer."

That is being done all over the country. You may not be guilty of a sin as black and as foul as this, but I tell you, every sin grows, and if you have sin in your heart you cannot tell where it will land you. Nothing separates a son from his mother or a man from his wife like sin. The grace of God binds men together, but sin tears them apart and separates them.

Come, my friend, what kind of seed are you sowing? What will the harvest be? Will it be a black harvest, or are you going to have a joyful harvest? If you think that, when you have sown tares, wheat will come up, you are greatly mistaken. If you think you can give a loose rein to your passions and lusts, and yet have eternal life, you are being deceived. For God says, "He that soweth to his flesh shall of the flesh reap corruption; but he that soweth to the Spirit shall of the Spirit reap life everlasting."

Choose Carefully

I beg of you to choose carefully your path. The farmer is careful in the choice of seed. He does not want bad seed or inferior seed, because he knows that such will give a poor crop. He looks for the best seed he can buy. If you choose to sow to the flesh, you will have a corrupted harvest. If you commit a sinful deed, it may land you into a dishonored grave.

Choice is a solemn thing. You can make this moment a turning-point in your life. Once during the conquest of Peru, Pizzaro's followers threatened to desert him. They gathered on the shore to embark for home. Drawing his sword, he traced a line with it in the sand from east to west. Then turning toward the south he said:

"Friends and comrades, on that side are toil, hunger, nakedness, the drenching storm, and death; on this side, ease and pleasure. There lies Peru with all its riches; here Panama and its poverty. Choose each man as becomes a brave Castilian. For my part, I go south."

So saying, he stepped across the line, and one after another his comrades followed him, and the destiny of South America was decided.

Napoleon was once offered a position as officer in the Turkish artillery. He declined it; but had he chosen to accept it, the history of Europe would have been different.

On your choice in spiritual things depends your eternity. On the one side there is Christ; on the other, the world. Between them you must choose. Do not wish to grow both wheat and tares. Oh, choose Christ! Let there be no half-heartedness. Give Him your whole heart. He died to redeem you from the curse of sin, and He lives to save you from the power of sin.

"No man can serve two masters." You can not belong to two kingdoms at once. Lord Brougham grew to be so fond of Cannes that he sought to be naturalized as a Frenchman, but found it was impossible to be both a peer of England and a citizen of a French town; he must renounce the one to become the other.

Now this is where the will comes in It is easy to follow other people's lead, to swim with the tide; but it requires character, moral back-bone, to stand against the current of popular opinion and practice. During the late war a deserter came into the Federal lines before Pittsburg. He was asked:

"What did you go into secession for?"

His answer was: "Because they all did."

That reason will account for many a man's action. He will act according to the saying: "While you are in Rome, do as the Romans do," neglecting to investigate and determine whether or not the Romans do right. If they do wrong, a man should stand against a whole nation, if need be, like another Daniel.

Almighty God set two sides before the children of Israel, and I set them now before you. Remember, as you choose, that your eternity is in the balance.

"See, I have set before thee this day life and good, and death and evil; in that I command thee this day to love the Lord thy God, to walk in His ways, and to keep His commandments, and His statutes, and His judgments, that thou mayest live and multiply; and the Lord thy God shall bless thee in the land whither thou goest to possess it.

But if thine heart turn away, so that thou wilt not hear, but shalt be drawn away, and worship other gods, and serve them: I denounce unto you this day that ye shall surely perish, and that ye shall not prolong your days upon the land whither thou passest over Jordan to go to possess it.

I call heaven and earth to record this day against you, that I have set before you life and death, blessing and cursing: therefore CHOOSE LIFE that both thou and thy seed may live: that thou mayest love the Lord thy God, and that thou mayest obey His voice, and that thou mayest cleave unto Him: for He is thy life and the length of thy days."

CHAPTER VII
FORGIVENESS AND RETRIBUTION

"Thou renderest to every man according to his work."—Psalms lxii: 12.

"For we must all appear before the judgment seat of Christ; that every one may receive the things done in his body, according to that he hath done, whether it be good or bad."—II Cor. v: 10.

Forgiveness and Retribution

I can imagine some one saying, "I attend church, and have heard that if we confess our sin, God will forgive us; now I hear that I must reap the same kind of seed that I have sown. How can I harmonize the doctrine of forgiveness with the doctrine of retribution? 'All we like sheep have gone astray; we have turned every one to his own way; and the Lord hath laid on him the iniquity of us all.' And yet you say that I must reap what I have sown."

Suppose I send my hired man to sow wheat. When it grows up, there are thistles mixed with the wheat. There wasn't a thistle a year ago. I say to my man:

"Do you know anything about the thistles in the field?"

He says: "Yes, I do; you sent me to sow that wheat, and I was angry and mixed some thistles with the wheat. But you promised me that if I ever did wrong and confessed it, you would forgive me; now I hold you to that promise, and expect you to forgive me."

"Yes," I say, "you are quite right; I forgive you for sowing the thistles; but I will tell you what you must do—you must reap the thistles along with the wheat when harvest time comes."

Many a Christian man is reaping thistles with his wheat. Twenty years ago you sowed thistles with the wheat and are reaping them now. Perhaps it was an obscene story, the memory of which keeps coming back to distress you, even at the most solemn moments. Perhaps some hasty word or deed that you have never been able to recall.

I heard John B. Gough say that he would rather cut off his hand than have committed a certain sin. He didn't say what it was, but I have always supposed it was the way he treated his mother. He was a wretched, drunken sot in the gutter when his mother died; the poor woman couldn't stand it, and died of a broken heart. God had forgiven him, but he never forgave himself. A great many have done things that they will never forgive themselves for to their dying day. "At this moment," said one, "from many a harlot's dishonored grave there arises a mute appeal for righteous retribution. From many a drunkard's miserable home, from heartbroken wife, from starving children, there rings up a terrible appeal into the ears of God."

I believe that God forgives sin fully and freely for Christ's sake; but He allows certain penalties to remain. If a man has wasted years in riotous living, he can never hope to live them over again. If he has violated his conscience, the scars will remain through life. If he has soiled his reputation, the effect of it can never be washed away. If he shatters his body through indulgence and vice, he must suffer until death. As Talmage says, "The grace of God gives a new heart, but not a new body."

"John," said a father to his son, "I wish you would get me the hammer."

"Yes, sir."

"Now a nail and a piece of pine board."

"Here they are, sir."

"Will you drive the nail into the board?"

It was done.

"Please pull it out again."

"That's easy, sir."

"Now, John," and the father's voice dropped to a lower key, "pull out the nail hole."

Every wrong act leaves a scar. Even if the board be a living tree the scar remains.

For our worst sins there is plenteous redemption. My sin may become white as snow, and pass away altogether, in so far as it has power to disturb or sadden my relation to God. Yet our least sins leave in our lives, in our characters, in our memories, in our consciences, sometimes in our weakness, often in our worldly position, in our reputation, in our success, in our health, in a thousand ways leave their traces and consequences. God will not put out His little finger to remove these, but lets them stop.

Let no man fancy that the Gospel which proclaims forgiveness can be vulgarized into a mere proclamation of impunity. Not so. It was to Christian men that Paul said, 'Be not deceived, God is not mocked: whatsoever a man soweth, that shall he also reap.' God loves us too well not to punish His children when they sin, and He loves us too well to annihilate (were it possible) the secondary consequences of our transgressions. The two sides of the truth must be recognized—that the deeper and (as we call them) the primary penalties of our evil, which are separation from God and the painful consciousness of guilt, are swept away; and also that other results are allowed to remain, which, being allowed, may be blessed and salutary for the transgressors.

MacLaren says, "If you waste your youth, no repentance will send the shadow back upon the dial, or recover the ground lost by idleness, or restore the constitution shattered by dissipation, or give back the resources wasted upon vice, or bring back the fleeting opportunities. The wounds can all be healed, for the Good Physician, blessed be His name! has lancets and bandages, and balm and anodynes for the deadliest; but scars remain even when the gash is closed."

God forgave Moses and Aaron for their sins, but both suffered the penalty. Neither one was permitted to enter the promised land. Jacob became a "prince of God" at the ford of Jabbok, but to the end of his days he carried in his body the mark of the struggle. Paul's thorn in the flesh was not removed, even after most earnest and repeated prayer. It lost its sting, however, and became a means of grace.

Perhaps that is one reason why God does not remove these penalties of sin. He may intend them to be used as tokens of His chastening. "Whom the Lord loveth He chasteneth." And if the temporal consequences were completely removed we would be liable to fall back again into sin. The penalty is a continual reminder of our weakness, and of the need of caution and dependence upon God.

One night in Chicago at the close of a meeting in the Y. M. C. A. rooms, a young man sprang to his feet and said: "Mr. Moody, would you let me speak a few words?"

I said, "Certainly."

Then for about five minutes he pleaded with those men to break from sin. He said:

"If you have anyone who takes any interest in your spiritual welfare, treat them kindly, for they are the best friends you have. I was an only child, and my mother and father took great interest in me. Every morning at the family altar father used to pray for me, and every night he would commend me to God. I was wild and reckless and didn't like the restraint of home. When my father died my mother took up the family worship. Many a time she came to me and said, Oh, my boy, if you would stay to family worship I should be the happiest mother on earth; but when I pray, you don't even stay in the house. Sometimes I would go in at midnight from a night of dissipation and hear my mother praying for me. Sometimes in the small hours of morning I heard her voice pleading for me. At last I felt that I must either become a Christian or leave home, and one day I gathered a few things together and stole away from home without letting my mother know.

"Some time after I heard indirectly that my mother was ill. Ah, I thought, it is my conduct that is making her ill! My first impulse was to go home and cheer her last days; but the thought came that if I did I should have to become a Christian. My proud heart revolted and I said: 'No, I will not become a Christian.'"

Months rolled by, and at last he heard again that his mother was worse. Then he thought:

"If my mother should not live I would never forgive myself."

That thought took him home. He reached the old village about dark, and started on foot for the home, which was about a mile and a half distant. On the way he passed the graveyard, and thought he would go to his father's grave to see if there was a newly-made grave beside it. As he drew near the spot, his heart began to beat faster, and when he came near enough, the light of the moon shone on a newly-made grave. With a great deal of emotion he said:

"Young men, for the first time in my life this question came over me—who is going to pray for my lost soul now? Father is gone, and mother is gone, and they are the only two who ever cared for me. If I could have called my mother back that night and heard her breathe my name in prayer, I would have given the world if it had been mine to give. I spent all that night by her grave, and God for Christ's sake heard my mother's prayers, and I became a child ot God. But I never forgave myself for the way I treated my mother, and never will."

Where is my wandering boy to-night—
The boy of my tenderest care,
The boy that was once my joy and light.
The child of my love and prayer?
Once he was pure as morning dew,
As he knelt at his mother's knee;

No face was so bright, no heart more true,
And none was so sweet as he.
O, could I see you now, my boy,
As fair as in olden time,
When prattle and smile made home a joy,
And life was a merry chime.
Go for my wandering boy to-night,
Go, search for him where you will;
But bring him to me with all his blight,
And tell him I love him still.

My dear friends, God may forgive you, but the consequences of your sin are going to be bitter even if you are forgiven.

A few years ago I was preaching in Chicago on that text, "Arise, go up to Bethel and dwell there." After the meeting a man asked to see me alone. I went into a private room. The perspiration stood in beads on his forehead. I said:

"What is it?"

He replied: "I am a fugitive from justice. I am in exile, in disguise. The government of my state has offered a reward for me. I have been hidden here for months. They tell me there is no hell, but it seems as though I have been in hell for months."

He had been a business man, and having, as he thought, plenty of money, he forged some bonds, thinking that he could give his check any time and call them in, but he got beyond his depth and fell.

He said, "I have been here for six months. I have a wife and three children, but I cannot write to them or hear from them." The poor man was in terrible mental agony.

I said, "Why don't you go back and give yourself up and face the law, and ask God to forgive you?"

He said, "I would take the first train to-morrow and give myself up, except for one thing. I have a wife and three children; how can I bring the disgrace upon them?"

I, too, have a wife and three children, and when he said that, the thing looked very different.

Ah! if we could do our own reaping, it would not be so bitter, but when we make our little children or the wife of our bosom, or our old gray-haired mother, or our old father reap with us, isn't the reaping pretty bitter? I don't fear any pestilence or any disease as much as I fear sin. If God will only keep sin out of thy family, I will praise Him in time and in eternity. The worst enemy that ever crossed a man's path is sin.

If a man comes to me for advice I always try to put myself in the place of the one to whom I am talking, and then to give the best advice I can. I said to this man,

"I don't know what to say, but it is safe to pray."

After I had prayed, I urged him to pray; but he said:

"If I do, it means the penitentiary."

I asked him to come the next day at twelve. He met me at the appointed hour, and said:

"It is all settled; if I ever meet the God of Bethel I must go through the prison to meet Him, and God helping me, I will give myself up. I am going back, and I should like to have you keep quiet until I give myself over into the hands of the law; then you may hold me up as a warning. Little did I think when I started out in life that I was coming to this! Little did I think when I married a girl from one of the first families in the state that I should bring such disgrace on her."

At four o'clock that afternoon he went back to Missouri. He reached home a little past midnight, and spent a week with his family. In a letter he said that he didn't dare let his children know he was there, lest they should tell the neighbor's children. At night he would creep out and look at his children, but he couldn't take them in his arms or kiss them. Oh, there is the result of sin! Would to God we could every one of us just turn from sin to-day!

One day, when this man was in hiding, he heard his little boy say:

"Mamma, doesn't papa love us any more?"

"Yes," his mother replied. "Why do you ask?" "Why," the little fellow said, "he has been gone so long and he never writes us any letters and never comes to see us."

The last night he came out from hiding and took a long look at those innocent, sleeping children; then he took his wife and kissed her again and again, and leaving that once happy home he gave himself up to the sheriff. The next morning he pleaded guilty, and was sent to the penitentiary for nineteen years. I believe that God had forgiven him, but he couldn't forgive himself, and he had to reap what he sowed. I pleaded with the governor for mercy, and the man was pardoned.

Some time ago I was telling this story, and some one doubted it, but the governor who pardoned him happened to be in the meeting, and rose and said, "I pardoned that man myself." The governor pardoned him, and he lived a few years, but from the time he committed that sin he had to reap. Oh, reader, I plead with you, overcome your besetting sin, whatever it is.

Future Punishment

I can imagine some one saying, "I am glad Mr. Moody hasn't tried to scare us about the future state. I agree with him that we shall receive all our reward and punishment in this life."

If you think I believe that, you are greatly mistaken. One sentence from the lips of the Son of God in regard to the future state has forever settled it in my mind. "If ye die in your sins, where I am, there ye cannot go." If a man has not given up his drunkenness, his profanity, his licentiousness, his covetousness, heaven would be hell to him. Heaven is a prepared place for prepared people. What would a man do in heaven who cannot bear to be in the society of the pure and holy down here?

Sowing and Reaping

It is not true that all reward and punishment is reaped in this life. Look how many crimes are committed, and the perpetrators are never caught. It often happens that the worst criminal uses his experience to escape detection, while a more innocent hand is captured. A man ruins a girl. Does he always reap punishment here? No. He holds his head as high as ever in society, while the unfortunate victim of his lust, who, perhaps, was innocently beguiled into sin by him, becomes an outcast. His punishment, however is, at the latest, only adjourned to another world.

Eternity!
Oh, the clanging bells of Time!
Night and day they never cease;
We are wearied with their chime,
For they do not bring us peace.
And we hush our breath to hear,
And we strain our eyes to see
If thy shores are drawing near—

Eternity! Eternity!
Oh, the clanging bells of Time!
How their changes rise and fall,
But in undertone sublime,
Sounding clearly through them all,
Is a voice that must be heard,
As our moments onward flee,
And it speaketh aye one word—

Eternity! Eternity!
Oh, the clanging bells of Time!

To their voices loud and low,
In a long, unresting line
We are marching to and fro;
And we yearn for sight or sound,
Of the life that is to be,
For thy breath doth wrap us round—

Eternity! Eternity!
Oh, the clanging bells of Time!
Soon their notes will all be dumb,
And in joy and peace sublime
We shall feel the silence come;
And our souls their thirst will slake,
And our eyes the King will see,
When thy glorious morn shall break—
Eternity! Eternity!
—Ellen M. H. Gates

CHAPTER VIII
WARNING

"Take heed that no man deceive you."—Matt. xxiv: 4.

"Christ in you, the hope of glory, whom we preach, warning every man, and teaching every man in all wisdom; that we may present every man perfect in Christ Jesus."—Col. i: 27, 28.

WARNING

To give a warning is a sign of love. Who warns like a mother, and who loves like a mother? Your mother, perhaps, is gone, and your father is gone. Let me take the place of those who have departed, and lift up a warning voice. With Paul I would say: "I write not these things to shame you, but as my beloved sons I warn you."

A pilot guiding a steamer down the Cumberland saw a light, apparently from a small craft, in the middle of the narrow channel. His impulse was to disregard the signal and run down the boat. As he came near, a voice shouted: "Keep off, keep off."

In great anger he cursed what he supposed to be a boatman in his way. On arriving at his next landing he learned that a huge rock had fallen from the mountain into the bed of the stream, and that a signal was placed there to warn the coming boats of the unknown danger. Alas! many regard God's warnings in the same way, and are angry with any who tell them of the rocks in their course. They will understand better at the end.

The children of Israel had no truer friend than Moses. They

never went astray but he warned them; and trouble never came upon them except when his warnings were unheeded. Elijah was the best friend Ahab had.

I wish I could warn as Jesus Christ did. As he went up Mount Olivet, His heart seemed to be greatly moved and He cried, "Oh, Jerusalem, Jerusalem, thou that killest the prophets, and stonest them which are sent unto thee, how often would I have gathered thy children together, even as a hen gathereth her chickens under her wings, and ye would not!" Did He not warn?

If a friend of mine were about to invest in a worthless silver-mine, do you think I would be true to him if I did not caution him against it? And do I show less love for him because I warn him against actions that will bring a harvest of misery and despair?

"Whosoever heareth the sound of the trumpet, and taketh not warning; if the sword come, and take him away, his blood shall be upon his own head; he heard the sound of the trumpet, and took not warning; his blood shall be upon him. But he that taketh warning shall deliver his soul."

Be sure that the seed you are sowing is good seed. Sow to the flesh, and a good harvest will be impossible. Good seed and bad seed cannot both succeed if allowed to grow together. One prospers at the expense of the other; and the likelihood is that the bad will get the upper hand. Weeds always seem to grow and spread more rapidly than good seed.

The longer they live, the firmer hold the weeds are gaining. Delay is dangerous. In the year 1691, a proclamation was sent through the Highlands of Scotland, that every one who had been guilty of rebellion against the constituted government would be pardoned, if, before the last day of the year, he laid down his arms and promised to cease his rebellion. Many did so; but one chief named Maclan put off submission from week to week, always intending to submit before it was too late. But when, at last, he started to accept pardon, he was hindered by a great storm and did not arrive until the time had expired. The day of pardon had passed and the day of vengeance had come; Maclan and his men were put to death.

Hence, it is wise to exterminate the weeds at once. And beware of remaining longer in sin. The deeper you sink, the more bitter will be your restoration. Why continue to sear you conscience, and sow the seeds of keener remorse? No matter how painful it may be, break with sin at once. Severe operations are often necessary, for the skilful surgeon knows that the disease cannot be cured by surface applications. The farmer takes his hoe and his spade and his axe, and he cuts away the obnoxious growths, and burns the roots out of the ground with fire.

If thy right eye offend thee, pluck it out, and cast it from thee: for it is profitable for thee that one of thy members should perish, and not that thy whole body should be cast into hell. And if thy right hand offend thee, cut it off, and cast it from thee: for it is profitable for thee that one of thy members should perish, and not that thy whole body should be cast into hell.

Remember that the tares and the wheat will be separated at the judgment day, if not before. Sowing to the flesh and sowing to the spirit inevitably lead in diverging paths. The axe will be laid at the root of the trees, and every tree that bringeth not forth good fruit will be hewn down and cast into the fire. The threshing-floor will be thoroughly purged, and the wheat will be gathered into the garner, while the chaff will be burned with unquenchable fire.

Beware of your habits. A recent writer has said: "Could the young but realize how soon they will become mere walking bundles of habits, they would give more heed to their conduct while in the plastic state. We are spinning our own fates, good or evil, and never to be undone. Every smallest stroke of virtue or of vice leaves its never so little scar. The drunken Rip Van Winkle, in Jefferson's play, excuses himself for every fresh dereliction by saying, 'I won't count this time.' Well, he may not count it, and a kind heaven may not count it, but it is being counted none the less. Down among his nerve cells and fibres the molecules are counting it, registering and storing it up, to be used against him when the next temptation comes. Nothing we ever do is, in strict scientific literalness, wiped out. Of course, this has its good side as well as its bad one. As we become permanent drunkards by so many separate drinks, so we become saints in the moral sphere, and authorities and experts in the practical and scientific spheres, by so many separate acts and hours of work."

Beware of temptations. "Lead us not into temptation," our Lord taught us to pray: and again he said, "Watch and pray, lest ye enter into temptation." We are weak and sinful by nature, and it is a good deal better for us to pray for deliverance rather than for strength to resist when temptation has overtaken us. Prevention is better than cure. Hidden under the soil may be seeds of passion and wickedness that only wait for a favorable opportunity to shoot up.

Young men pretend that it is necessary to see both sides of life. What foolishness! I am not called upon to put my hand in the fire to see if it will burn.

A steamboat was stranded on the Mississippi river, and the captain could not get her off. Eventually a hard-looking fellow came on board and said:

"Captain, I understand you want a pilot to take you out of this difficulty?"

The captain said, "Are you a pilot?"

"Well, they call me one."

"Do you know where the snags and sand-bars are?"

"No sir,"

"Well, how do you expect to take me out of here if you don't know where the snags and sand-bars are?"

"I know where they ain't!" was the reply.

Begin to sow the good seed while the children are young, and thus prevent the weeds getting a start. Satan does not wait till they grow up, and no more should we.

There are many fishing nets so constructed as to allow none but full grown fish to be caught, the immature escaping. Satan has none such. He catches the weakest and youngest.

"We must care for our boys or the devil will," said a young Sabbath School teacher.

"The devil will care for them anyway," answered the old superintendent: "The devil will not neglect them even though we do."

It is a master-piece of the devil to make us believe that children can not understand religion. Would Christ have made a child the standard of faith if He had known that it was not capable of understanding His words? It is far easier for children to love and trust than for grown-up persons, and so we should set Christ before them as the supreme object of their choice.

Do not neglect opportunities. Napoleon used to say: "There is a crisis in every battle—ten or fifteen minutes—on which the issue of the battle depends. To gain this is victory; to lose it is defeat."

Beware of sin. Its wages are Death, and (as has been said) the wages have never been reduced. It deceives men as to the satisfaction to be found in it, the excuses to be made for it, and the certainty of the punishment that must follow. If it was not deceitful, it would never be delightful. It comes in innocent guise, and saps the life blood, depriving one of the moral capacity to do good. Canon Wilberforce walking in the Isle of Skye, saw a magnificent eagle soaring upward. He halted and watched its flight. Soon he observed something was wrong. It began to fall, and presently lay dead at his feet. Eager to know the reason of its death, he examined it and found no trace of gunshot wound; but he saw in its talons a small weazel, which, in its flight, drawn near its body, had sucked the life blood from the eagle's-breast. Such is the end of every one who persistently clings to sin.

Do not be deceived by the attractiveness of this world. It will cheat you and destroy you. "The Redoubtable" was the name of a French ship that Lord Nelson spared twice from destruction; and it was from the rigging of that very ship that the fatal ball that killed him was fired. The devil administers many a sin in honey; but there is poison mixed with it. The truest pleasures spring from the good seed of righteousness—none else are profitable.

Beware of ignorance and indifference. You cannot afford to neglect your soul. There is too much at stake. I never knew an idle man to be converted. Until he wakes up and realizes his lost and hopeless condition, God Almighty will not reach down and take him by the hand. A ship was once in great danger at sea, and all but one man were on their knees. They called to him to come and join them in prayer, but he replied:

"Not I; it's your business to look after the ship. I'm only a passenger."

Remember that mere knowledge is not enough. Many a man knows the gospel precepts and promises by heart who is not touched by saving grace. Knowledge is often useless or positively harmful, and what we want is to know God's will and observe it. Even good resolutions are not enough. No doubt they are helpful in their way, but the Bible does not lead us to believe that they can save a man. It does not say: "As many as resolved to receive Him, to them gave He power to become the sons of God, even to them that resolve to believe on His name"; it says: "As many as received Him -- believe on His name."

Be watchful! There is constant need to be on guard lest we fall into sin. "Set a double guard upon that point to-night," was the command of a prudent officer when an attack was expected. At the best there will be some tares among the wheat. We, all of us, carry around with us material that Satan can work on. Paul said:

"For I know that in me (that is, in my flesh) dwelleth no good thing: for to will is present with me; but how to perform that which is good I find not. For the good that I would, I do not: but the evil which I would not, that I do. Now if I do that I would not, it is no more I that do it, but sin that dwelleth in me. I find then a law, that, when I would do good, evil is present with me. For I delight in the law of God after the inward man: but I see another law in my members, warring against the law of my mind, and bringing me into captivity to the law of sin which is in my members. O wretched man that I am! who shall deliver me from the body of this death?"

Blessed be God, he could add: "I thank God through Jesus Christ our Lord."

The issue that God has placed before us is clear-cut: "He that believeth on the Son hath everlasting life; and he that believeth not the Son shall not see life; but the wrath of God abideth on him." There is no middle course—"he that believeth"—"he that believeth not." He leaves us to choose, and the responsibility rests upon ourselves.

It may cost you many a sacrifice, and wrench many a heartstring to choose aright, but I plead with you to take the decisive step now. The salvation of your soul outweighs all other considerations. Will you imperil your eternity for the sake of some present gain or pleasure? Bow your head and say: "Heavenly Father, I now choose to come unto Thee as a poor, suppliant sinner. I believe on Thy Son, whom Thou didst send to be my Savior; and trusting in the merits of His blood, which was shed as a propitiation for my sins, I rest in the assurance of sins forgiven."

There is hope for the vilest sinner. Wherever weeds grow, there is the possibility of good seed growing. The greater your need, the more welcome will you be to Jesus. The proud and the self-confident He knoweth afar off, but the faintest whisper of the contrite sinner commands His attention.

Our Lord gave us a simple test to help us in our choice. He said, "Every tree is known by its fruit. A good tree bringeth not forth corrupt fruit, neither doth a corrupt tree bring forth good fruit." Many of us have not the time or ability to unravel intricate arguments, or grasp profound doctrines. Certain phases of truth are often inaccessible to the ordinary mind. But the test Christ gave is short and practical, and within the reach of any one of us.

"Have you ever heard the gospel?" asked a missionary of a Chinaman, whom he had not seen in his mission before.

"No," he replied, "but I have seen it. I know a man who used to be the terror of his neighborhood. He was a bad opium smoker and dangerous as a wild beast; but he became wholly changed. He is now gentle and good and has left off opium."

Apply this test to infidelity. What are its fruits? Crime follows in its track. Society becomes disorganized. Chastity, honesty and the other virtues are underminined. The whole life is blighted.

The following brief extract from a letter written in an english prison, is a tremendous arraignment of that system of belief which does not acknowledge God:

"I am one of thirteen infidels. Where are my friends? Four have been hanged. One became a Christian. Six have been sentenced to various terms of imprisonment, and one is now confined in a cell just over my head, sentenced to imprisonment for life."

With all reverence we may apply this text to our Lord Himself. We have His own authority for it. On one occasion when the jews cavilled at His actions, He said: "The works which the Father hath given me to finish, the same works that I do, bear witness of me, that the Father hath sent me." On another occasion they gathered round Him and asked, "How long dost thou hold us in suspense? If thou be the Christ, tell us plainly." Jesus answered: "I told you, and ye believed not. The works that I do in my Father's name, they bear witness of me. * * * If I do not the works of my Father, believe me not. But if I do, though you believe not me, believe the works: that ye may know and believe that the Father is in me, and I in Him." Well might the ruler Nicodemus say, "Rabbi, we know that thou art a teacher come from God: for no man can do these miracles that thou doest, except God be with him." And Peter: "Ye men of Israel, hear these words: Jesus of Nazareth, a man approved of God among you by miracles and wonders and signs, which God did by Him in the midst of you, as ye yourselves know."

What are the fruits of extravagance, of pride, of covetousness? And on the other hand, of prayer, of fearing God and doing His commandments? What are the fruits of heathenism? Look at Africa and China and India and the islands of the seas with their gods of wood and stone. What must be the intelligence and moral sense of people who will worship such things?

Even the best of non-Christian religions must always prove a failure. It cannot be denied that many of the highest virtues are enjoined in the writings of heathen philosophers. How could it be otherwise? Morality is universal as humanity, and it is only to be expected that here and there some thinker should pierce beyond the average and read deeper into the foundation-truths of ethics. This fact only proves, in my mind, the intimate connection between the human and the divine. Christianity never claimed to introduce a brand-new system of morality.

Referring to another matter, Christ said: "Think not that I am come to destroy the law and the prophets: I am not come to destroy, but to fulfill." And so the fulness and perfection of His own system could not fail to embrace many principles that had already appeared in heathen morality. But in the hands of our Savior they became broader and brighter and fuller of power and meaning.

Will these non-Christian religions bear the test? Stoicism was perhaps the noblest of the Greek philosophies, but it rapidly developed into utter cynicism, and culminated in the asserted impossibility of attaining to virtue. Epicureanism started out fairly well, but its founder was not dead before it earned for itself the opprobrious epithet that it was a doctrine worthy only of swine. Look at Buddhism, with its filthy ceremonies and cruel tortures. All these systems exhibit a conflict between theory and practice. They failed in their object, because they approached the difficulty on the wrong side. They trimmed away at the branch, not recognizing that the tree was rotten at heart.

Christianity alone will stand the test of raising man out of the pit. And how does it propose to do it? Not by minimizing the danger and need. It says: "The whole head is sick, and the whole heart faint. From the sole of the foot even unto the head there is no soundness in it; but wounds and bruises and putrefying sores." It demands as the first necessity a new birth, regeneration by the Holy Spirit. "Ye must be born again." It does not place sanctification before justification, but having first imparted life from above, it throws around the redeemed sinner the love of Christ and the fellowship and guidance of the Holy Spirit.

A converted Chinaman once said: "I was down in a deep pit, half sunk in the mire, crying for some one to help me out. As I looked up I saw a venerable, grayhaired man looking down at me.

"'My son,' he said, 'this is a dreadful place.'

'Yes,' I answered, 'I fell into it; can't you help me out?'

'My son,' was his reply, 'I am Confucius. If you had read my books and followed what they taught, you would never have been here.'

'Yes, father,' I said, 'but can't you help me out?'

As I looked he was gone. Soon I saw another form approaching, and another man bent over me, this time with closed eyes and folded arms. He seemed to be looking to some far-off place.

'My son,' Buddha said, 'just close your eyes and fold your arms, and forget all about yourself. Get into a state of rest. Don't think about anything that can disturb. Get so still that nothing can move you. Then, my child, you will be in such delicious rest as I am.'

'Yes, father,' I answered, 'I will when I am above ground. Can't you help me out?' But Buddha, too, was gone.

I was just beginning to sink into despair when I saw another figure above me, different from the others. There were marks of suffering on His face. I cried out to Him:

'O, Father! can you help me?'

'My child,' He said, 'what is the matter?'

Before I could answer Him, He was down in the mire by my side. He folded His arms about me and lifted me up; then He fed me and rested me. When I was well He did not say: Now, don't do that again, but He said: 'We will walk on together now'; and we have been walking together until this day."

This was a poor Chinaman's way of telling of the compassionate love and help of the Lord Jesus.

I was reading, some time ago, of a young man who had just come out of a saloon, and had mounted his horse. As a certain deacon passed on his way to church, he followed and said,

"Deacon, can you tell me how far it is to hell?"

The deacon's heart was pained to think that a young man like that should talk so lightly; he passed on and said nothing. When he came round the corner to the church, he found that the horse had thrown that young man, and he was dead. So you may be nearer the Judgment than you think.

When I was in Switzerland many years ago, I learned some solemn lessons about the suddenness with which death may overtake us. I saw several places where land-slides had occurred, completely destroying whole villages; or where avalanches had swept down the mountain sides, leaving destruction in their wake. A terrible calamity happened in the year 1806 to a village, called Goldau, situated in a fertile valley at the foot of the Rossberg mountain. The season had been unusually wet, and this had made the crops all the more abundant.

Early one morning a young peasant, passing the cottage of an old man whom he knew, saw him sitting at the door in the full rays of the sun.

"Good morning, neighbor," said he; "we are likely to have a fine day."

"Time we should have a fine day," growled the old man; "it has been wet enough lately."

"Have you heard the report?" said the other. "Those who were up the earliest this morning declare they saw the top of old Rossberg move."

"Indeed! like enough," said the old man. "Mark my words, and I have often said it before; I shan't live to see it, but those who are now young will not live to be as old as I am before the top of yonder mountain lies at its foot."

"I hope it will not be in my day," said the young man; and he passed on, little thinking how near the prediction was to a fulfilment, and that the ripening fields of corn and the abundant clusters of luscious grapes would never be gathered; but so it was.

The springs of water in the mountain had been overcharged by the excessive rains, and these, in forcing their way to the surface and toward the valley below, had loosened the masses of rounded rock which had been cemented together by a kind of clay, of which material the upper part of the mountain was formed. These huge masses at length gave way and fell headlong into the valley, burying the entire village and about eight hundred of its inhabitants beneath their weight.

But what became of the old man? Alas! he did not escape. He believed the mountain would fall, but he did not think the fall was so near. He was sitting in his cottage, composedly smoking his pipe, when the young man came hastily back, and crying out:

"The mountain is falling!"

The old man composedly rose from his seat, looked out at his door, and saying:

"I shall have time to fill my pipe again," went back into his house.

The young man was saved. The old man perished before he had left his cottage, it and its owner were crushed, and swept to the bottom of the valley.

I was in the north of England, in 1881, when a fearful storm swept over that part of the country. A friend of mine, who was a minister at Eyemouth, had a great many of the fishermen of the place in his congregation. It had been very stormy weather, and the fishermen had been detained in the harbor for a week. One day, however, the sun shone out in a clear blue sky; it seemed as if the storm had passed away, and the boats started out for the fishing-ground. Forty-one boats left the harbor that day. Before they started, the harbor-master hoisted the storm signal, and warned them of the coming tempest. He begged of them not to go; but they disregarded his warning, and away they went. They saw no sign of the coming storm. In a few hours, however, it swept down on that coast, and very few of those fishermen returned. There were five or six men in each boat, and nearly all were lost in that dreadful gale. In the church of which my friend was pastor, I believe there were three male members left.

Those men were ushered into eternity because they did not give heed to the warning. I lift up the storm-signal now, and warn you to escape from the coming judgment!

There was a man living near one of the great trunk roads a number of years ago, who one night saw that a landside had obstructed the track. He saw by the clock that he hadn't time to reach the telegraph office to stop the night express, so he caught up a lantern and started up the track, thinking he might be in time to stop the train. As he ran he fell and put out his light. He hadn't another match, and he could hear the train coming in the distance. He didn't know what to do. As a last resort he stood on the bank, and the moment the train come abreast of him he hurled the lantern with all his might at the engineer. The engineer saw that something must be wrong, took the warning, whistled down the brakes, and stopped the train within a few yards of the obstruction.

I throw the broken lantern at your feet now! I beg you to take warning, make a clear work of sin, cost what it may. Take warning! You must either give up sin, or give up the hope of heaven. Put yourself in the way of being blessed. Make up your mind now that by the grace of God you will obtain the mastery.

"Let the wicked forsake his way, and the unrighteous man his thoughts: and let him return unto the Lord, and He will have mercy upon him; and to our God, for he will abundantly pardon."

THE WAY TO GOD AND HOW TO FIND IT

TO THE READER

In this small volume I have endeavored to point out the Way to God.

I have embodied in the little book a considerable part of several addresses which have been delivered in different cities, both of Great Britain and my own country. God has graciously owned them when spoken from the pulpit, and I trust will none the less add his blessing now they have been put into the printed page with additional matter.

I have called attention first to the Love of God, the source of all Gifts of Grace; have then endeavored to present truths to meet the special needs of representative classes, answering the question, "How man can be just with God," hoping thereby to lead souls to Him who is "the Way, the Truth and the Life."

The last chapter is specially addressed to Backsliders—a class, alas, far too numerous amongst us.

With the earnest prayer and hope that by the blessing of God on these pages the reader may be strengthened, established and settled in the faith of Christ,

I am, yours in His service,

D. L. Moody

CONTENTS

To The Reader	182
Chapter I – "Love that passeth Knowledge"	184
Chapter II – The Gateway into the Kingdom	195
Chapter III – The Two Classes	210
Chapter IV – Words of Counsel	219
Chapter V – A Divine Saviour	227
Chapter VI – Repentance and Restitution	233
Chapter VII – Assurance of Salvation	243
Chapter VIII – Christ All and in All	256
Chapter IX – Backsliding	265

CHAPTER I

"LOVE THAT PASSETH KNOWLEDGE."

"To know the love of Christ which passeth knowledge."
(Ephesians iii. 19.)

If I could only make men understand the real meaning of the words of the apostle John—"God is love," I would take that single text, and would go up and down the world proclaiming this glorious truth. If you can convince a man that you love him you have won his heart. If we really make people believe that God loves them, how we should find them crowding into the kingdom of heaven! The trouble is that men think God hates them; and so they are all the time running away from Him.

We built a church in Chicago some years ago; and were very anxious to teach the people the love of God. We thought if we could not preach it into their hearts we would try and burn it in; so we put right over the pulpit in gas-jets these words—God is Love. A man going along the streets one night glanced through the door, and saw the text. He was a poor prodigal. As he passed on he thought to himself, "God is Love! No! He does not love me; for I am a poor miserable sinner." He tried to get rid of the text; but it seemed to stand out right before him in letters of fire. He went on a little further; then turned round, went back, and went into the meeting. He did not hear the sermon; but the words of that short text had got deeply lodged in his heart, and that was enough. It is of little account what men say if the Word of God only gets an entrance into the sinner's heart. He staid after the first meeting was over; and I found him there weeping like a child. As I unfolded the Scriptures and told him how God had loved him all the time, although he had wandered so far away, and how God was waiting to receive him and forgive him, the light of the Gospel broke into his mind, and he went away rejoicing.

There is nothing in this world that men prize so much us they do Love. Show me a person who has no one to care for or love him, and I will show you one of the most wretched beings on the face of the earth. Why do people commit suicide? Very often it is because this thought steals in upon them—that no one loves them; and they would rather die than live.

I know of no truth in the whole Bible that ought to come home to us with such power and tenderness as that of the Love of God; and there is no truth in the Bible that Satan would so much like to blot out. For more than six thousand years he has been trying to persuade men that God does not love them. He succeeded in making our first parents believe this lie; and he too often succeeds with their children.

The idea that God does not love us often comes from false teaching. Mothers make a mistake in teaching children that God does not love them when they do wrong; but only when they do right. That is not taught in Scripture. You do not teach your children that when they do wrong you hate them. Their wrong-doing does not change your love to hate; if it did, you would change your love a great many times. Because your child is fretful, or has committed some act of disobedience, you do not cast him out as though he did not belong to you! No! he is still your child; and you love him. And if men have gone astray from God it does not follow that He hates them. It is the sin that He hates.

I believe the reason why a great many people think God does not love them is because they are measuring God by their own small rule, from their own standpoint. We love men as long as we consider them worthy of our love; when they are not we cast them off. It is not so with God. There is a vast difference between human love and Divine love.

In Ephesians iii. 18, we are told of the breadth, and length, and depth, and height, of God's love. Many of us think we know something of God's love; but centuries hence we shall admit we have never found out much about it. Columbus discovered America; but what did he know about its great lakes, rivers, forests, and the Mississippi Valley? He died, without knowing much about what he had discovered. So, many of us have discovered something of the love of God; but there are heights, depths and lengths of it we do not know. That Love is a great ocean; and we require to plunge into it before we really know anything of it. It is said of a Roman Catholic Archbishop of Paris, that when he was thrown into prison and condemned to be shot, a little while before he was led out to die, he saw a window in his cell in the shape of a cross. Upon the top of the cross he wrote "height," at the bottom "depth," and at the end of each arm "length." He had experienced the truth conveyed in the hymn—

"When I survey the wondrous Cross,
On which the Prince of Glory died."

When we wish to know the love of God we should go to Calvary. Can we look upon that scene, and say God did not love us? That cross speaks of the love of God. Greater love never has been taught than that which the cross teaches. What prompted God to give up Christ?—what prompted Christ to die?—if it were not love? "Greater love hath no man than this, that a man lay down his life for his friends." Christ laid down His life for His enemies; Christ laid down His life for His murderers; Christ laid down His life for them that hated Him; and the spirit of the cross, the spirit of Calvary, is love. When they were mocking Him and deriding Him, what did He say? "Father, forgive them, for they know not what they do." That is love. He did not call down fire from heaven to consume them; there was nothing but love in His heart.

If you study the Bible you will find that the love of God is unchangeable. Many who loved you at one time have perhaps grown cold in their affection, and turned away from you: it may be that their love is changed to hatred. It is not so with God. It is recorded of Jesus Christ, just when He was about to be parted from His disciples and led away to Calvary, that: "having loved His own which were in the world, He loved them unto the end" (John xiii. 1). He knew that one of His disciples would betray Him; yet He loved Judas. He knew that another disciple would deny Him, and swear that he never knew Him; and yet He loved Peter. It was the love which Christ had for Peter that broke his heart, and brought him back in penitence to the feet of his Lord. For three years Jesus had been with the disciples trying to teach them His love, not only by His life and words, but by His works. And, on the night of His betrayal, He takes a basin of water, girds Himself with a towel, and taking the place of a servant, washes their feet; He wanted to convince them of His unchanging love.

There is no portion of Scripture I read so often as John xiv; and there is none that is more sweet to me. I never tire of reading it. Hear what our Lord says, as He pours out His heart to His Disciples: "At that day ye shall know that I am in My Father, and ye in Me, and I in you. He that hath My commandments, and keepeth them, he it is that loveth Me: and he that loveth Me shall be loved by My Father" (xiv. 20,21). Think of the great God who created heaven and earth loving you and me! . . . "If a man love Me, he will keep My words; and My Father will love him; and We will come unto him, and make Our abode with him" (v. 23).

Would to God that our puny minds could grasp this great truth, that the Father and the Son so love us that They desire to come and abide with us. Not to tarry for a night, but to come and abide in our hearts.

We have another passage more wonderful still in John xvii. 23. "I in them, and thou in Me, that they may be made perfect in one; and that the world may know that Thou hast sent Me, and hast loved them as Thou hast loved Me." I think that is one of the most remarkable sayings that ever fell from the lips of Jesus Christ. There is no reason why the Father should not love him. He was obedient unto death; He never transgressed the Father's law, or turned aside from the path of perfect obedience by one hair's breadth. It is very different with us; and yet, notwithstanding all our rebellion and foolishness, He says that if we are trusting in Christ, the Father loves us as He loves the Son. Marvellous love! Wonderful love! That God can possibly love us as He loves His own Son seems too good to be true. Yet that is the teaching of Jesus Christ.

It is hard to make a sinner believe in this unchangeable love of God. When a man has wandered away from God he thinks that God hates him. We must make a distinction between sin and the sinner. God loves the sinner; but He hates the sin. He hates sin, because it mars human life. It is just because God loves the sinner that He hates sin.

God's love is not only unchangeable, but unfailing. In Isaiah xlix. 15, 16 we read: "Can a woman forget her sucking child that she should not have compassion on the son of her womb? yea, they may forget; yet will I not forget thee. Behold I have graven thee upon the palms of My hands; thy walls are continually before Me."

Now the strongest human love that we know of is a mother's love. Many things will separate a man from his wife. A father may turn his back on his child; brothers and sisters may become inveterate enemies; husbands may desert their wives; wives, their husbands. But a mother's love endures through all. In good repute, in bad repute, in the face of the world's condemnation, a mother loves on, and hopes that her child may turn from his evil ways and repent. She remembers the infant smiles, the merry laugh of childhood, the promise of youth; and she can never be brought to think him unworthy. Death cannot quench a mother's love; it is stronger than death.

You have seen a mother watching over her sick child. How willingly she would take the disease into her own body if she could thus relieve her child! Week after week she will keep watch; she will let no one else take care of that sick child.

A friend of mine, some time ago, was visiting in a beautiful home where he met a number of friends. After they had all gone away, having left something behind, he went back to get it. There he found the lady of the house, a wealthy lady, sitting behind a poor fellow who looked like a tramp. He was her own son. Like the prodigal, he had wandered far away: yet the mother said, "This is my boy; I love him still." Take a mother with nine or ten children, if one goes astray, she seems to love that one more than any of the rest.

A leading minister in the state of New York once told me of a father who was a very bad character. The mother did all she could to prevent the contamination of the boy; but the influence of the father was stronger, and he led his son into all kinds of sin until the lad became one of the worst of criminals. He committed murder, and was put on his trial. All through the trial, the widowed mother (for the father had died) sat in the court. When the witnesses testified against the boy it seemed to hurt the mother much more than the son. When he was found guilty and sentenced to die, every one else feeling the justice of the verdict, seemed satisfied at the result. But the mother's love never faltered. She begged for a reprieve; but that was denied. After the execution she craved for the body; and this also was refused. According to custom, it was buried in the prison yard. A little while afterwards the mother herself died; but, before she was taken away, she expressed a desire to be buried by the side of her boy. She was not ashamed of being known as the mother of a murderer.

The story is told of a young woman in Scotland, who left her home, and became an outcast in Glasgow. Her mother sought her far and wide, but in vain. At last, she caused her picture to be hung upon the walls of the Midnight Mission rooms, where abandoned women resorted. Many gave the picture a passing glance. One lingered by the picture. It is the same dear face that looked down upon her in her childhood. She has not forgotten nor cast off her sinning child; or her picture would never have been hung upon those walls. The lips seemed to open, and whisper, "Come home; I forgive you, and love you still." The poor girl sank down overwhelmed with her feelings. She was the prodigal daughter. The sight of her mother's face had broken her heart. She became truly penitent for her sins, and with a heart full of sorrow and shame, returned to her forsaken home; and mother and daughter were once more united.

But let me tell you that no mother's love is to be compared with the love of God; it does not measure the height of the depth of God's love. No mother in this world ever loved her child as God loves you and me. Think of the love that God must have had when He gave His Son to die for the world. I used to think a good deal more of Christ than I did of the Father. Somehow or other I had the idea that God was a stern judge; that Christ came between me and God, and appeased the anger of God. But after I became a father, and for years had an only son, as I looked at my boy I thought of the Father giving His Son to die; and it seemed to me as if it required more love for the Father to give His Son than for the Son to die. Oh, the love that God must have had for the world when He gave His Son to die for it! "God so loved the world, that He gave His only begotten Son, that whosoever believeth in Him should not perish, but have everlasting life" (John iii. 16). I have never been able to preach from that text. I have often thought I would; but it is so high that I can never climb to its height; I have just quoted it and passed on. Who can fathom the depth of those words: "God so loved the world?" We can never scale the heights of His love or fathom its depths. Paul prayed that he might know the height, the depth, the length, and the breadth, of the love of God; but it was past his finding out. It "passeth knowledge" (Eph. iii. 19).

Nothing speaks to us of the love of God, like the cross of Christ. Come with me to Calvary, and look upon the Son of God as He hangs there. Can you hear that piercing cry from His dying lips: "Father, forgive them; for they know not what they do!" and say that He does not love you? "Greater love hath no man than this, that a man lay down his life for his friends" (John xv. 13). But Jesus Christ laid down His life for his enemies.

Another thought is this: He loved us long before we ever thought of Him. The idea that he does not love us until we first love Him is not to be found in Scripture. In 1 John iv. 10, it is written: "Herein is love, not that we loved God, but that He loved us, and sent His Son to be the propitiation for our sins." He loved us before we ever thought of loving Him. You loved your children before they knew anything about your love. And so, long before we ever thought of God, we were in His thoughts.

What brought the prodigal home? It was the thought that his father loved him. Suppose the news had reached him that he was cast off, and that his father did not care for him any more, would he have gone back? Never! But the thought dawned upon him that his father loved him still: so he rose up, and went back to his home. Dear reader, the love of the Father ought to bring us back to Him. It was Adam's calamity and sin that revealed God's love. When Adam fell God came down and dealt in mercy with him. If any one is lost it will not be because God does not love him: it will be because he has resisted the love of God.

What will make Heaven attractive? Is it the pearly gates or the golden streets? No. Heaven will be attractive, because there we shall behold Him who loved us so much as to give His only-begotten Son to die for us. What makes home attractive? Is it the beautiful furniture and stately rooms? No; some homes with all these are like whited sepulchres. In Brooklyn a mother was dying; and it was necessary to take her child from her, because the little child could not understand the nature of the sickness, and disturbed her mother. Every night the child sobbed herself to sleep in a neighbor's house, because she wanted to go back to her mother's; but the mother grew worse, and they could not take the child home. At last the mother died; and after her death they thought it best not to let the child see her dead mother in her coffin. After the burial the child ran into one room crying "Mamma! mamma!" and then into another crying "Mamma! mamma!" and so went over the whole house: and when the little creature failed to find that loved one she cried to be taken back to the neighbors. So what makes heaven attractive is the thought that we shall see Christ who has loved us and given Himself for us.

If you ask me why God should love us, I cannot tell. I suppose it is because He is a true Father. It is His nature to love; just as it is the nature of the sun to shine. He wants you to share in that love. Do not let unbelief keep you away from Him. Do not think that, because you are a sinner, God does not love you, or care for you. He does! He wants to save you and bless you.

"When we were yet without strength, in due time Christ died for the ungodly" (Rom. v. 6). Is that not enough to convince you that He loves you? He would not have died for you if He had not loved you. Is your heart so hard that you can brace yourself up against His love, and spurn and despise it? You can do it; but it will be at your peril.

I can imagine some saying to themselves, "Yes, we believe that God loves us, if we love Him; we believe that God loves the pure and the holy." Let me say, my friend, not only does God love the pure and the holy: He also loves the ungodly. "God commendeth His love toward us, in that, while we were yet sinners, Christ died for us" (Rom. v. 8). God sent him to die for the sins of the whole world. If you belong to the world, then you have part and lot in this love that has been exhibited in the cross of Christ.

There is a passage in Revelation (i. 5.) which I think a great deal of—"Unto Him that loved us, and washed us." It might be thought that God would first wash us, and then love us. But no, He first loved us. About eight years ago the whole country was intensely excited about Charlie Ross, a child of four years old, who was stolen. Two men in a gig asked him and an elder brother if they wanted some candy. They then drove away with the younger boy, leaving the elder one. For many years a search has been made in every State and territory. Men have been over to Great Britain, France, and Germany, and have hunted in vain for the child. The mother still lives in the hope that she will see her long lost Charlie. I never remember the whole country to have been so much agitated about any event unless it was the assassination of President Garfield. Well, suppose the mother of Charlie Ross were in some meeting; and that while the preacher was speaking, she happened to look down amongst the audience and see her long lost son. Suppose that he was poor, dirty and ragged, shoeless and coatless, what would she do? Would she wait till he was washed and decently clothed before she would acknowledge him? No, she would get off the platform at once, rush towards him and take him in her arms. After that she would cleanse and clothe him. So it is with God. He loved us, and washed us. I can imagine one saying, "If God loves me, why does He not make me good?" God wants sons and daughters in heaven; He does not want machines or slaves. He could break our stubborn hearts, but He wants to draw us towards Himself by the cords of love.

He wanted you to sit down with Him at the marriage supper of the Lamb; to wash you, and make you whiter than snow. He wants you to walk with Him the crystal pavement of yonder blissful world. He wants to adopt you into His family; and to make you a son or a daughter of heaven. Will you trample His love under your feet? or will you, this hour, give yourself to Him?

When our terrible civil war was going on, a mother received the news that her boy had been wounded in the battle of the Wilderness. She took the first train, and started for her boy, although the order had gone forth from the War Department that no more women should be admitted within the lines. But a mother's love knows nothing about orders so she managed by tears and entreaties to get through the lines to the Wilderness. At last she found the hospital where her boy was. Then she went to the doctor and she said: "Will you let me go to the ward and nurse my boy?"

The doctor said: "I have just got your boy to sleep; he is in a very critical state; and I am afraid if you wake him up the excitement will be so great that it will carry him off. You had better wait awhile, and remain without until I tell him that you have come, and break the news gradually to him." The mother looked into the doctor's face and said: "Doctor, supposing my boy does not wake up, and I should never see him alive! Let me go and sit down by his side; I won't speak to him." "If you will not speak to him you may do so," said the doctor.

She crept to the cot and looked into the face of her boy. How she had longed to look at him! How her eyes seemed to be feasting as she gazed upon his countenance! When she got near enough she could not keep her hands off; she laid that tender, loving hand upon his brow. The moment the hand touched the forehead of her boy, he, without opening his eyes, cried out: "Mother, you have come!" He knew the touch of that loving hand. There was love and sympathy in it.

Ah, sinner, if you feel the loving touch of Jesus you will recognize it; it is so full of tenderness. The world may treat you unkindly; but Christ never will. You will never have a better Friend in this world. What you need is—to come today to Him. Let His loving arm be underneath you; let His loving hand be about you; and He will hold you with mighty power. He will keep you, and fill that heart of yours with His tenderness and love.

I can imagine some of you saying, "How shall I go to Him?" Why, just as you would go to your mother. Have you done your mother a great injury and a great wrong? If so, you go to her and you say, "Mother, I want you to forgive me." Treat Christ in the same way. Go to Him to-day and tell Him that you have not loved Him, that you have not treated Him right; confess you sins, and see how quickly He will bless you.

I am reminded of another incident—that of a boy who had been tried by court-martial and ordered to be shot. The hearts of the father and mother were broken when they heard the news. In that home was a little girl. She had read the life of Abraham Lincoln, and she said: "Now, if Abraham Lincoln knew how my father and mother loved their boy, he would not let my brother be shot." She wanted her father to go to Washington to plead for his boy. But the father said: "No; there is no use; the law must take its course. They have refused to pardon one or two who have been sentenced by that court-martial, and an order has gone forth that the President is not going to interfere again; if a man has been sentenced by court-martial he must suffer the consequences." That father and mother had not faith to believe that their boy might be pardoned.

But the little girl was strong in hope; she got on the train away up in Vermont, and started off to Washington. When she reached the White House the soldiers refused to let her in; but she told her pitiful story, and they allowed her to pass. When she got to the Secretary's room, where the President's private secretary was, he refused to allow her to enter the private office of the President. But the little girl told her story, and it touched the heart of the private secretary; so he passed her in. As she went into Abraham Lincoln's room, there were United States senators, generals, governors and leading politicians, who were there about important business about the war; but the President happened to see that child standing at his door. He wanted to know what she wanted, and she went right to him and told her story in her own language. He was a father, and the great tears trickled down Abraham Lincoln's cheeks. He wrote a dispatch ard sent it to the army to have that boy sent to Washington at once. When he arrived, the President pardoned him, gave him thirty days furlough, and sent him home with the little girl to cheer the hearts of the father and mother.

Do you want to know how to go to Christ? Go just as that little girl went to Abraham Lincoln. It may be possible that you have a dark story to tell. Tell it all out; keep nothing back. If Abraham Lincoln had compassion on that little girl, heard her petition and answered it, do you think the Lord Jesus will not hear your prayer? Do, you think that Abraham Lincoln, or any man that ever lived on earth, had as much compassion as Christ? No! He will be touched when no one else will; He will have mercy when no one else will; He will have pity when no one else will. If you will go right to Him, confessing your sin and your need, He will save you.

A few years ago a man left England and went to America. He was an Englishman; but he was naturalized, and so became an American citizen. After a few years he felt restless and dissatisfied, and went to Cuba; and after he had been in Cuba a little while civil war broke out there; it was in 1867; and this man was arrested by the Spanish government as a spy. He was tried by court-martial, found guilty and ordered to be shot. The whole trial was conducted in the Spanish language, and the poor man did not know what was going on. When they told him the verdict, that he was found guilty and had been condemned to be shot, he sent to the American Consul and the English Consul, and laid the whole case before them, proving his innocence and claiming protection. They examined the case, and found that this man whom the Spanish officers had condemned to be shot was perfectly innocent; they went to the Spanish General and said, "Look here, this man whom you have condemned to death is an innocent man; he is not guilty." But the Spanish General said, "He has been tried by our law; he has been found guilty; he must die." There was no electric cable; and these men could not consult with their governments.

The morning came on which the man was to be executed. He was brought out sitting on his coffin in a cart, and drawn to the place where he was to be executed. A grave was dug. They took the coffin out of the cart, placed the young man upon it, took the black cap, and were just pulling it down over his face. The Spanish soldiers awaited the order to fire. But just then the American and English Consuls rode up. The English Consul sprang out of the carriage and took the union jack, the British flag, and wrapped it around the man, and the American Consul wrapped around him the star-spangled banner, and then turning to the Spanish officers they said: "Fire upon those flags if you dare." They did not dare to fire upon the flags. There were two great governments behind those flags. That was the secret of it.

"He brought me to the banqueting house, and His banner over me was love. . . . His left hand is under my head, and His right hand doth embrace me" (Song Sol. ii. 4, 6). Thank God we can come under the banner to-day if we will. Any, poor sinner can come under that banner to-day. His banner of love is over us. Blessed Gospel; blessed, precious, news. Believe it to-day; receive it into your heart; and enter into a new life. Let the love of God be shed abroad in your heart by the Holy Ghost to-day: it will drive away darkness; it will drive away gloom; it will drive away sin; and peace and joy shall be yours.

CHAPTER II

THE GATEWAY INTO THE KINGDOM.

"Except a man be born again he cannot enter the kingdom of God."

(John iii. 3.)

There is no portion of the Word of God, perhaps, with which we are more familiar than this passage. I suppose if I were to ask those in any audience if they believed that Jesus Christ taught the doctrine of the New Birth, nine tenths of them would say: "Yes, I believe He did."

Now if the words of this text are true they embody one of the most solemn questions that can come before us. We can afford to be deceived about many things rather than about this one thing. Christ makes it very plain. He says, "Except a man be born again, he cannot see the Kingdom of God"—much less inherit it. This doctrine of the New Birth is therefore the foundation of all our hopes for the world to come. It is really the A B C of the Christian religion. My experience has been this—that if a man is unsound on this doctrine he will be unsound on almost every other fundamental doctrine in the Bible. A true understanding of this subject will help a man to solve a thousand difficulties that he may meet with in the Word of God. Things that before seemed very dark and mysterious will become very plain.

The doctrine of the New Birth upsets all false religion—all false views about the Bible and about God. A friend of mine once told me that in one of his after-meetings, a man came to him with a long list of questions written out for him to answer. He said: "If you can answer these questions satisfactorily, I have made up my mind to be a Christian." "Do you not think," said my friend, "that you had better come to Christ first? Then you can look into these questions." The man thought that perhaps he had better do so. After he had received Christ, he looked again at his list of questions; but then it seemed to him as if they had all been answered. Nicodemus came with his troubled mind, and Christ said to him, "Ye must be born again." He was treated altogether differently from what he expected; but I venture to say that was the most blessed night in all his life. To be "born again" is the greatest blessing that will ever come to us in this world.

Notice how the Scripture puts it. "Except a man be born again," "born from above,"[Note: John iii. 3. Marginal reading] "born of the Spirit." From amongst a number of other passages where we find this word "except," I would just name three. "Except ye repent, ye shall all likewise perish." (Luke xiii. 3, 5.) "Except ye be converted, and become as little children, ye shall not enter into the kingdom of heaven." (Matt. xviii. 3.) "Except your righteousness shall exceed the righteousness of the Scribes and Pharisees, ye shall in no case enter into the kingdom of heaven." (Matt. v. 20.) They all really mean the same thing.

I am so thankful that our Lord spoke of the New Birth to this ruler of the Jews, this doctor of the law, rather than to the woman at the well of Samaria, or to Matthew the publican, or to Zaccheus. If He had reserved his teaching on this great matter for these three, or such as these, people would have said: "Oh yes, these publicans and harlots need to be converted: but I am an upright man; I do not need to be converted." I suppose Nicodemus was one of the best specimens of the people of Jerusalem: there was nothing on record against him.

I think it is scarcely necessary for me to prove that we need to be born again before we are meet for heaven. I venture to say that there is no candid man but would say he is not fit for the kingdom of God, until he is born of another Spirit. The Bible teaches us that man by nature is lost and guilty, and our experience confirms this. We know also that the best and holiest man, if he turn away from God, will very soon fall into sin.

Now, let me say what Regeneration is not. It is not going to church. Very often I see people, and ask them if they are Christians. "Yes, of course I am; at least, I think I am: I go to church every Sunday." Ah, but this is not Regeneration. Others say, "I am trying to do what is right—am I not a Christian? Is not that a new birth?" No. What has that to do with being born again? There is yet another class—those who have "turned over a new leaf," and think they are regenerated. No; forming a new resolution is not being born again.

Nor will being baptized do you any good. Yet you hear people say, "Why, I have been baptized; and I was born again when I was baptized." They believe that because they were baptized into the church, they were baptized into the Kingdom of God. I tell you that it is utterly impossible. You may be baptized into the church, and yet not be baptized into the Son of God. Baptism is all right in its place. God forbid that I should say anything against it. But if you put that in the place of Regeneration—in the place of the New Birth—it is a terrible mistake. You cannot be baptized into the Kingdom of God. "Except a man be born again, he cannot see the Kingdom of God." If any one reading this rests his hopes on anything else—on any other foundation—I pray that God may sweep it away.

Another class say, "I go to the Lord's Supper; I partake uniformly of the Sacrament." Blessed ordinance! Jesus hath said that as often as ye do it ye commemorate His death. Yet, that is not being "born again;" that is not passing from death unto life. Jesus says plainly—and so plainly that there need not be any mistake about it—"Except a man be born of the Spirit, he cannot enter into the Kingdom of God." What has a sacrament to do with that? What has going to church to do with being born again?

Another man comes up and says, "I say my prayers regularly." Still I say that is not being born of the Spirit. It is a very solemn question, then, that comes up before us; and oh! that every reader would ask himself earnestly and faithfully: "Have I been born again? Have I been born of the Spirit? Have I passed from death unto life?"

There is a class of men who say that special religious meetings are very good for a certain class of people. They would be very good if you could get the drunkard there, or get the gambler there, or get other vicious people there—that would do a great deal of good. But "we do not need to be converted." To whom did Christ utter these words of wisdom? To Nicodemus. Who was Nicodemus? Was he a drunkard, a gambler, or a thief? No! No doubt he was one of the very best men in Jerusalem. He was an honorable Councillor; he belonged to the Sanhedrim; he held a very high position; he was an orthodox man; he was one of the very soundest men. And yet what did Christ say to him? "Except a man be born again, he cannot see the kingdom of God."

But I can imagine some one saying, "What am I to do? I cannot create life. I certainly cannot save myself." You certainly cannot; and we do not claim that you can. We tell you it is utterly impossible to make a man better without Christ; but that is what men are trying to do. They are trying to patch up this "old Adam" nature. There must be a new creation. Regeneration is a new creation; and if it is a new creation it must be the work of God. In the first chapter of Genesis man does not appear. There is no one there but God. Man is not there to take part. When God created the earth He was alone. When Christ redeemed the world He was alone.

"That which is born of the flesh is flesh; and that which is born of the Spirit is spirit." (John iii. 6.) The Ethiopian cannot change his skin, and the leopard cannot change his spots. You might as well try to make yourselves pure and holy without the help of God. It would be just as easy for you to do that as for the black man to wash himself white. A man might just as well try to leap over the moon as to serve God in the flesh. Therefore, "that which is born of the flesh is flesh; and that which is born of the Spirit is spirit."

Now God tells us in this chapter how we are to get into His kingdom. We are not to work our way in—not but that salvation is worth working for. We admit all that. If there were rivers and mountains in the way, it would be well worth while to swim those rivers, and climb those mountains. There is no doubt that salvation is worth all that effort; but we do not obtain it by our works. It is "to him that worketh not, but believeth" (Rom. iv. 5). We work because we are saved; we do not work to be saved. We work from the cross; but not towards it. It is written, "Work out your own salvation with fear and trembling" (Phil. ii. 12). Why, you must have your salvation before you can work it out. Suppose I say to my little boy, "I want you to spend that hundred dollars carefully." "Well," he says, "let me have the hundred dollars; and I will be careful how I spend it." I remember when I first left home and went to Boston; I had spent all my money, and I went to the post-office three times a day. I knew there was only one mail a day from home; but I thought by some possibility there might be a letter for me. At last I received a letter from my little sister; and oh, how glad I was to get it. She had heard that there were a great many pickpockets in Boston, and a large part of that letter was to urge me to be very careful not to let anybody pick my pocket. Now I required to have something in my pocket before I could have it picked. So you must have salvation before you can work it out.

When Christ cried out on Calvary, "It is finished!" He meant what

He said. All that men have to do now is just to accept of the work of Jesus Christ. There is no hope for man or woman so long as they are trying to work out salvation for themselves. I can imagine there are some people who will say, as Nicodemus possibly did, "This is a very mysterious thing." I see the scowl on that Pharisee's brow as he says, "How can these things be?" It sounds very strange to his ear. "Born again; born of the Spirit! How can these things be?" A great many people say, "You must reason it out; but if you do not reason it out, do not ask us to believe it." I can imagine a great many people saying that. When you ask me to reason it out, I tell you frankly I cannot do it. "The wind bloweth where it listeth, and thou hearest the sound thereof, but canst not tell whence it cometh and whither it goeth: so is every one that is born of the Spirit." (John 8.) I do not understand everything about the wind. You ask me to reason it out. I cannot. It may blow due north here, and a hundred miles away due south. I may go up a few hundred feet, and find it blowing in an entirely opposite direction from what it is down here. You ask me to explain these currents of wind; but suppose that, because I cannot explain them, and do not understand them, I were to take my stand and assert, "Oh, there is no such thing as wind." I can imagine some little girl saying, "I know more about it than that man does; often have I heard the wind, and felt it blowing against my face;" and she might say, "Did not the wind blow my umbrella out of my hands the other day? and did I not see it blow a man's hat off in the street? Have I not seen it blow the trees in the forest, and the growing corn in the country?"

You might just as well tell me that there is no such thing as wind, as tell me there is no such thing as a man being born of the Spirit. I have felt the spirit of God working in my heart, just as really and as truly as I have felt the wind blowing in my face. I cannot reason it out. There are a great many things I cannot reason out, but which I believe. I never could reason out the creation. I can see the world, but I cannot tell how God made it out of nothing. But almost every man will admit there was a creative power.

There are a great many things that I cannot explain and cannot reason out, and yet that I believe. I heard a commercial traveler say that he had heard that the ministry and religion of Jesus Christ were matters of revelation and not of investigation. "When it pleased God to reveal His Son in Me," says Paul (Gal. i, 15, 16). There was a party of young men together, going up the country; and on their journey they made up their minds not to believe anything they could not reason out. An old man heard them; and presently he said, "I heard you say you would not believe anything you could not reason out." "Yes," they said, "that is so." "Well," he said, "coming down on the train to-day, I noticed some geese, some sheep, some swine, and some cattle all eating grass. Can you tell me by what process that same grass was turned into hair, feathers, bristles and wool? Do you believe it is a fact?" "Oh yes," they said, "we cannot help believing that, though we fail to understand it." "Well," said the old man, "I cannot help believing in Jesus Christ." And I cannot help believing in the regeneration of man, when I see men who have been reclaimed, when I see men who have been reformed. Have not some of the very worst men been regenerated—been picked up out of the pit, and had their feet set upon the Rock, and a new song put in their mouths? Their tongues were cursing and blaspheming; and now are occupied in praising God. Old things have passed away, and all things have become new. They are not reformed only, but regenerated—new men in Christ Jesus.

Down there in the dark alleys of one of our great cities is a poor drunkard. I think if you want to get near hell, you should go to a poor drunkard's home. Go to the house of that poor miserable drunkard. Is there anything more like hell on earth? See the want and distress that reign there. But hark! A footstep is heard at the door, and the children run and hide themselves. The patient wife waits to meet the man. He has been her torment. Many a time she has borne about the marks of his blows for weeks. Many a time that strong right hand has been brought down on her defenseless head. And now she waits expecting to hear his oaths and suffer his brutal treatment. He comes in and says to her: "I have been to the meeting; and I heard there that if I will I can be converted. I believe that God is able to save me." Go down to that house again in a few weeks: and what a change! As you approach you hear some one singing. It is not the song of a reveller, but the strains of that good old hymn, "Rock of Ages." The children are no longer afraid of the man, but cluster around his knee. His wife is near him, her face lit up with a happy glow. Is not that a picture of Regeneration? I can take you to many such homes, made happy by the regenerating power of the religion of Christ. What men want is the power to overcome temptation, the power to lead a right life.

The only way to get into the kingdom of God is to be "born" into it. The law of this country requires that the President should be born in the country. When foreigners come to our shores they have no right to complain against such a law, which forbids them from ever becoming Presidents. Now, has not God a right to make a law that all those who become heirs of eternal life must be "born" into His kingdom?

An unregenerated man would rather be in hell than in heaven. Take a man whose heart is full of corruption and wickedness, and place him in heaven among the pure, the holy and the redeemed; and he would not want to stay there. Certainly, if we are to be happy in heaven we must begin to make a heaven here on earth. Heaven is a prepared place for a prepared people. If a gambler or a blasphemer were taken out of the streets of New York and placed on the crystal pavement of heaven and under the shadow of the tree of life, he would say, "I do not want to stay here." If men were taken to heaven just as they are by nature, without having their hearts regenerated, there would be another rebellion in heaven. Heaven is filled with a company of those who have been twice born.

In the 14th and 15th verses of this chapter we read "As Moses lifted up the serpent in the wilderness, even so must the Son of Man be lifted up; that whosoever believeth in Him should not perish, but have eternal life." "WHOSOEVER." Mark that! Let me tell you who are unsaved what God has done for you. He has done everything that He could do toward your salvation. You need not wait for God to do anything more. In one place he asks the question, what more could he have done (Isaiah v. 4). He sent His prophets, and they killed them; then He sent His beloved Son, and they murdered Him. Now He has sent the Holy Spirit to convince us of sin, and to show how we are to be saved.

In this chapter we are told how men are to be saved, namely, by Him who was lifted up on the cross. Just as Moses lifted up the brazen serpent in the wilderness, so must the Son of Man be lifted up, "that whosoever believeth in Him should not perish, but have eternal life." Some men complain and say that it is very unreasonable that they should be held responsible for the sin of a man six thousand years ago. It was not long ago that a man was talking to me about this injustice, as he called it. If a man thinks he is going to answer God in that way, I tell you it will not do him any good. If you are lost, it will not be on account of Adam's sin.

Let me illustrate this; and perhaps you will be better able to understand it. Suppose I am dying of consumption, which I inherited from my father or mother. I did not get the disease by any fault of my own, by any neglect of my health; I inherited it, let us suppose. A friend happens to come along: he looks at me, and says: "Moody, you are in a consumption." I reply, "I know it very well; I do not want any one to tell me that." "But," he says, "there is a remedy." "But, sir, I do not believe it. I have tried the leading physicians in this country and in Europe; and they tell me there is no hope." "But you know me, Moody; you have known me for years." "Yes, sir." "Do you think, then, I would tell you a falsehood?" "No." "Well, ten years ago I was as far gone. I was given up by the physicians to die; but I took this medicine and it cured me. I am perfectly well: look at me." I say that it is "a very strange case." "Yes, it may be strange; but it is a fact. This medicine cured me: take this medicine, and it will cure you. Although it has cost me a great deal, it shall not cost you anything. Do not make light of it, I beg of you." "Well," I say, "I should like to believe you; but this is contrary to my reason."

Hearing this, my friend goes away and returns with another friend, and that one testifies to the same thing. I am still disbelieving; so he goes away, and brings in another friend, and another, and another, and another; and they all testify to the same thing. They say they were as bad as myself; that they took the same medicine that has been offered to me; and that it has cured them. My friend then hands me the medicine. I dash it to the ground; I do not believe in its saving power; I die. The reason is then that I spurned the remedy. So, if you perish, it will not be because Adam fell; but because you spurned the remedy offered to save you. You will choose darkness rather than light. "How then shall ye escape, if ye neglect so great salvation?" There is no hope for you if you neglect the remedy. It does no good to look at the wound. If we had been in the Israelitish camp and had been bitten by one of the fiery serpents, it would have done us no good to look at the wound. Looking at the wound will never save any one. What you must do is to look at the Remedy—look away to Him who hath power to save you from your sin.

Behold the camp of the Israelites; look at the scene that is pictured to your eyes! Many are dying because they neglect the remedy that is offered. In that arid desert is many a short and tiny grave; many a child has been bitten by the fiery serpents. Fathers and mothers are bearing away their children. Over yonder they are just burying a mother; a loved mother is about to be laid in the earth. All the family, weeping, gather around the beloved form. You hear the mournful cries; you see the bitter tears. The father is being borne away to his last resting place. There is wailing going up all over the camp. Tears are pouring down for thousands who have passed away; thousands more are dying; and the plague is raging from one end of the camp to the other.

I see in one tent an Israelitish mother bending over the form of a beloved boy just coming into the bloom of life, just budding into manhood. She is wiping away the sweat of death that is gathering upon his brow. Yet a little while, and his eyes are fixed and glassy, for life is ebbing fast away. The mother's heart-strings are torn and bleeding. All at once she hears a noise in the camp. A great shout goes up. What does it mean? She goes to the door of the tent. "What is the noise in the camp?" she asks those passing by. And some one says: "Why, my good woman, have you not heard the good news that has come into the camp?" "No," says the woman, "Good news! What is it?" "Why, have you not heard about it? God has provided a remedy." "What! for the bitten Israelites? Oh, tell me what the remedy is!" "Why, God has instructed Moses to make a brazen serpent, and to put it on a pole in the middle of the camp; and He has declared that whosoever looks upon it shall live. The shout that you hear is the shout of the people when they see the serpent lifted up." The mother goes back into the tent, and she says: "My boy, I have good news to tell you. You need not die! My boy, my boy, I have come with good tidings; you can live!" He is already getting stupefied; he is so weak he cannot walk to the door of the tent. She puts her strong arms under him and lifts him up. "Look yonder; look right there under the hill!" But the boy does not see anything; he says—"I do not see anything; what is it, mother?" And she says: "Keep looking, and you will see it." At last he catches a glimpse of the glistening serpent; and lo, he is well! And thus it is with many a young convert. Some men say, "Oh, we do not believe in sudden conversions." How long did it take to cure that boy? How long did it take to cure those serpent-bitten Israelites? It was just a look; and they were well.

That Hebrew boy is a young convert. I can fancy that I see him now calling on all those who were with him to praise God. He sees another young man bitten as he was; and he runs up to him and tells him, "You, need not die." "Oh," the young man replies, "I cannot live; it is not possible. There is not a physician in Israel who can cure me." He does not know that he need not die. "Why, have you not heard the news? God has provided a remedy." "What remedy?" "Why, God has told Moses to lift up a brazen serpent, and has said that none of those who look upon that serpent shall die." I can just imagine the young man. He may be what you call an intellectual young man. He says to the young convert "You do not think I am going to believe anything like that? If the physicians in Israel cannot cure me, how do you think that an old brass serpent on a pole is going to cure me?" "Why, sir, I was as bad as yourself!" "You do not say so!" "Yes, I do." "That is the most astonishing thing I ever heard," says the young man: "I wish you would explain the philosophy of it." "I cannot. I only know that I looked at that serpent, and I was cured: that did it. I just looked; that is all. My mother told me the reports that were being heard through the camp; and I just believed what my mother said, and I am perfectly well." "Well, I do not believe you were bitten as badly as I have been." The young man pulls up his sleeve. "Look there! That mark shows where I was bitten; and I tell you I was worse than you are." "Well, if I understood the philosophy of it I would look and get well." "Let your philosophy go: look and live." "But, sir, you ask me to do an unreasonable thing. If God had said, Take the brass and rub it into the wound, there might be something in the brass that would cure the bite. Young man, explain the philosophy of it." I have often seen people before me who have talked in that way. But the young man calls in another, and takes him into the tent, and says: "Just tell him how the Lord saved you;" and he tells just the same story; and he calls in others, and they all say the same thing.

The young man says it is a very strange thing. "If the Lord had told Moses to go and get some herbs, or roots, and stew them, and take the decoction as a medicine, there would be something in that. But it is so contrary to nature to do such a thing as look at the serpent, that I cannot do it." At length his mother, who has been out in the camp, comes in, and she says, "My boy, I have just the best news in the world for you. I was in the camp, and I saw hundreds who were very far gone, and they are all perfectly well now." The young man says: "I should like to get well; it is a very painful thought to die; I want to go into the promised land, and it is terrible to die here in this wilderness; but the fact is—I do not understand the remedy. It does not appeal to my reason. I cannot believe that I can get well in a moment." And the young man dies in consequence of his own unbelief.

God provided a remedy for this bitten Israelite—"Look and live!" And there is eternal life for every poor sinner, Look, and you can be saved, my reader, this very hour. God has provided a remedy; and it is offered to all. The trouble is, a great many people are looking at the pole. Do not look at the pole; that is the church. You need not look at the church; the church is all right, but the church cannot save you. Look beyond the pole. Look at the Crucified One. Look to Calvary. Bear in mind, sinner, that Jesus died for all. You need not look at ministers; they are just God's chosen instruments to hold up the Remedy, to hold up Christ. And so, my friends, take your eyes off from men; take your eyes off from the church. Lift them up to Jesus; who took away the sin of the world, and there will be life for you from this hour.

Thank God, we do not require an education to teach us how to look. That little girl, that little boy, only four years old, who cannot read, can look. When the father is coming home, the mother says to her little boy, "Look! look! look!" and the little child learns to look long before he is a year old. And that is the way to be saved. It is to look at the Lamb of God "who taketh away the sin of the world;" and there is life this moment for every one who is willing to look.

Some men say, "I wish I knew how to be saved." Just take God at His word and trust His Son this very day—this very hour—this very moment. He will save you, if you will trust Him. I imagine I hear some one saying, "I do not feel the bite as much as I wish I did. I know I am a sinner, and all that; but I do not feel the bite enough." How much does God want you to feel it?

When I was in Belfast I knew a doctor who had a friend, a leading surgeon there; and he told me that the surgeon's custom was, before performing any operation, to say to the patient, "Take a good look at the wound, and then fix your eyes on me; and do not take them off till I get through." I thought at the time that was a good illustration. Sinner, take a good look at your wound; and then fix your eyes on Christ, and do not take them off. It is better to look at the Remedy than at the wound. See what a poor wretched sinner you are; and then look at the Lamb of God who "taketh away the sin of the world." He died for the ungodly and the sinner. Say "I will take Him!" And may God help you to lift your eye to the Man on Calvary. And as the Israelites looked upon the serpent and were healed, so may you look and live.

After the battle of Pittsburgh Landing I was in a hospital at Murfreesbro. In the middle of the night I was aroused and told that a man in one of the wards wanted to see me. I went to him and he called me "chaplain"—I was not the chaplain—and said he wanted me to help him die. And I said, "I would take you right up in my arms and carry you into the kingdom of God if I could; but I cannot do it: I cannot help you die!" And he said, "Who can?" I said, "The Lord Jesus Christ can—He came for that purpose." He shook his head, and said, "He cannot save me; I have sinned all my life." And I said, "But He came to save sinners." I thought of his mother in the north, and I was sure that she was anxious that he should die in peace; so I resolved I would stay with him. I prayed two or three times, and repeated all the promises I could; for it was evident that in a few hours he would be gone. I said I wanted to read him a conversation that Christ had with a man who was anxious about his soul. I turned to the third chapter of John. His eyes were riveted on me; and when I came to the 14th and 15th verses—the passage before us—he caught up the words, "As Moses lifted up the serpent in the wilderness, even so must the Son of Man be lifted up; that whosoever believeth in Him should not perish, but have eternal life." He stopped me and said, "Is that there?" I said "Yes." He asked me to read it again; and I did so. He leant his elbows on the cot and clasping his hands together, said, "That's good; won't you read it again?" I read it the third time; and then went on with the rest of the chapter. When I had finished, his eyes were closed, his hands were folded, and there was a smile on his face. Oh, how it was lit up! What change had come over it! I saw his lips quivering, and leaning over him I heard in a faint whisper, "As Moses lifted up the serpent in the wilderness, even so must the Son of Man be lifted up; that whosoever believeth in Him should not perish, but have eternal life." He opened his eyes and said, "That's enough; don't read any more." He lingered a few hours, pillowing his head on those two verses; and then went up in one of Christ's chariots, to take his seat in the kingdom of God.

Christ said to Nicodemus: "Except a man be born again, he cannot see the kingdom of God." You may see many countries; but there is one country—the land of Beulah, which John Bunyan saw in vision—you shall never behold, unless you are born again—regenerated by Christ. You can look abroad and see many beautiful trees; but the tree of life, you shall never behold, unless your eyes are made clear by faith in the Saviour. You may see the beautiful rivers of the earth—you may ride upon their bosoms; but bear in mind that your eye will never rest upon the river which bursts out from the Throne of God and flows through the upper Kingdom, unless you are born again. God has said it; and not man. You will never see the kingdom of God except you are born again. You may see the kings and lords of the earth; but the King of kings and Lord of lords you will never see except you are born again. When you are in London you may go to the Tower and see the crown of England, which is worth thousands of dollars, and is guarded there by soldiers; but bear in mind that your eye will never rest upon the crown of life except you are born again.

You may hear the songs of Zion which are sung here; but one song—that of Moses and the Lamb—the uncircumcised ear shall never hear; its melody will only gladden the ear of those who have been born again. You may look upon the beautiful mansions of earth, but bear in mind the mansions which Christ has gone to prepare you shall never see unless you are born again. It is God who says it. You may see ten thousand beautiful things in this world; but the city that Abraham caught a glimpse of—and from that time became a pilgrim and sojourner—you shall never see unless you are born again (Heb. xi. 8, 10-16). You may often be invited to marriage feasts here; but you will never attend the marriage supper of the Lamb except you are born again. It is God who says it, dear friend. You may be looking on the face of your sainted mother to-night, and feel that she is praying for you; but the time will come when you shall never see her more unless you are born again.

The reader may be a young man or a young lady who has recently stood by the bedside of a dying mother; and she may have said, "Be sure and meet me in heaven," and you made the promise. Ah! you shall never see her more, except you are born again. I believe Jesus of Nazareth, sooner than those infidels who say you do not need to be born again. Parents, if you hope to see your children who have gone before, you must be born of the Spirit. Possibly you are a father or a mother who has recently borne a loved one to the grave; and how dark your home seems! Never more will you see your child, unless you are born again. If you wish to be re-united to your loved one, you must be born again. I may be addressing a father or a mother who has a loved one up yonder. If you could hear that loved one's voice, it would say, "Come this way." Have you a sainted friend up yonder? Young man or young lady, have you not a mother in the world of light? If you could hear her speak, would not she say, "Come this way, my son,"—"Come this way, my daughter?" If you would ever see her more you must be born again.

We all have an Elder Brother there. Nearly nineteen hundred years ago He crossed over, and from the heavenly shores He is calling you to heaven. Let us turn our backs upon the world. Let us give a deaf ear to the world. Let us look to Jesus on the Cross and be saved. Then we shall one day see the King in His beauty, and we shall go no more out.

CHAPTER III

THE TWO CLASSES.

"Two men went up into the temple to pray."—Luke xvii. 10.

I now want to speak of two classes: First, those who do not feel their need of a Saviour who have not been convinced of sin by the Spirit; and Second, those who are convinced of sin and cry, "What must I do to be saved?"

All inquirers can be ranged under two heads: they have either the spirit of the Pharisee, or the spirit of the publican. If a man having the spirit of the Pharisee comes into an after-meeting, I know of no better portion of Scripture to meet his case than Romans iii. 10: "As it is written, There is none righteous, no, not one: there is none that understandeth; there is none that seeketh after God." Paul is here speaking of the natural man. "They are all gone out of the way, they are together become unprofitable; there is none that doeth good, no, not one." And in the 17th verse and those which follow, we have "And the way of peace have they not known; there is no fear of God before their eyes. Now we know what things soever the law saith, it saith to them who are under the law; that every mouth may be stopped, and all the world may become guilty before God."

Then observe the last clause of verse 22: "For there is no difference; for all have sinned, and come short of the glory of God." Not part of the human family—but all—"have sinned, and come short of the glory of God." Another verse which has been very much used to convict men of their sin is 1 John i. 8: "If we say that we have no sin, we deceive ourselves, and the truth is not in us."

I remember that on one occasion we were holding meetings in an eastern city of forty thousand inhabitants; and a lady came and asked us to pray for her husband, whom she purposed bringing into the after meeting. I have traveled a good deal and met many pharisaical men; but this man was so clad in self-righteousness that you could not get the point of the needle of conviction in anywhere. I said to his wife: "I am glad to see your faith; but we cannot get near him; he is the most self-righteous man I ever saw." She said: "You must! My heart will break if these meetings end without his conversion." She persisted in bringing him; and I got almost tired of the sight of him.

But towards the close of our meetings of thirty days, he came up to me and put his trembling hand on my shoulder. The place in which the meetings were held was rather cold, and there was an adjoining room in which only the gas had been lighted; and he said to me, "Can't you come in here for a few minutes?" I thought that he was shaking from cold, and I did not particularly wish to go where it was colder. But he said: "I am the worst man in the State of Vermont. I want you to pray for me." I thought he had committed a murder, or some other awful crime; and I asked: "Is there any one sin that particularly troubles you?" And he said: "My whole life has been a sin. I have been a conceited, self-righteous Pharisee. I want you to pray for me." He was under deep conviction. Man could not have produced this result; but the Spirit had. About two o'clock in the morning light broke in upon his soul: and he went up and down the business street of the city and told what God had done for him; and has been a most active Christian ever since.

There are four other passages in dealing with inquirers, which were used by Christ Himself. "Verily, verily, I say unto thee, Except a man be born again, he cannot see the kingdom of God." (John iii. 3.)

In Luke xiii. 3, we read: "Except ye repent, ye shall all likewise perish."

In Matthew xviii., when the disciples came to Jesus to know who was to be the greatest in the kingdom of heaven, we are told that He took a little child and set him in the midst and said, "Verily I say unto you, Except ye be converted, and become as little children, ye shall not enter the kingdom of heaven" (xviii. 1-3).

There is another important "Except" in Matthew v. 20: "Except your righteousness shall exceed the righteousness of the Scribes and Pharisees, ye shall in no case enter the kingdom of heaven."

A man must be made meet before he will want to go into the kingdom of God. I would rather go into the kingdom with the younger brother than stay outside with the elder. Heaven would be hell to such an one. An elder brother who could not rejoice at his younger brother's return would not be "fit" for the kingdom of God. It is a solemn thing to contemplate; but the curtain drops and leaves him outside, and the younger brother within. To him the language of the Saviour under other circumstances seems appropriate: "Verily I say unto you, That the publicans and the harlots go into the kingdom of God before you" (Matt. xxi. 31).

A lady once came to me and wanted a favor for her daughter. She said: "You must remember I do not sympathize with you in your doctrine." I asked: "What is your trouble?" She said: "I think your abuse of the elder brother is horrible. I think he is a noble character." I said that I was willing to hear her defend him; but that it was a solemn thing to take up such a position; and that the elder brother needed to be converted as much as the younger. When people talk of being moral it is well to get them to take a good look at the old man pleading with his boy who would not go in.

But we will pass on now to the other class with which we have to deal. It is composed of those who are convinced of sin and from whom the cry comes as from the Philippian jailer, "What must I do to be saved?" To those who utter this penitential cry there is no necessity to administer the law. It is well to bring them straight to the Scripture: "Believe on the Lord Jesus Christ, and thou shalt be saved." (Acts xvi. 31). Many will meet you with a scowl and say, "I don't know what it is to believe;" and though it is the law of heaven that they must believe, in order to be saved—yet they ask for something besides that. We are to tell them what, and where, and how, to believe.

In John iii. 35 and 36 we read: "The Father loveth the Son, and hath given all things into His hand. He that believeth on the Son hath everlasting life; and he that believeth not the Son shall not see life; but the wrath of God abideth on him."

Now this looks reasonable. Man lost life by unbelief—by not believing God's word; and we got life back again by believing—by taking God at His word. In other words we get up where Adam fell down. He stumbled and fell over the stone of unbelief; and we are lifted up and stand upright by believing. When people say they cannot believe, show them chapter and verse, and hold them right to this one thing: "Has God ever broken His promise for these six thousand years?" The devil and men have been trying all the time and have not succeeded in showing that He has broken a single promise; and there would be a jubilee in hell to-day if one word that He has spoken could be broken. If a man says that he cannot believe it is well to press him on that one thing.

I can believe God better to-day than I can my own heart. "The heart is deceitful above all things, and desperately wicked: who can know it?" (Jer. xxii. 9). I can believe God better than I can myself. If you want to know the way of Life, believe that Jesus Christ is a personal Saviour; cut away from all doctrines and creeds, and come right to the heart of the Son of God. If you have been feeding on dry doctrine there is not much growth on that kind of food. Doctrines are to the soul what the streets which lead to the house of a friend who has invited me to dinner are to the body. They will lead me there if I take the right one; but if I remain in the streets my hunger will never be satisfied. Feeding on doctrines is like trying to live on dry husks; and lean indeed must the soul remain which partakes not of the Bread sent down from heaven.

Some ask: "How am I to get my heart warmed?" It is by believing. You do not get power to love and serve God until you believe.

The apostle John says "If we receive the witness of men, the witness of God is greater: for this is the witness of God which He hath testified of His Son. He that believeth on the Son of God hath the witness in himself: he that believeth not God hath made Him a liar; because he believeth not the record that God gave of His Son. And this is the record, that God hath given to us eternal life, and this life is in His Son. He that hath the Son hath life; and he that hath not the Son of God hath not life" (1 John v. 9).

Human affairs would come to a standstill if we did not take the testimony of men. How should we get on in the ordinary intercourse of life, and how would commerce get on, if we disregarded men's testimony? Things social and commercial would come to a dead-lock within forty-eight hours! This is the drift of the apostle's argument here. "If we receive the witness of men, the witness of God is greater." God has borne witness to Jesus Christ. And if man can believe his fellow men who are frequently telling untruths and whom we are constantly finding unfaithful, why should we not take God at His word and believe His testimony?

Faith is a belief in testimony. It is not a leap in the dark, as some tell us. That would be no faith at all. God does not ask any man to believe without giving him something to believe. You might as well ask a man to see without eyes; to hear without ears; and to walk without feet—as to bid him believe without giving him something to believe.

When I started for California I procured a guide-book. This told me, that after leaving the State of Illinois, I should cross the Mississippi, and then the Missouri; get into Nebraska; then over the Rocky Mountains to the Mormon settlement at Salt Lake City, and by the way of the Sierra Nevada into San Francisco. I found the guide book all right as I went along; and I should have been a miserable sceptic if, having proved it to be correct three-fourths of the way, I had said that I would not believe it for the remainder of the journey.

Suppose a man, in directing me to the Post Office, gives me ten landmarks; and that, in my progress there, I find nine of them to be as he told me; I should have good reason to believe that I was coming to the Post Office.

And if, by believing, I get a new life, and a hope, a peace, a joy, and a rest to my soul, that I never had before; if I get self-control, and find that I have a power to resist evil and to do good, I have pretty good proof that I am in the right road to the "city which hath foundations, whose builder and maker is God." And if things have taken place, and are now taking place, as recorded in God's Word, I have good reason to conclude that what yet remains will be fulfilled. And yet people talk of doubting. There can be no true faith where there is fear. Faith is to take God at His word, unconditionally. There cannot be true peace where there is fear. "Perfect love casteth out fear." How wretched a wife would be if she doubted her husband! and how miserable a mother would feel if after her boy had gone away from home she had reason, from his neglect, to question that son's devotion! True love never has a doubt.

There are three things indispensable to faith—knowledge, assent, and appropriation.

We must know God. "And this is life eternal, that they might know Thee, the only true God, and Jesus Christ whom Thou hast sent" (John xvii. 3). Then we must not only give our assent to what we know; but we must lay hold of the truth. If a man simply give his assent to the plan of salvation, it will not save him: he must accept Christ as his Saviour. He must receive and appropriate Him.

Some say they cannot tell how a man's life can be affected by his belief. But let some one cry out that some building in which we happen to be sitting, is on fire; and see how soon we should act on our belief and get out. We are all the time influenced by what we believe. We cannot help it. And let a man believe the record that God has given of Christ, and it will very quickly affect his whole life.

Take John v. 24. There is enough truth in that one verse for every soul to rest upon for salvation. It does not admit the shadow of a doubt. "Verily, verily"—which means truly, truly—"I say unto you, He that heareth My word, and believeth on Him that sent Me, hath—hath—everlasting life, and shall not come into condemnation; but is passed from death unto life."

Now if a person really hears the word of Jesus and believes with the heart on God who sent the Son to be the Saviour of the world, and lays hold of and appropriates this great salvation, there is no fear of judgment. He will not be looking forward with dread to the Great White Throne; for we read in 1 John iv. 17: "Herein is our love made perfect, that we may have boldness in the day of judgment: because as He is, so are we in this world."

If we believe, there is for us no condemnation, no judgment. That is behind us, and passed; and we shall have boldness in the day of judgment.

I remember reading of a man who was on trial for his life. He had friends with influence; and they procured a pardon for him from the king on condition that he was to go through the trial, and be condemned. He went into court with the pardon in his pocket. The feeling ran very high against him, and the judge said that the court was shocked that he was so much unconcerned. But, when the sentence was pronounced, he pulled out the pardon, presented it, and walked out a free man. He has been pardoned; and so have we. Then let death come, we have nought to fear. All the grave-diggers in the world cannot dig a grave large enough and deep enough to hold eternal life; all the coffin makers in the world cannot make a coffin large enough and tight enough to hold eternal life. Death has had his hand on Christ once, but never again.

Jesus said: "I am the Resurrection, and the Life: he that believeth in Me, though he were dead, yet shall he live: and whosoever liveth and believeth in Me shall never die" (John xi. 25, 26). And in the Apocalypse we read that the risen Saviour said to John, "I am He that liveth, and was dead; and, behold, I am alive for evermore" (Rev i. 18). Death cannot touch Him again.

We get life by believing. In fact we get more than Adam lost; for the redeemed child of God is heir to a richer and more glorious inheritance than Adam in Paradise could ever have conceived; yea, and that inheritance endures forever—it is inalienable.

I would much rather have my life hid with Christ in God than have lived in Paradise; for Adam might have sinned and fallen after being there ten thousand years. But the believer is safer, if these things become real to him. Let us make them a fact, and not a fiction. God has said it; and that is enough. Let us trust Him even where we cannot trace Him. Let the same confidence animate us that was in little Maggie as related in the following simple but touching incident which I read in the Bible Treasury:—

"I had been absent from home for some days, and was wondering, as I again draw near the homestead, if my little Maggie, just able to sit alone, would remember me. To test her memory, I stationed myself where I could see her, but could not be seen by her, and called her name in the familiar tone, 'Maggie!' She dropped her playthings, glanced around the room, and then looked down upon her toys. Again I repeated her name, 'Maggie!' when she once more surveyed the room; but, not seeing her father's face, she looked very sad, and slowly resumed her employment. Once more I called, 'Maggie!' when, dropping her playthings, and bursting into tears, she stretched out her arms in the direction whence the sound proceeded, knowing that, though she could not see him, her father must be there, for she knew his voice."

Now, we have power to see and to hear, and we have power to believe. It is all folly for the inquirers to take the ground that they cannot believe. They can, if they will. But the trouble with most people is that they have connected feeling with believing. Now Feeling has nothing whatever to do with Believing. The Bible does not say—He that feeleth, or he that feeleth and believeth, hath everlasting life. Nothing of the kind. I cannot control my feelings. If I could, I should never feel ill, or have a headache or toothache. I should be well all the while. But I can believe God; and if we get our feet on that rock, let doubts and fears come and the waves surge around us, the anchor will hold.

Some people are all the time looking at their faith. Faith is the hand that takes the blessing. I heard this illustration of a beggar. Suppose you were to meet a man in the street whom you had known for years as being accustomed to beg; and you offered him some money, and he were to say to you: "I thank you; I don't want your money: I am not a beggar." "How is that?" "Last night a man put a thousand dollars into my hands." "He did! How did you know it was good money?" "I took it to the bank and deposited it and have got a bank book." "How did you get this gift?" "I asked for alms; and after the gentleman talked with me he took out a thousand dollars in money and put it in my hand." "How do you know that he put it in the right hand?" "What do I care about which hand; so that I have got the money." Many people are always thinking whether the faith by which they lay hold of Christ is the right kind—but what is far more essential is to see that we have the right kind of Christ.

Faith is the eye of the soul; and who would ever think of taking out an eye to see if it were the right kind so long as the sight was perfect? It is not my taste, but it is what I taste, that satisfies my appetite. So, dear friends, it is taking God at His Word that is the means of our salvation. The truth cannot be made too simple.

There is a man living in the city of New York who has a home on the Hudson River. His daughter and her family went to spend the winter with him: and in the course of the season the scarlet fever broke out. One little girl was put in quarantine, to be kept separate from the rest. Every morning the old grandfather used to go and bid his grandchild, "Goodbye," before going to his business. On one of these occasions the little thing took the old man by the hand, and, leading him to a corner of the room, without saying a word she pointed to the floor where she had arranged some small crackers so they would spell out, "Grandpa, I want a box of paints." He said nothing. On his return home he hung up his overcoat and went to the room as usual: when his little grandchild, without looking to see if her wish had been complied with, took him into the same corner, where he saw spelled out in the same way, "Grandpa, I thank you for the box of paints." The old man would not have missed gratifying the child for anything. That was faith.

Faith is taking God at His Word; and those people who want some token are always getting into trouble. We want to come to this: God says it—let us believe it.

But some say, Faith is the gift of God. So is the air; but you have to breathe it. So is bread; but you have to eat it. So is water; but you have to drink it. Some are wanting a miraculous kind of feeling. That is not faith. "Faith cometh by hearing, and hearing by the Word of God" (Rom. x. 17). That is whence faith comes. It is not for me to sit down and wait for faith to come stealing over me with a strange sensation; but it is for me to take God at His Word. And you cannot believe, unless you have something to believe. So take the Word as it is written, and appropriate it, and lay hold of it.

In John vi. 47, 48 we read: "Verily, verily, I say unto you, He that believeth on Me hath everlasting life. I am that Bread of life." There is the bread right at hand. Partake of it. I might have thousands of loaves within my home, and as many hungry men in waiting. They might assent to the fact that the bread was there; but unless they each took a loaf and commenced eating, their hunger would not be satisfied. So Christ is the Bread of heaven; and as the body feeds on natural food, so the soul must feed on Christ.

If a drowning man sees a rope thrown out to rescue him he must lay hold of it; and in order to do so he must let go everything else. If a man is sick he must take the medicine—for simply looking at it will not cure him. A knowledge of Christ will not help the inquirer, unless he believes in Him, and takes hold of Him, as his only hope. The bitten Israelites might have believed that the serpent was lifted up; but unless they had looked they would not have lived (Num. xxi. 6-9).

I believe that a certain line of steamers will convey me across the ocean, because I have tried it: but this will not help another man who may want to go, unless he acts upon my knowledge. So a knowledge of Christ does not help us unless we act upon it. That is what it is to believe on the Lord Jesus Christ. It is to act on what we believe. As a man steps on board a steamer to cross the Atlantic, so we must take Christ and make a commitment of our souls to Him; and He has promised to keep all who put their trust in Him. To believe on the Lord Jesus Christ, is simply to take Him at His word.

CHAPTER IV

WORDS OF COUNSEL.

"A bruised reed shall He not break."—Isaiah xlii. 3; Matt. xii. 20.

It is dangerous for those who are seeking salvation to lean upon the experience of other people. Many are waiting for a repetition of the experience of their grandfather or grandmother. I had a friend who was converted in a field; and he thinks the whole town ought to go down into that meadow and be converted. Another was converted under a bridge; and he thinks that if any enquirer were to go there he would find the Lord. The best thing for the anxious is to go right to the Word of God. If there are any persons in the world to whom the Word ought to be very precious it is those who are asking how to be saved.

For instance a man may say, "I have no strength." Let him turn to Romans v. 6. "For when we were yet without strength, in due time Christ died for the ungodly." It is because we have no strength that we need Christ. He has come to give strength to the weak.

Another may say, "I cannot see." Christ says, "I am the Light of the world" (John viii. 12). He came, not only to give light, but "to open the blind eyes" (Isa. xlii. 7).

Another may say, "I do not think a man can be saved all at once." A person holding that view was in the Enquiry-room one night; and I drew his attention to Romans vi. 23. "The wages of sin is death; but the gift of God is eternal life through Jesus Christ our Lord." How long does it take to accept a gift? There must be a moment when you have it not, and another when you have it—a moment when it is another's, and the next when it is yours. It does not take six months to get eternal life. It may however in some cases be like the mustard seed, very small at the commencement. Some people are converted so gradually that, like the morning light, it is impossible to tell when the dawn began; while, with others, it is like the flashing of a meteor, and the truth bursts upon them suddenly.

I would not go across the street to prove when I was converted;

but what is important is for me to know that I really have been.

It may be that a child has been so carefully trained that it is impossible to tell when the new birth began; but there must have been a moment when the change took place, and when he became a partaker of the Divine nature.

Some people do not believe in sudden conversion. But I will challenge any one to show a conversion in the New Testament that was not instantaneous. "As Jesus passed by He saw Levi, the son of Alpheus, sitting at the receipt of custom, and said unto him, 'Follow Me': and he arose and followed Him" (Matt. ix. 9). Nothing could be more sudden than that.

Zaccheus, the publican, sought to see Jesus; and because he was little of stature he climbed up a tree. When Jesus came to the place He looked up and saw him, and said, "Zaccheus, make haste, and come down" (Luke xix. 5). His conversion must have taken place somewhere between the branch and the ground. We are told that he received Jesus joyfully, and said, "Behold, Lord, the half of my goods I give to the poor; and if I have taken anything from any man by false accusation, I restore him fourfold" (Luke xix. 8). Very few in these days could say that in proof of their conversion.

The whole house of Cornelius was converted suddenly; for so Peter preached Christ to him and his company the Holy Ghost fell on them, and they were baptized. (Acts x.)

On the day of Pentecost three thousand gladly received the Word. They were not only converted, but they were baptized the same day. (Acts ii.)

And when Philip talked to the eunuch, as they went on their way, the eunuch said to Philip, "See, here is water: what doth hinder me to be baptized?" Nothing hindered. And Philip said, "If thou believest with all thine heart, thou mayest." And they both went down into the water; and the man of great authority under Candace, the queen of the Ethiopians, was baptized, and went on his way rejoicing. (Acts viii. 26-38.) You will find all through Scripture that conversions were sudden and instantaneous.

A man has been in the habit of stealing money from his employer. Suppose he has taken $1,000 in twelve months; should we tell him to take $500 the next year, and less the next year, and the next, until in five years the sum taken would be only $50? That would be upon the same principle as gradual conversion.

If such a person were brought before the court and pardoned, because he could not change his mode of life all at once, it would be considered a very strange proceeding.

But the Bible says, "Let him that stole steal no more" (Eph. iv. 28). It is "right about face!" Suppose a person is in the habit of cursing one hundred times a day: should we advise him not to utter more than ninety oaths the following day, and eighty the next day; so that in the course of time he would get rid of the habit? The Saviour says, "Swear not at all." (Matt. v. 34.)

Suppose another man is in the habit of getting drunk and beating his wife twice a month; if he only did so once a month, and then only once in six months, that would be, upon the same ground, as reasonable as gradual conversion. Suppose Ananias had been sent to Paul, when he was on his way to Damascus breathing out threatenings and slaughter against the disciples, and casting them into prison, to tell him not to kill so many as he intended; and to let enmity die out of his heart gradually, but not all at once. Suppose he had been told that it would not do to stop breathing out threatenings and slaughter, and to commence preaching Christ all at once, because the philosophers would say that the change was so sudden it would not hold out; this would be the same kind of reasoning as is used by those who do not believe in instantaneous conversion.

Then another class say that they are afraid that they will not hold out. This is a numerous and very hopeful class. I like to see a man distrust himself. It is a good thing to get such to look to God, and to remember that it is not he who holds God, but that it is God who holds him. Some want to get hold of Christ; but the thing is to get Christ to take hold of you in answer to prayer. Let such read Psalm cxxi.; "I will lift up mine eyes unto the hills, from whence cometh my help. My help cometh from the Lord, which made heaven and earth. He will not suffer thy foot to be moved: He that keepeth thee will not slumber. Behold, He that keepeth Israel shall neither slumber nor sleep. The Lord is thy keeper; the Lord is thy shade upon thy right hand. The sun shall not smite thee by day, nor the moon by night. The Lord shall preserve thee from all evil: He shall preserve thy soul. The Lord shall preserve thy going out and thy coming in, from this time forth, and even for evermore."

Some one calls that the traveler's psalm. It is a beautiful psalm for those of us who are pilgrims through this world; and one with which we should be well acquainted.

God can do what He has done before. He kept Joseph in Egypt; Moses before Pharaoh; Daniel in Babylon; and enabled Elijah to stand before Ahab in that dark day. And I am so thankful that these I have mentioned were men of like passions with ourselves. It was God who made them so great. What man wants is to look to God. Real true faith is man's weakness leaning on God's strength. When man has no strength, if he leans on God he becomes powerful. The trouble is that we have too much strength and confidence in ourselves.

Again in Hebrews vi. 17, 18: "Wherein God, willing more abundantly to show unto the heirs of promise the immutability of His counsel, confirmed it by an oath that by two immutable things, in which it was impossible for God to lie, we might have a strong consolation, who have fled for refuge to lay hold upon the hope set before us: which hope we have as an anchor of the soul, both sure and steadfast, and which entereth into that within the vail; whither the Forerunner is for us entered, even Jesus, made an high priest for ever after the order of Melchisedec."

Now these are precious verses to those who are afraid of falling, who fear that they will not hold out. It is God's work to hold. It is the Shepherd's business to keep the sheep. Who ever heard of the sheep going to bring back the shepherd? People have an idea that they have to keep themselves and Christ too. It is a false idea. It is the work of the Shepherd to look after them, and to take care of those who trust Him. And He has promised to do it. I once heard that when a sea captain was dying he said, "Glory to God; the anchor holds." He trusted in Christ. His anchor had taken hold of the solid rock. An Irishman said, on one occasion, that "he trembled; but the Rock never did." We want to get sure footing.

In 2 Timothy i. 12 Paul says: "I know whom I have believed, and am persuaded that He is able to keep that which I have committed unto Him against that day." That was Paul's persuasion.

During the late war of the rebellion, one of the chaplains, going through the hospitals, came to a man who was dying. Finding that he was a Christian, he asked to what persuasion he belonged, and was told "Paul's persuasion." "Is he a Methodist?" he asked; for the Methodists all claim Paul. "No." "Is he a Presbyterian?" for the Presbyterians lay special claim to Paul. "No," was the answer.

"Does he belong to the Episcopal Church?" for all the Episcopalian brethren contend that they have a claim to the Chief Apostle. "No," he was not an Episcopalian. "Then, to what persuasion does he belong?" "I am persuaded that He is able to keep that which I have committed unto Him against that day." It is a grand persuasion; and it gave the dying soldier rest in a dying hour.

Let those who fear that they will not hold out turn to the 24th verse of the Epistle of Jude: "Now unto Him that is able to keep you from falling, and to present you faultless before the presence of His glory with exceeding joy."

Then look at Isaiah xli. 10: "Fear thou not; for I am with thee: be not dismayed; for I am thy God: I will strengthen thee; yea, I will help thee; yea, I will uphold thee with the right hand of My righteousness."

Then see verse 13: "For I the Lord thy God will hold thy right hand, saying unto thee, Fear not; I will help thee."

Now if God has got hold of my right hand in His, cannot He hold me and keep me? Has not God the power to keep? The great God who made heaven and earth can keep a poor sinner like you and like me if we trust Him. To refrain from feeling confidence in God for fear of falling—would be like a man who refused a pardon, for fear that he should get into prison again; or a drowning man who refused to be rescued, for fear of falling into the water again.

Many men look forth at the Christian life, and fear that they will not have sufficient strength to hold out to the end. They forget the promise that "as thy days, thy strength" (Deut. xxxiii. 25). It reminds me of the pendulum to the clock which grew disheartened at the thought of having to travel so many thousands of miles; but when it reflected that the distance was to be accomplished by "tick, tick, tick," it took fresh courage to go its daily journey. So it is the special privilege of the Christian to commit himself to the keeping of his heavenly Father and to trust Him day by day. It is a comforting thing to know that the Lord will not begin the good work without also finishing it.

There are two kinds of sceptics—one class with honest difficulties; and another class who delight only in discussion. I used to think that this latter class would always be a thorn in my flesh; but they do not prick me now. I expect to find them right along the journey. Men of this stamp used to hang around Christ to entangle Him in His talk. They come into our meetings to hold a discussion. To all such I would commend Paul's advice to Timothy: "But foolish and unlearned questions avoid; knowing that they do gender strifes." (2 Tim. ii. 23.) Unlearned questions: Many young converts make a woful mistake. They think they are to defend the whole Bible. I knew very little of the Bible when I was first converted; and I thought that I had to defend it from beginning to end against all comers; but a Boston infidel got hold of me, floored all my arguments at once, and discouraged me. But I have got over that now. There are many things in the Word of God that I do not profess to understand.

When I am asked what I do with them. I say, "I don't do anything."

"How do you explain them?" "I don't explain them."

"What do you do with them?" "Why, I believe them."

And when I am told, "I would not believe anything that I do not understand," I simply reply that I do.

There are many things which were dark and mysterious five years ago, on which I have since had a flood of light; and I expect to be finding out something fresh about God throughout eternity. I make a point of not discussing disputed passages of Scripture. An old divine has said that some people, if they want to eat fish, commence by picking the bones. I leave such things till I have light on them. I am not bound to explain what I do not comprehend. "The secret things belong unto the Lord our God: but those things which are revealed belong unto us, and to our children, for ever" (Deut. xxii. 29); and these I take, and eat, and feed upon, in order to get spiritual strength.

Than there is a little sound advice in Titus iii. 9. "But avoid foolish questions, and genealogies, and contentions, and strivings about the law; for they are unprofitable and vain."

But now here comes an honest sceptic. With him I would deal as tenderly as a mother with her sick child. I have no sympathy with those people who, because a man is sceptical, cast him off and will have nothing to do with him.

I was in an Inquiry-meeting, some time ago, and I handed over to a Christian lady, whom I had known some time, one who was sceptical. On looking round soon after I noticed the enquirer marching out of the hall. I asked, "Why have you let her go?" "Oh, she is a sceptic!" was the reply. I ran to the door and got her to stop, and introduced her to another Christian worker who spent over an hour in conversation and prayer with her. He visited her and her husband; and, in the course of a week, that intelligent lady cast off her scepticism and came out an active Christian. It took time, tact, and prayer; but if a person of this class is honest we ought to deal with such an one as the Master would have us.

Here are a few passages for doubting enquirers:

"If any man will do His will, he shall know of the doctrine, whether it be of God, or whether I speak of myself" (John vii. 17). If a man is not willing to do the will of God he will not know the doctrine. There is no class of sceptics who are ignorant of the fact that God desires them to give up sin; and if a man is willing to turn from sin and take the light and thank Him for what He does give, and not expect to have light on the whole Bible all at once, he will get more light day by day; make progress step by step; and be led right out of darkness into the clear light of heaven.

In Daniel xii. 10 we are told: "Many shall be purified, and made white, and tried: but the wicked shall do wickedly; and none of the wicked shall understand; but the wise shall understand."

Now God will never reveal His secrets to His enemies. Never! And if a man persists in living in sin he will not know the doctrines of God.

"The secret of the Lord is with them that fear Him; and He will show them His covenant" (Ps. xxv. 14).

And in John xv. 15 we read: "Henceforth I call you not servants; for the servant knoweth not what his Lord doeth: but I have called you friends; for all things that I have heard of my Father I have made known unto you." When you become friends of Christ you will know His secrets. The Lord said, "Shall I hide from Abraham the things which I do?" (Gen. xviii. 17).

Now those who resemble God are the most likely to understand God. If a man is not willing to turn from sin he will not know God's will, nor will God reveal His secrets to him. But if a man is willing to turn from sin he will be surprised to see how the light will come in!

I remember one night when the Bible was the driest and darkest book in the universe to me. The next day it became entirely different. I thought I had the key to it. I had been born of the Spirit. But before I knew anything of the mind of God I had to give up my sin. I believe God meets every soul on the spot of self-surrender; and when they are willing to let Him guide and lead. The trouble with many sceptics is their self-conceit. They know more than the Almighty! and they do not come in a teachable spirit. But the moment a man comes in a receptive spirit he is blessed; for "If any of you lack wisdom, let him ask of God, that giveth to all men liberally, and upbraideth not; and it shall be given him" (James i. 5).

CHAPTER V

A DIVINE SAVIOUR.

"Thou art the Christ, the Son of the living God."
(Matthew xvi. 1; John vi. 69.)

We meet with a certain class of Enquirers who do not believe in the Divinity of Christ. There are many passages that will give light on this subject.

In 1 Corinthians xv. 47, we are told: "The first man is of the earth earthy: the second man is the Lord from heaven."

In 1 John v. 20: "We know that the Son of God is come, and hath given us an understanding, that we may know Him that is true; and we are in Him that is true, even in His Son Jesus Christ. This is the true God, and eternal life."

Again in John xvii. 3: "And this is life eternal, that they might know Thee, the only true God; and Jesus Christ, whom Thou hast sent."

And then, in Mark xiv. 60: "The high priest stood up in the midst, and asked Jesus, saying, Answerest Thou nothing? What is it which these witness against thee? But He held His peace, and answered nothing. Again the high priest asked Him, and said unto Him, Art Thou the Christ, the Son of the Blessed? And Jesus said, I am: and ye shall see the Son of Man sitting on the right hand of power, and coming in the clouds of heaven. Then the high priest rent his clothes, and saith, What need we any further witnesses? Ye have heard the blasphemy: what think ye? And they all condemned Him to be guilty of death."

Now what brought me to believe in the Divinity of Christ was this: I did not know where to place Christ, or what to do with Him, if He were not divine. When I was a boy I thought that He was a good man like Moses, Joseph, or Abraham. I even thought that He was the best man who had ever lived on the earth. But I found that Christ had a higher claim. He claimed to be God-Man, to be divine; to have come from heaven. He said: "Before Abraham was I am" (John viii. 58). I could not understand this; and I was driven to the conclusion—and I challenge any candid man to deny the inference, or meet the argument—that Jesus Christ is either an impostor or deceiver, or He is the God-Man—God manifest in the flesh. And for these reasons. The first commandment is, "Thou shalt have no other gods before Me" (Exod. xx. 2). Look at the millions throughout Christendom who worship Jesus Christ as God. If Christ be not God this is idolatry. We are all guilty of breaking the first commandment if Jesus Christ were mere man—if He were a created being, and not what He claims to be.

Some people, who do not admit His divinity, say that He was the best man who ever lived; but if He were not Divine, for that very reason He ought not to be reckoned a good man, for He laid claim to an honor and dignity to which these very people declare He had no right or title. That would rank Him as a deceiver.

Others say that He thought He was divine, but that He was deceived. As if Jesus Christ were carried away by a delusion and deception, and thought that He was more than He was! I could not conceive of a lower idea of Jesus Christ than that. This would not only make Him out an impostor; but that He was out of His mind, and that He did not know who He was, or where He came from. Now if Jesus Christ was not what He claimed to be, the Saviour of the world; and if He did not come from heaven, He was a gross deceiver.

But how can any one read the life of Jesus Christ and make Him out a deceiver? A man has generally some motive for being an impostor. What was Christ's motive? He knew that the course He was pursuing would conduct Him to the cross; that His name would be cast out as vile; and that many of His followers would be called upon to lay down their lives for His sake. Nearly every one of the apostles were martyrs; and they were considered as offscouring and refuse in the midst of the people. If a man is an impostor, he has a motive at the back of his hypocrisy. But what was Christ's object? The record is that "He went about doing good." This is not the work of an impostor. Do not let the enemy of your soul deceive you.

In John v. 21 we read: "For as the Father raiseth up the dead, and quickeneth them; even so the Son quickeneth whom He will. For the Father judgeth no man, but hath committed all judgment unto the Son: that all men should honor the Son, even as they honor the Father. He that honoureth not the Son, honoureth not the Father which hath sent Him."

Now notice: by the Jewish law if a man were a blasphemer he was to be put to death; and supposing Christ to be merely human if this be not blasphemy I do not know where you will find it. "He that honoureth not the Son, honoureth not the Father." That is downright blasphemy if Christ be not divine. If Moses, or Elijah, or Elisha, or any other mortal had said, "You must honour me as you honor God;" and had put himself on a level with God, it would have been downright blasphemy.

The Jews put Christ to death because they said that He was not what He claimed to be. It was on that testimony He was put under oath. The high priest said: "I adjure Thee by the living God, that Thou tell us whether Thou be the Christ, the Son of God" (Matt. xxvi. 63). And when the Jews came round Him and said, "How long dost Thou make us to doubt? If Thou be the Christ tell us plainly." Jesus said, "I and My Father are one." Then the Jews took up stones again to stone Him. (John x. 24-33.) They said they did not want to hear more, for that was blasphemy. It was for declaring Himself to be the Son of God that He was condemned and put to death. (Matt. xxvi. 63-66).

Now if Jesus Christ were mere man the Jews did right, according to their law, in putting Him to death. In Leviticus xxiv. 16, we read: "And he that blasphemeth the name of the Lord, he shall surely be put to death, and all the congregation shall certainly stone him: as well the stranger, as he that is born in the land, when he blasphemeth the name of the Lord, shall be put to death."

This law obliged them to put to death every one who blasphemed. It was making the statement that He was divine that cost Him His life; and by the Mosaic law He ought to have suffered the death penalty. In John xvi. 15, Christ says, "All things that the Father hath are Mine: therefore said I, that He shall take of Mine, and shall show it unto you." How could He be merely a good man and use language as that?

No doubt has ever entered my mind on the point since I was converted.

A notorious sinner was once asked how he could prove the divinity of Christ. His answer was, "Why, He has saved me; and that is a pretty good proof, is it not?"

An infidel on one occasion said to me, "I have been studying the life of John the Baptist, Mr. Moody. Why don't you preach him? He was a greater character than Christ. You would do a greater work." I said to him, "My friend, you preach John the Baptist; and I will follow you and preach Christ: and we will see who will do the most good." "You will do the most good," he said, "because the people are so superstitious." Ah! John was beheaded; and his disciples begged his body and buried it: but Christ has risen from the dead; He has "ascended on high; He has led captivity captive; and received gifts for men." (Ps. lxviii. 18.)

Our Christ lives. Many people have not found out that Christ has risen from the grave. They worship a dead Saviour, like Mary, who said, "They have taken away my Lord; and I know not where they have laid Him." (John xx. 13.) That is the trouble with those who doubt the divinity of our Lord.

Then look at Matthew xviii. 20. "Where two or three are gathered together in My name, there am I in the midst of them." "There am I." Well now, if He is a mere man, how can He be there? All these are strong passages.

Again in Matthew xxviii. 18. "And Jesus came and spake unto them, saying, All power is given unto Me in heaven and in earth." Could He be a mere man and talk in that way? "All power is given unto Me in heaven and in earth!"

Then again in Matthew xxviii. 20. "Teaching them to observe all things whatsoever I have commanded you; and, lo, I am with you alway, even unto the end of the world." If He were mere man, how could He be with us? Yet He says, "I am with you away, even unto the end of the world!"

Then again in Mark ii. 7. "Why doth this Man thus speak blasphemies? who can forgive sins but God only? And immediately when Jesus perceived in His Spirit that they reasoned within themselves, He said unto them, Why reason ye these things in your hearts? Whether is it easier to say to the sick of the palsy, Thy sins be forgiven thee, or to say, Arise and take up thy bed and walk?"

Some men will meet you and say, "Did not Elisha also raise the dead?" Notice that in the rare instances in which men have raised the dead, they did it by the power of God. They called on God to do it. But when Christ was on earth He did not call upon the Father to bring the dead to life, When He went to the house of Jairus He said, "Damsel, I say unto thee, Arise." (Mark v. 41.)

He had power to impart life. When they were carrying the young man out of Nain He had compassion on the widowed mother and came and touched the bier and said, "Young man, I say unto thee, Arise." (Luke vii. 14.)

He spake; and the dead arose.

And when He raised Lazarus He called with a loud voice, "Lazarus, come forth!" (John xi. 43.) And Lazarus heard, and came forth.

Some one has said, It was a good thing that Lazarus was mentioned by name, or all the dead within the sound of Christ's voice would immediately have risen.

In John v. 25, Jesus says: "Verily, verily, I say unto you, The hour is coming, and now is, when the dead shall hear the voice of the Son of God; and they that hear shall live." What blasphemy would this have been, had He not been divine! The proof is overwhelming, if you will but examine the Word of God.

And then another thing—no good man except Jesus Christ has ever allowed anybody to worship him. When this was done He never rebuked the worshiper. In John ix. 38, we read that when the blind man was found by Christ he said, "Lord, I believe. And he worshiped Him." The Lord did not rebuke him.

Then again, Revelation xxii. 6, runs thus: "And he said unto me, These things are faithful and true; and the Lord God of the holy prophets sent His angel to show unto His servants the things which must shortly be done. Behold, I come quickly: blessed is he that keepeth the sayings of the prophecy of this book. And I John saw these things and heard them. And when I had heard and seen, I fell down to worship before the feet of the angel which showed me these things. Then saith He unto me, See thou do it not; for I am thy fellow-servant and of thy brethren the prophets, and of them which keep the sayings of this book, worship God."

We see here that even that angel would not allow John to worship him. Even an angel from heaven! And if Gabriel came down here from the presence of God it would be a sin to worship him, or any seraph, or any cherub, or Michael, or any archangel.

"Worship God!" And if Jesus Christ were not God manifest in the flesh we are guilty of idolatry in worshiping Him. In Matthew xiv. 33, we read: "Then they that were in the ship came and worshiped

Him, saying, Of a truth Thou art the Son of God." He did not rebuke them.

And in Matthew viii. 2, we also read: "And, behold, there came a leper and worshiped Him, saying, Lord, if Thou wilt, Thou canst make me clean."

In Matthew xv. 25: "Then came she, and worshiped Him, saying, Lord, help me!"

There are many other passages; but I give these as sufficient in my opinion to prove beyond any doubt the Divinity of our Lord.

In the 14th chapter of Acts we are told the heathen at Lystra came with garlands and would have done sacrifice to Paul and Barnabas because they had cured an impotent man; but the evangelists rent their clothes and told these Lystrans that they were but men, and not to be worshipped; as if it were a great sin. And if Jesus Christ is a mere man, we are all guilty of a great sin in worshipping Him.

But if He is, as we believe, the only-begotten and well-beloved Son of God, let us yield to His claims upon us; let us rest on His all-atoning work, and go forth to serve Him all the days of our life.

CHAPTER VI

REPENTANCE AND RESTITUTION.

"God commandeth all men everywhere to repent."—Acts xvii. 30.

Repentance is one of the fundamental doctrines of the Bible. Yet I believe it is one of those truths that many people little understand at the present day. There are more people to-day in the mist and darkness about Repentance, Regeneration, the Atonement, and such-like fundamental truths, than perhaps on any other doctrines. Yet from our earliest years we have heard about them. If I were to ask for a definition of Repentance, a great many would give a very strange and false idea of it.

A man is not prepared to believe or to receive the Gospel, unless he is ready to repent of his sins and turn from them. Until John the Baptist met Christ, he had but one text, "Repent ye; for the kingdom of heaven is at hand" (Matt. iii. 2). But if he had continued to say this, and had stopped there without pointing the people to Christ the Lamb of God, he would not have accomplished much.

When Christ came, He took up the same wilderness cry, "Repent; for the kingdom of heaven is at hand" (Matt. iv. 17). And when our Lord sent out His disciples, it was with the same message, "that men should repent" (Mark vi. 12). After He had been glorified, and when the Holy Ghost came down, we find Peter on the day of Pentecost raising the same cry, "Repent!" It was this preaching—Repent, and believe the Gospel—that wrought such marvellous results then. (Acts ii. 38-47). And we find that, when Paul went to Athens, he uttered the same cry, "Now God commandeth all men, everywhere, to repent" (Acts xvii. 30).

Before I speak of what Repentance is, let me briefly say what it is not. Repentance is not fear. Many people have confounded the two. They think they have to be alarmed and terrified; and they are waiting for some kind of fear to come down upon them. But multitudes become alarmed who do not really repent. You have heard of men at sea during a terrible storm. Perhaps they have been very profane men; but when the danger came they suddenly grew quiet, and began to cry to God for mercy. Yet you would not say they repented. When the storm had passed away, they went on swearing the same as before. You might think that the king of Egypt repented when God sent the terrible plagues upon him and his land. But it was not repentance at all. The moment God's hand was removed Pharaoh's heart was harder than ever. He did not turn from a single sin; he was the same man. So that there was no true repentance there.

Often, when death comes into a family, it looks as if the event would be sanctified to the conversion of all who are in the house. Yet in six months' time all may be forgotten. Some who read this have perhaps passed through that experience. When God's hand was heavy upon them it looked as if they were going to repent; but the trial has been removed—and lo and behold, the impression has all gone.

Then again, Repentance is not feeling. I find a great many people are waiting for a certain kind of feeling to come. They would like to turn to God; but think they cannot do it until this feeling comes. When I was in Baltimore I used to preach every Sunday in the Penitentiary to nine hundred convicts. There was hardly a man there who did not feel miserable enough: they had plenty of feeling. For the first week or ten days of their imprisonment many of them cried half the time. Yet, when they were released, most of them would go right back to their old ways. The truth was, that they felt very bad because they had got caught; that was all. So you have seen a man in the time of trial show a good deal of feeling: but very often it is only because he has got into trouble; not because he has committed sin, or because his conscience tells him he has done evil in the sight of God. It seems as if the trial were going to result in true repentance; but the feeling too often passes away.

Once again, Repentance is not fasting and afflicting the body. A man may fast for weeks and months and years, and yet not repent of one sin. Neither is it remorse. Judas had terrible remorse—enough to make him go and hang himself; but that was not repentance. I believe if he had gone to his Lord, fallen on his face, and confessed his sin, he would have been forgiven. Instead of this he went to the priests, and then put an end to his life. A man may do all sorts of penance—but there is no true repentance in that. Put that down in your mind. You cannot meet the claims of God by offering the fruit of your body for the sin of your soul. Away with such a delusion!

Repentance is not conviction of sin. That may sound strange to some. I have seen men under such deep conviction of sin that they could not sleep at night; they could not enjoy a single meal. They went on for months in this state; and yet they were not converted; they did not truly repent. Do not confound conviction of sin with Repentance.

Neither is praying—Repentance. That too may sound strange. Many people, when they become anxious about their soul's salvation, say, "I will pray, and read the Bible;" and they think that will bring about the desired effect. But it will not do it. You may read the Bible and cry to God a great deal, and yet never repent. Many people cry loudly to God, and yet do not repent.

Another thing: it is not breaking off some one sin. A great many people make that mistake. A man who has been a drunkard signs the pledge, and stops drinking. Breaking off one sin is not Repentance. Forsaking one vice is like breaking off one limb of a tree, when the whole tree has to come down. A profane man stops swearing; very good: but if he does not break off from every sin it is not Repentance—it is not the work of God in the soul. When God works He hews down the whole tree. He wants to have a man turn from every sin. Supposing I am in a vessel out at sea, and I find the ship leaks in three or four places. I may go and stop up one hole; yet down goes the vessel. Or suppose I am wounded in three or four places, and I get a remedy for one wound: if the other two or three wounds are neglected, my life will soon be gone. True Repentance is not merely breaking off this or that particular sin.

Well then, you will ask, what is Repentance? I will give you a good definition: it is "right about face!" In the Irish language the word "Repentance" means even more than "right about face!" It implies that a man who has been walking in one direction has not only faced about, but is actually walking in an exactly contrary direction. "Turn ye, turn ye; for why will ye die?" A man may have little feeling or much feeling; but if he does not turn away from sin, God will not have mercy on him. Repentance has also been described as "a change of mind." For instance, there is the parable told by Christ: "A certain man had two sons; and he came to the first, and said, Son, go work to-day in my vineyard. He answered and said, I will not" (Matt. xxi. 28, 29). After he had said "I will not" he thought over it, and changed his mind. Perhaps he may have said to himself, "I did not speak very respectfully to my father. He asked me to go and work, and I told him I would not go. I think I was wrong." But suppose he had only said this, and still had not gone, he would not have repented. He was not only convinced that he was wrong; but he went off into the fields, hoeing, or mowing or whatever it was. That is Christ's definition of repentance. If a man says, "By the grace of God I will forsake my sin, and do His will," that is Repentance—a turning right about.

Some one has said, man is born with his face turned away from God. When he truly repents he is turned right around towards God; he leaves his old life.

Can a man at once repent? Certainly he can. It does not take a long while to turn around. It does not take a man six months to change his mind. There was a vessel that went down some time ago on the Newfoundland coast. As she was bearing towards the shore, there was a moment when the captain could have given orders to reverse the engines and turn back. If the engines had been reversed then, the ship would have been saved. But there was a moment when it was too late. So there is a moment, I believe, in every man's life when he can halt and say, "By the grace of God I will go no further towards death and ruin. I repent of my sins and turn from them." You may say you have not got feeling enough; but if you are convinced that you are on the wrong road, turn right about, and say, "I will no longer go on in the way of rebellion and sin as I have done."

Just then, when you are willing to turn towards God, salvation may be yours.

I find that every case of conversion recorded in the Bible was instantaneous. Repentance and faith came very suddenly. The moment a man made up his mind, God gave him the power. God does not ask any man to do what he has not the power to do. He would not command "all men everywhere to repent" (Acts xvii. 30) if they were not able to do so. Man has no one to blame but himself if he does not repent and believe the Gospel. One of the leading ministers of the Gospel in Ohio wrote me a letter some time ago describing his conversion; it very forcibly illustrates this point of instantaneous decision. He said:

"I was nineteen years old, and was reading law with a Christian lawyer in Vermont. One afternoon when he was away from home, his good wife said to me as I came into the house, 'I want you to go to class-meeting with me to-night and become a Christian, so that you can conduct family worship while my husband is away.' 'Well, I'll do it,' I said, without any thought. When I came into the house again she asked me if I was honest in what I had said. I replied, 'Yes, so far as going to meeting with you is concerned; that is only courteous.'

"I went with her to the class-meeting, as I had often done before. About a dozen persons were present in a little school-house. The leader had spoken to all in the room but myself and two others. He was speaking to the person next me, when the thought occurred to me: he will ask me if I have anything to say. I said to myself: I have decided to be a Christian sometime; why not begin now? In less time than a minute after these thoughts had passed through my mind he said, speaking to me familiarly—for he knew me very well—'Brother Charles, have you anything to say?' I replied, with perfect coolness, 'Yes, sir. I have just decided, within the last thirty seconds, that I will begin a Christian life, and would like to have you pray for me.'

"My coolness staggered him; I think he almost doubted my sincerity. He said very little, but passed on and spoke to the other two. After a few general remarks, he turned to me and said, 'Brother Charles, will you close the meeting with prayer?' He knew I had never prayed in public. Up to this moment I had no feeling. It was purely a business transaction. My first thought was: I cannot pray, and I will ask him to excuse me. My second was: I have said I will begin a Christian life; and this is a part of it. So I said, 'Let us pray.' And somewhere between the time I started to kneel and the time my knees struck the floor the Lord converted my soul.

"The first words I said were, 'Glory to God!' What I said after that I do not know, and it does not matter, for my soul was too full to say much but Glory! From that hour the devil has never dared to challenge my conversion. To Christ be all the praise."

Many people are waiting, they cannot exactly tell for what, but for some sort of miraculous feeling to come stealing over them—some mysterious kind of faith. I was speaking to a man some years ago, and he always had one answer to give me. For five years I tried to win him to Christ, and every year he said, "It has not 'struck me' yet." "Man, what do you mean? What has not struck you?" "Well," he said, "I am not going to become a Christian until it strikes me; and it has not struck me yet. I do not see it in the way you see it." "But don't you know you are a sinner?" "Yes, I know I am a sinner." "Well, don't you know that God wants to have mercy on you—that there is forgiveness with God? He wants you to repent and come to Him." "Yes, I know that; but—it has not struck me yet." He always fell back on that. Poor man! he went down to his grave in a state of indecision. Sixty long years God gave him to repent; and all he had to say at the end of those years was that it "had not struck him yet."

Is any reader waiting for some strange feeling—you do not know what? Nowhere in the Bible is a man told to wait; God is commanding you now to repent.

Do you think God can forgive a man when he does not want to be forgiven? Would he be happy if God forgave him in this state of mind? Why, if a man went into the kingdom of God without repentance, heaven would be hell to him. Heaven is a prepared place for a prepared people. If your boy has done wrong, and will not repent, you cannot forgive him. You would be doing him an injustice. Suppose he goes to your desk, and steals $10, and squanders it. When you come home your servant tells you what your boy has done. You ask if it is true, and he denies it. But at last you have certain proof. Even when he finds he cannot deny it any longer, he will not confess the sin, but says he will do it again the first chance he gets. Would you say to him, "Well, I forgive you," and leave the matter there? No! Yet people say that God is going to save all men, whether they repent or not—drunkards, thieves, harlots, whoremongers, it makes no difference. "God is so merciful," they say. Dear friend, do not be deceived by the god of this world. Where there is true repentance and a turning from sin unto God, He will meet and bless you; but He never blesses until there is sincere repentance.

David made a woful mistake in this respect with his rebellious son, Absalom. He could not have done his son a greater injustice than to forgive him when his heart was unchanged. There could be no true reconciliation between them when there was no repentance. But God does not make these mistakes. David got into trouble on account of his error of judgment. His son soon drove his father from the throne.

Speaking on repentance, Dr. Brooks, of St. Louis, well remarks: "Repentance, strictly speaking, means a 'change of mind or purpose;' consequently it is the judgment which the sinner pronounces upon himself, in view of the love of God displayed in the death of Christ, connected with the abandonment of all confidence in himself and with trust in the only Saviour of sinners. Saving repentance and saving faith always go together; and you need not be worried about repentance if you will believe."

"Some people are no sure that they have 'repented enough.' If you mean by this that you must repent in order to incline God to be merciful to you, the sooner you give over such repentance the better. God is already merciful, as He has fully shown at the Cross of Calvary; and it is a grievous dishonor to His heart of love if you think that your tears and anguish will move Him, not knowing that 'the goodness of God leadeth thee to repentance.' It is not your badness, therefore, but His goodness that leads to repentance; hence the true way to repent is to believe on the Lord Jesus Christ, 'who was delivered for our offences, and was raised again for our justification.'"

Another thing. If there is true repentance it will bring forth fruit. If we have done wrong to any one we should never ask God to forgive us, until we are willing to make restitution. If I have done any man a great injustice and can make it good, I need not ask God to forgive me until I am willing to make it good. Suppose I have taken something that does not belong to me. I have no right to expect forgiveness until I make restitution.

I remember preaching in one of our large cities, when a fine-looking man came up to me at the close. He was in great distress of mind. "The fact is," he said, "I am a defaulter. I have taken money that belonged to my employers. How can I become a Christian without restoring it?" "Have you got the money?" He told me he had not got it all. He had taken about $1,500, and he still had about $900. He said "Could I not take that money and go into business, and make enough to pay them back?" I told him that was a delusion of Satan; that he could not expect to prosper on stolen money; that he should restore all he had, and go and ask his employers to have mercy upon him and forgive him. "But they will put me in prison," he said: "cannot you give me any help?" "No, you must restore the money before you can expect to get any help from God." "It is pretty hard," he said. "Yes. it is hard; but the great mistake was in doing the wrong at first."

His burden became so heavy that it got to be insupportable. He handed me the money—950 dollars and some cents—and asked me to take it back to his employers. The next evening the two employers and myself met in a side room of the church. I laid the money down, and informed them it was from one of their employes. I told them the story, and said he wanted mercy from them, not justice. The tears trickled down the cheeks of these two men, and they said, "Forgive him! Yes, we will be glad to forgive him." I went down stairs and brought him up. After he had confessed his guilt and been forgiven, we all got down on our knees and had a blessed prayer-meeting. God met us and blessed us there.

There was a friend of mine who some time ago had come to Christ and wished to consecrate himself and his wealth to God. He had formerly had transactions with the government, and had taken advantage of them. This thing came up when he was converted, and his conscience troubled him. He said, "I want to consecrate my wealth, but it seems as if God will not take it." He had a terrible struggle; his conscience kept rising up and smiting him. At last he drew a check for $1,500 and sent it to the United States Treasury. He told me he received such a blessing when he had done it. That was bringing forth "fruits meet for repentance." I believe a great many men are crying to God for light; and they are not getting it because they are not honest.

I was once preaching, and a man came to me who was only thirty-two years old, but whose hair was very grey. He said, "I want you to notice that my hair is grey, and I am only thirty-two years old. For twelve years I have carried a great burden." "Well," I said, "what is it?" He looked around as if afraid some one would hear him. "Well," he answered, "my father died and left my mother with the county newspaper, and left her only that: that was all she had. After he died the paper begun to waste away; and I saw my mother was fast sinking into a state of need. The building and the paper were insured for a thousand dollars, and when I was twenty years old I set fire to the building, and obtained the thousand dollars, and gave it to my mother. For twelve years that sin has been haunting me. I have tried to drown it by indulgence in pleasure and sin; I have cursed God; I have gone into infidelity; I have tried to make out that the Bible is not true; I have done everything I could: but all these years I have been tormented." I said, "There is a way out of that." He inquired "How?" I said, "Make restitution. Let us sit down and calculate the interest, and then you pay the Company the money." It would have done you good to see that man's face light up when he found there was mercy for him. He said he would be glad to pay back the money and interest if he could only be forgiven.

There are men to-day who are in darkness and bondage because they are not willing to turn from their sins and confess them; and I do not know how a man can hope to be forgiven if he is not willing to confess his sins.

Bear in mind that now is the only day of mercy you will ever have. You can repent now, and have the awful record blotted out. God waits to forgive you; He is seeking to bring you to Himself. But I think the Bible teaches clearly that there is no repentance after this life. There are some who tell you of the possibility of repentance in the grave; but I do not find that in Scripture. I have looked my Bible over very carefully, and I cannot find that a man will have another opportunity of being saved.

Why should he ask for any more time? You have time enough to repent now. You can turn from your sins this moment if you will. God says: "I have no pleasure in the death of him that dieth; wherefore turn, and live ye" (Ezek. xviii. 32).

Christ said, He "came not to call the righteous, but sinners to repentance." Are you a sinner? Then the call to repent is addressed to you. Take your place in the dust at the Saviour's feet, and acknowledge your guilt. Say, like the publican of old, "God be merciful to me a sinner!" and see how quickly He will pardon and bless you. He will even justify you and reckon you as righteous, by virtue of the righteousness of Him who bore your sins in His own body on the Cross.

There are some perhaps who think themselves righteous; and that, therefore, there is no need for them to repent and believe the Gospel. They are like the Pharisee in the parable, who thanked God that he was not as other men—"extortioners, unjust, adulterers, or even as this publican;" and who went on to say, "I fast twice a week; I give tithes of all I possess." What is the judgment about such self-righteous persons? "I tell you this man [the poor, contrite, repenting publican] went down to his house justified rather than the other" (Luke xviii. 11-14). "There is none righteous; no, not one." "All have sinned, and come short of the glory of God" (Rom. iii. 10, 23). Let no one say he does not need to repent. Let each one take his true place—that of a sinner; then God will lift him up to the place of forgiveness and justification. "Whosoever exalteth himself shall be abased: and he that humbleth himself shall be exalted" (Luke xiv. 11).

Wherever God sees true repentance in the heart He meets that soul.

I was in Colorado, preaching the gospel some time ago, and I heard something that touched my heart very much. The governor of the State was passing through the prison, and in one cell he found a boy who had his window full of flowers, that seemed to have been watched with very tender care. The governor looked at the prisoner, and then at the flowers, and asked whose they were, "These are my flowers," said the poor convict. "Are you fond of flowers?" "Yes, sir." "How long have you been here?" He told him so many years: he was in for a long sentence. The governor was surprised to find him so fond of the flowers, and he said, "Can you tell me why you like these flowers so much?" With much emotion he replied, "While my mother was alive she thought a good deal of flowers; and when I came here I thought if I had these they would remind me of mother." The governor was so pleased that he said, "Well, young man, if you think so much of your mother I think you will appreciate your liberty," and he pardoned him then and there.

When God finds that beautiful flower of true repentance springing up in a man's heart, then salvation comes to that man.

CHAPTER VII

ASSURANCE OF SALVATION.

"These things have I written unto you that believe on the name of the Son of God; that ye may knew that ye have eternal life, and that ye may believe on the name of the Son of God."

(1 John v. 13.)

There are two classes who ought not to have Assurance. First: those who are in the Church, but who are not converted, having never been born of the Spirit. Second: those not willing to do God's will; who are not ready to take the place that God has mapped out for them, but want to fill some other place.

Some one will ask "Have all God's people Assurance?" No; I think a good many of God's dear people have no Assurance; but it is the privilege of every child of God to have beyond doubt a knowledge of his own salvation. No man is fit for God's service who is filled with doubts. If a man is not sure of his own salvation, how can he help any one else into the kingdom of God? If I seem in danger of drowning and do not know whether I shall ever reach the shore, I cannot assist another. I must first get on the solid rock myself; and then I can lend my brother a helping hand. If being myself blind I were to tell another blind man how to get sight, he might reply, "First get healed yourself; and then you can tell me." I recently met with a young man who was a Christian: but he had not attained to victory over sin. He was in terrible darkness. Such an one is not fit to work for God, because he has besetting sins; and he has not the victory over his doubts, because he has not the victory over his sins.

None will have time or heart to work for God, who are not assured as to their own salvation. They have as much as they can attend to; and being themselves burdened with doubts, they cannot help others to carry their burdens. There is no rest, joy, or peace—no liberty, nor power—where doubts and uncertainty exist.

Now it seems as if there are three wiles of Satan against which we ought to be on our guard. In the first place he moves all his kingdom to keep us away from Christ; then he devotes himself to get us into "Doubting Castle:" but if we have, in spite of him, a clear ringing witness for the Son of God, he will do all he can to blacken our characters and belie our testimony.

Some seem to think that it is presumption not to have doubts; but doubt is very dishonoring to God. If any one were to say that they had known a person for thirty years and yet doubted him, it would not be very creditable; and when we have known God for ten, twenty or thirty years does it not reflect on His veracity to doubt Him.

Could Paul and the early Christians and martyrs have gone through what they did if they had been filled with doubts, and had not known whether they were going to heaven or to perdition after they had been burned at the stake? They must have had Assurance.

Mr. Spurgeon says: "I never heard of a stork that when it met with a fir tree demurred as to its right to build its nest there; and I never heard of a coney yet that questioned whether it had a permit to run into the rock. Why, these creatures would soon perish if they were always doubting and fearing as to whether they had a right to use providential provisions.

"The stork says to himself, 'Ah, here is a fir tree:' he consults with his mate, 'Will this do for the nest in which we may rear our young?' 'Aye,' says she; and they gather the materials, and arrange them. There is never any deliberation, 'May we build here?' but they bring their sticks and make their nest.

"The wild goat on the crag does not say, 'Have I a right here?' No, he must be somewhere: and there is a crag which exactly suits him; and he springs upon it.

"Yet, though these dumb creatures know the provision of their God, the sinner does not recognize the provision of his Saviour. He quibbles and questions, 'May I?' and am 'I am afraid it is not for me;' and 'I think it cannot be meant for me;' and 'I am afraid it is too good to be true.'

"And yet nobody ever said to the stork, 'Whosoever buildeth on this fir tree shall never have his nest pulled down.' No inspired word has ever said to the coney, 'Whosoever runs into this rock cleft shall never be driven out of it.' If it had been so it would make assurance doubly sure."

"And yet here is Christ provided for sinners, just the sort of a Saviour sinners need; and the encouragement is added, 'Him that cometh unto Me I will in no wise cast out;' 'Whosoever will, let him take the water of life freely.'"

Now let us come to the Word. John tells us in his Gospel what Christ did for us on earth. In his Epistle He tells us what He is doing for us in heaven as our Advocate. In his Gospel there are only two chapters in which the word "believe" does not occur. With these two exceptions, every chapter in John is "Believe! Believe!! Believe!!!" He tells us in xx. 31, "But these are written, that ye might believe that Jesus is the Christ, the son of God, and that, believing, ye might have life through His name." That is the purpose for which he wrote the Gospel—"that we might believe that Jesus is the Christ, the Son of God: and that, believing, we might have life through His name" (John xx. 31).

Turn to 1 John v. 13, he there tells us why he wrote this Epistle: "These things have I written unto you that believe on the name of the Son of God." Notice to whom he writes it "You that believe on the name of the Son of God; that ye may know that ye have eternal life, and that ye may believe on the name of the Son of God." There are only five short chapters in this first Epistle, and the word "know" occurs over forty times. It is "Know! Know!! KNOW!!!" The Key to it is Know! and all through the Epistle there rings out the refrain—"that we might know that we have eternal life."

I went twelve hundred miles down the Mississippi in the spring some years ago; and every evening, just as the sun went down, you might have seen men, and sometimes women, riding up to the banks of the river on either side on mules or horses, and sometimes coming on foot, for the purpose of lighting up the Government lights; and all down that mighty river there were landmarks which guided the pilots in their dangerous navigation. Now God has given us lights or landmarks to tell us whether we are His children or not; and what we need to do is to examine the tokens He has given us.

In the third chapter of John's first Epistle there are five things worth knowing.

In the fifth verse we read the first: "And ye know that He was manifested to take away our sins; and in Him is no sin." Not what I have done, but what HE has done. Has He failed in His mission?

Is He not able to do what He came for? Did ever any heaven-sent man fail yet? and could God's own Son fail? He was manifested to take away our sins.

Again, in the nineteenth verse, the second thing worth knowing: "And hereby we know that we are of the truth, and shall assure our hearts before Him." We know that we are of the truth. And if the truth make us free, we shall be free indeed. "If the Son therefore shall make you free, ye shall be free indeed." (John viii. 36.)

The third thing worth knowing is in the fourteenth verse, "We know that we have passed from death unto life, because we love the brethren." The natural man does not like godly people, nor does he care to be in their company. "He that loveth not his brother abideth in death." He has no spiritual life.

The fourth thing worth knowing we find in verse twenty-four: "And he that keepeth His commandments dwelleth in Him, and He in him. And hereby we know that He abideth in us, by the Spirit which He hath given us." We can tell what kind of Spirit we have if we possess the Spirit of Christ—a Christ-like spirit—not the same in degree, but the same in kind. If I am meek, gentle, and forgiving; if I have a spirit filled with peace and joy; if I am long-suffering and gentle, like the Son of God—that is a test: and in that way we are to tell whether we have eternal life or not.

The fifth thing worth knowing, and the best of all, is "Beloved, now." Notice the word "Now." It does not say when you come to die. "Beloved, now are we the sons of God; and it doth not yet appear what we shall be: but we know that, when He shall appear; we shall be like Him; for we shall see Him as He is" (v. 2).

But some will say, "Well, I believe all that; but then I have sinned since I became a Christian." Is there a man or a woman on the face of the earth who has not sinned since becoming a Christian? Not one! There never has been, and never will be, a soul on this earth who has not sinned, or who will not sin, at some time of their Christian experience. But God has made provision for believers' sins. We are not to make provision for them; but God has. Bear that in mind.

Turn to 1 John ii. 1: "My little children, these things write I unto you, that ye sin not. And if any man sin, we have an Advocate with the Father, Jesus Christ the righteous." He is here writing to the righteous. "If any man sin, we"—John put himself in—"we have an Advocate with the Father, Jesus Christ the righteous." What an

Advocate! He attends to our interests at the very best place—the throne of God. He said, "Nevertheless, I tell you the truth; it is expedient for you that I go away" (John xvi. 7). He went away to become our High Priest, and also our Advocate. He has had some hard cases to plead; but he has never lost one: and if you entrust your immortal interests to Him, He will "present you faultless before the presence of His glory with exceeding joy" (Jude 24).

The past sins of Christians are all forgiven as soon as they are confessed; and they are never to be mentioned. That is a question which is not to be opened up again. If our sins have been put away, that is the end of them. They are not to be remembered; and God will not mention them any more. This is very plain. Suppose I have a son who, while I am from home, does wrong. When I go home he throws his arms around my neck and says, "Papa, I did what you told me not to do. I am very sorry. Do forgive me." I say: "Yes, my son," and kiss him. He wipes away his tears, and goes off rejoicing.

But the next day he says: "Papa, I wish you would forgive me for the wrong I did yesterday." I should say: "Why, my son, that thing is settled; and I don't want it mentioned again." "But I wish you would forgive me: it would help me to hear you say, 'I forgive you.'" Would that be honoring me? Would it not grieve me to have my boy doubt me? But to gratify him I say again, "I forgive you, my son."

And if, the next day, he were again to bring up that old sin, and ask forgiveness, would not that grieve me to the heart? And so, my dear reader, if God has forgiven us, never let us mention the past. Let us forget those things which are behind, and reach forth unto those which are before, and press toward the mark for the prize of the high calling of God in Christ Jesus. Let the sins of the past go; for "If we confess our sins, He is faithful and just to forgive us our sins, and to cleanse us from all unrighteousness" (1 John i. 9).

And let me say that this principle is recognized in courts of justice. A case came up in the courts of a country—I won't say where—in which a man had had trouble with his wife; but he forgave her, and then afterwards brought her into court. And, when it was known that he had forgiven her, the judge said that the thing was settled. The judge recognized the soundness of the principle, that if a sin were once forgiven there was an end of it. And do you think the Judge of all the earth will forgive you and me, and open the question again? Our sins are gone for time and eternity, if God forgives: and what we have to do is to confess and forsake our sins.

Again in 2 Corinthians xiii. 5: "Examine yourselves whether ye be in the faith; prove your own selves. Know ye not your own selves, how that Jesus Christ is in you, except ye be reprobates?" Now examine yourselves. Try your religion. Put it to the test. Can you forgive an enemy? That is a good way to know if you are a child of God. Can you forgive an injury, or take an affront, as Christ did? Can you be censured for doing well, and not murmur? Can you be misjudged and misrepresented, and yet keep a Christ-like spirit?

Another good test is to read Galatians v., and notice the fruits of the Spirit; and see if you have them. "The fruit of the Spirit is love, joy, peace, long suffering, gentleness, goodness, faith, meekness, temperance: against such there is no law." If I have the fruits of the Spirit I must have the Spirit. I could not have the fruits without the Spirit any more than there could be an orange without the tree. And Christ says "Ye shall know them by their fruits;" "for the tree is known by his fruits." Make the tree good, and the fruit will be good. The only way to get the fruit is to have the Spirit. That is the way to examine ourselves whether we are the children of God.

Then there is another very striking passage. In Romans viii. 9, Paul says: "Now, if any man have not the Spirit of Christ, he is none of His." That ought to settle the question, even though one may have gone through all the external forms that are considered necessary by some to constitute a member of a Church. Read Paul's life, and put yours alongside of it. If your life resembles his, it is a proof that you are born again—that you are a new creature in Christ Jesus.

But although you may be born again, it will require time to become a full-grown Christian. Justification is instantaneous; but sanctification is a life-work. We are to grow in wisdom. Peter says "Grow in grace, and in the knowledge of our Lord and Saviour Jesus Christ" (2 Pet. iii. 18); and in the first chapter of his Second Epistle, "Add to your faith virtue; and to virtue knowledge; and to knowledge temperance; and to temperance patience; and to patience godliness; and to godliness brotherly kindness; and to brotherly kindness charity. For if these things be in you and abound they make you that ye shall neither be barron nor unfruitful in the knowledge of our Lord Jesus Christ." So that we are to add grace to grace. A tree may be perfect in its first year of growth;

but it does not attain its maturity. So with the Christian: he may be a true child of God, but not a matured Christian. The eighth of Romans is very important, and we should be very familiar with it. In the fourteenth verse the apostle says: "For as many as are led by the Spirit of God they are the sons of God." Just as the soldier is led by his captain, the pupil by his teacher, or the traveller by his guide; so the Holy Spirit will be the guide of every true child of God.

Then let me call your attention to another fact. All Paul's teaching in nearly every Epistle rings out the doctrine of assurance. He says in 2 Corinthians v. 1: "For we know that if our earthly house of this tabernacle were dissolved, we have a building of God, a house not made with hands, eternal in the heavens." He had a title to the mansions above, and he says—I know it. He was not living in uncertainty. He said: "I have a desire to depart and be with Christ" (Phil. i. 23); and if he had been uncertain he would not have said that. Then in Colossians iii. 4, he says: "When Christ, who is our life, shall appear, then shall ye also appear with Him in glory." I am told that Dr. Watts' tombstone bears this same passage of Scripture. There is no doubt there.

Then turn to Colossians i. 12: "Giving thanks unto the Father, which hath made us meet to be partakers of the inheritance of the saints in light; who hath delivered us from the power of darkness, and hath translated us into the kingdom of His dear Son."

Three haths: "hath made us meet;" "hath delivered us;" and "hath translated us." It does not say that He is going to make us meet; that He is going to deliver; that He is going to translate.

Then again in verse 14th: "In whom we have redemption through His blood, even the forgiveness of sins." We are either forgiven or we are not, we should not give ourselves any rest until we get into the kingdom of God; nor until we can each look up and say, "I know that if my earthly house of this tabernacle were dissolved, I have a building of God, a house not made with hands, eternal in the heavens" (2 Cor. v. 1).

Look at Romans viii. 32: "He that spared not His own Son, but delivered Him up for us all, how shall He not with Him also freely give us all things?" If He gave us His Son, will He not give us the certainty that He is ours. I have heard this illustration. There was a man who owed $10,000, and would have been made a bankrupt, but a friend came forward and paid the sum. It was found afterwards that he owed a few dollars more; but he did not for a moment entertain a doubt that, as his friend had paid the larger amount, he would also pay the smaller. And we have high warrant for saying that if God has given us His Son He will with Him also freely give us all things; and if we want to realize our salvation beyond controversy He will not leave us in darkness.

Again in the 33d verse: "Who shall lay anything to the charge of God's elect? It is God that justifieth. Who is he that condemneth? It is Christ that died, yea rather, that is risen again, who is even at the right hand of God, who also maketh intercession for us. Who shall separate us from the love of Christ? shall tribulation, or distress, or persecution, or famine, or nakedness, or peril, or sword? As it is written, For Thy sake we are killed all the day long; we are accounted as sheep for the slaughter. Nay, in all these things we are more than conquerors through Him that loved us. For I am persuaded that neither death, nor life, nor angels, nor principalities, nor powers, nor things present, nor things to come, nor height, nor depth, nor any other creature, shall be able to separate us from the love of God, which is in Christ Jesus our Lord."

That has the right ring in it. There is Assurance for you. "I Know." Do you think that the God who has justified me will condemn me? That is quite an absurdity. God is going to save us so that neither men, angels, nor devils, can bring any charge against us or Him. He will have the work complete.

Job lived in a darker day than we do; but we read in Job xix. 25: "I know that my Redeemer liveth, and that He shall stand in the latter day upon the earth."

The same confidence breathes through Paul's last words to Timothy: "For the which cause I also suffer these things: nevertheless I am not ashamed; for I know whom I have believed, and am persuaded that He is able to keep that which I have committed unto Him against that day." It is not a matter of doubt, but of knowledge. "I know." "I am persuaded." The word "Hope," is not used in the Scripture to express doubt. It is used in regard to the second coming of Christ, or to the resurrection of the body. We do not say that we "hope" we are Christians. I do not say that I "hope" I am an American, or that I "hope" I am a married man. These are settled things. I may say that I "hope" to go back to my home, or I hope to attend such a meeting. I do not say that I "hope" to come to this country, for I am here. And so, if we are born of God we know it;

and He will not leave us in darkness if we search the Scriptures.

Christ taught this doctrine to His seventy disciples when they returned elated with their success, saying, "Lord, even the devils are subject unto us through Thy name." The Lord seemed to check them, and said that He would give them something to rejoice in. "Notwithstanding in this rejoice not, that the spirits are subject unto you; but rather rejoice because your names are written in heaven." (Luke x. 20.)

It is the privilege of every one of us to know, beyond a doubt, that our salvation is sure. Then we can work for others. But if we are doubtful of our own salvation, we are not fit for the service of God.

Another passage is John v. 24: "Verily, verily I say unto you: He that heareth my word, and believeth on Him that sent Me, hath everlasting life, and shall not come into 'judgment,'" (the new translation has it so), "but is passed from death unto life."

Some people say that you never can tell till you are before the great white throne of Judgment whether you are saved or not. Why, my dear friend, if your life is hid with Christ in God, you are not coming into judgment for your sins. We may come into judgment for reward. This is clearly taught where the lord reckoned with the servant to whom five talents had been given, and who brought other five talents saying, "Lord, thou deliveredst unto me five talents; behold, I have gained beside them five talents more. His lord said unto him, Well done, thou good and faithful servant: thou hast been faithful over a few things; I will make thee ruler over many things; enter thou into the joy of thy lord." (Matt. xxv. 20, 21.) We shall be judged for our stewardship. That is one thing; but salvation—eternal life—is another.

Will God demand payment twice of the debt which Christ has paid for us? If Christ bear my sins in His own body on the tree, am I to answer for them as well?

Isaiah tells us that, "He was wounded for our transgressions; He was bruised for our iniquities; the chastisement of our peace was upon Him: and with His stripes we are healed." In Romans iv. 25, we read: He "was delivered for our offences, and was raised again for our justification." Let us believe, and get the benefit of His finished work.

Then again in John x. 9: "I am the door: by Me if any man enter in he shall be saved, and shall go in and out, and find pasture."

That is the promise. Then the 27th verse, "My sheep hear my voice; and I know them, and they follow Me. And I give unto them eternal life; and they shall never perish, neither shall any man pluck them out of my hand. My father which gave them is greater than all; and no man is able to pluck them out of my Father's hand." Think of that! The Father, the Son, and the Holy Ghost, are pledged to keep us. You see that it is not only the Father, not only the Son, but the three persons of the Triune God.

Now, a great many people want some token outside of God's word. That habit always brings doubt. If I made a promise to meet a man at a certain hour and place to-morrow, and he were to ask me for my watch as a token of my sincerity, it would be a slur on my truthfulness. We must not question what God has said: He has made statement after statement, and multiplied figure upon figure. Christ says: "I am the door; by Me if any man enter in he shall be saved." "I am the Good Shepherd, and know My sheep, and am known of Mine." "I am the light of the world; he that followeth Me shall not walk in darkness, but shall have the light of life." "I am the truth;" receive Me, and you will have the truth; for I am the embodiment of truth. Do you want to know the way? "I am the way:" follow Me, and I will lead you into the kingdom. Are you hungering after righteousness? "I am the Bread of life:" if you eat of Me you shall never hunger. "I am the Water of life:" if you drink of this water it shall be within you "a well of water springing up unto everlasting life." "I am the resurrection and the life: he that believeth in Me, though he were dead, yet shall he live; and whosoever liveth and believeth in Me shall never die." (John xi. 25, 26.)

Let me remind you where our doubts come from. A good many of God's dear people never get beyond knowing themselves servants. He calls us "friends." If you go into a house you will soon see the difference between the servant and the son. The son walks at perfect liberty all over the house; he is at home. But the servant takes a subordinate place. What we want is to get beyond servants. We ought to realize our standing with God as sons and daughters. He will not "un-child" His children. God has not only adopted us, but we are His by birth: we have been born into His kingdom. My little boy was as much mine when he was a day old as now that he is fourteen. He was my son; although it did not appear what he would be when he attained manhood. He is mine; although he may have to undergo probation under tutors and governors. The children of God are not perfect; but we are perfectly His children.

Another origin of doubts is looking at ourselves. If you want to be wretched and miserable, filled with doubts from morning till night, look at yourselves. "Thou wilt keep him in perfect peace whose mind is stayed on Thee." (Isa. xxvi. 3.) Many of God's dear children are robbed of joy because they keep looking at themselves.

Some one has said: "There are three ways to look. If you want to be wretched, look within; if you wish to be distracted, look around; but if you would have peace, look up." Peter looked away from Christ, and he immediately began to sink. The Master said to him: "O thou of little faith! Wherefore didst thou doubt?" (Matt. xiv. 31.) He had God's eternal word, which was sure footing, and better than either marble, granite or iron; but the moment he took his eyes off Christ down he went. Those who look around cannot see how unstable and dishonoring is their walk. We want to look straight at the "Author and Finisher of our faith."

When I was a boy I could only make a straight track in the snow, by keeping my eyes fixed upon a tree or some object before me. The moment I took my eye off the mark set in front of me, I walked crooked. It is only when we look fixedly on Christ that we find perfect peace. After He rose from the dead He showed His disciples His hands and His feet. (Luke xxiv. 40.) That was the ground of their peace. If you want to scatter your doubts, look at the blood; and if you want to increase your doubts, look at yourself. You will get doubts enough for years by being occupied with yourself for a few days.

Then again: look at what He is, and at what He has done; not at what you are, and what you have done. That is the way to get peace and rest.

Abraham Lincoln issued a proclamation declaring the emancipation of three millions of slaves. On a certain day their chains were to fall off, and they were to be free. The proclamation was put up on the trees and fences wherever the Northern Army marched. A good many slaves could not read: but others read the proclamation, and most of them believed it; and on a certain day a glad shout went up, "We are free!" Some did not believe it, and stayed with their old masters; but it did not alter the fact that they were free. Christ, the Captain of our salvation, has proclaimed freedom to all who have faith in Him. Let us take Him at His word. Their feelings would not have made the slaves free. The power must come from the outside. Looking at ourselves will not make us free, but it is looking to Christ with the eye of faith.

Bishop Ryle has strikingly said: "Faith is the root, and Assurance the flower." Doubtless you can never have the flower without the root; but it is no less certain you may have the root, and not the flower.

"Faith is that poor trembling woman who came behind Jesus in the press, and touched the hem of His garment. (Mark v. 27.) Assurance is Stephen standing calmly in the midst of his murderers, and saying, 'I see the heavens opened, and the Son of Man standing on the right hand of God'" (Acts vii. 56).

"Faith is the penitent thief, crying, 'Lord, remember me' (Luke xxiii. 42). Assurance is Job sitting in the dust, covered with sores, and saying, 'I know that my Redeemer liveth;' 'Though He slay me, yet will I trust in Him'" (Job xix. 25; xiii. 15).

"Faith is Peter's drowning cry, as he began to sink, 'Lord, save me!' (Matt. xxiv. 30). Assurance is that same Peter declaring before the Council, in after-times, 'This is the stone which was set at nought of you builders, which is become the head of the corner: neither is there salvation in any other; for there is none other name under heaven given among men whereby we must be saved'" (Acts iv. 11, 12).

"Faith is the anxious, trembling voice, 'Lord, I believe; help Thou mine unbelief!' (Mark ix. 24). Assurance is the confident challenge, 'Who shall lay anything to the charge of God's elect? Who is he that condemneth?'" (Rom. viii. 33, 34).

Faith is Saul praying in the house of Judas at Damascus, sorrowful, blind, and alone. (Acts ix. 11.) Assurance is Paul, the aged prisoner, looking calmly into the grave, and saying, 'I know whom I have believed.' There is a crown laid up for me' (2 Tim. i. 12; iv. 8).

"Faith is Life. How great the blessing! Who can tell the gulf between life and death? And yet life may be weak, sickly, unhealthy, painful, trying, anxious, worn, burdensome, joyless, smileless, to the very end.

"Assurance is more than life. It is health, strength, power, vigor, activity, energy, manliness, beauty."

A minister once pronounced the benediction in this way: "The heart of God to make us welcome; the blood of Christ to make us clean, and the Holy Spirit to make us certain." The security of the believer is the result of the operation of the Spirit of God.

Another writer says: "I have seen shrubs and trees grow out of the rocks, and overhang fearful precipices, roaring cataracts, and deep running waters; but they maintained their position, and threw out their foliage and branches as much as if they had been in the midst of a dense forest." It was their hold on the rock that made them secure; and the influences of nature that sustained their life. So believers are oftentimes exposed to the most horrible dangers in their journey to heaven; but, so long as they are "rooted and grounded" in the Rock of Ages, they are perfectly secure. Their hold of Him is their guarantee; and the blessings of His grace give them life and sustain them in life. And as the tree must die, or the rock fall, before a dissolution can be effected between them, so either the believer must lose his spiritual life, or the Rock must crumble, ere their union can be dissolved.

Speaking of the Lord Jesus, Isaiah says: "I will fasten Him as a nail in a sure place; and He shall be for a glorious throne to His Father's house: and they shall hang upon Him all the glory of His father's house, the offspring and the issue, all vessels of small quantity, from the vessels of cups, even to all the vessels of flagons" (xxii. 23, 24).

There is one nail, fastened in a sure place; and on it hang all the flagons and all the cups. "Oh," says one little cup, "I am so small and so black, suppose I were to drop!" "Oh," says a flagon, "there is no fear of you; but I am so heavy, so very weighty, suppose I were to drop!" And a little cup says, "Oh, if I were only like the gold cup there, I should never fear falling." But the gold cup answers, "It is not because I am a gold cup that I keep up; but because I hang upon the nail." If the nail gives way we all come down, gold cups, china cups, pewter cups, and all; but as long as the nail keeps up, all that hang on Him hang safely.

I once read these words on a tombstone: "Born, died, kept." Let us pray God to keep us in perfect peace, and assured of salvation.

CHAPTER VIII

CHRIST ALL AND IN ALL.

Colossians iii. 11.)

Christ is all to us that we make Him to be. I want to emphasize that word "all." Some men make Him to be "a root out of a dry ground," "without form or comeliness." He is nothing to them; they do not want Him. Some Christians have a very small Saviour, for they are not willing to receive Him fully, and let Him do great and mighty things for them. Others have a mighty Saviour, because they make Him to be great and mighty.

If we would know what Christ wants to be to us, we must first of all know Him as our Saviour from sin. When the angel came down from heaven to proclaim that He was to be born into the world, you remember he gave His name, "He shall be called Jesus, for He shall save His people from their sins." Have we been delivered from sin? He did not come to save us in our sins, but from our sins. Now, there are three ways of knowing a man. Some men you know only by hearsay; others you merely know by having been once introduced to them, you know them very slightly; other again you know by having been acquainted with them for years, you know them intimately. So I believe there are three classes of people to-day in the Christian Church and out of it: those who know Christ only by reading or by hearsay, those who have a historical Christ; those who have a slight personal acquaintance with Him; and, those who thirst, as Paul did, to "know Him and the power of His resurrection." The more we know of Christ the more we shall love Him, and the better we shall serve Him.

Let us look at Him as He hangs upon the Cross, and see how He has put away sin. He was manifested that He might take away our sins; and if we really know Him we must first of all see Him as our Saviour from sin. You remember how the angels said to the shepherds on the plains of Bethlehem, "Behold, I bring you good tidings of great joy, which shall be to all people: for unto you is born this day, in the city of David, a Saviour, which is Christ the

Lord." (Luke ii. 10, 11.) Then if you go clear back to Isaiah, seven hundred years before Christ's birth, you will find these words: "I, even I, am the Lord; and beside me there is no Saviour" (xliii. 11).

Again, in the First Epistle of John (iv. 14) we read: "We have seen, and do testify, that the Father sent the Son to be the Saviour of the world." All the heathen religions, we read, teach men to work their way up to God; but the religion of Jesus Christ is God coming down to men to save them, to lift them up out of the pit of sin. In Luke xix. 10, we read that Christ Himself told the people what He had come for: "The Son of Man is come to seek and to save that which was lost." So we start from the Cross, not from the cradle. Christ has opened up a new and living way to the Father; He has taken all the stumbling-blocks out of the way, so that every man who accepts of Christ as his Saviour can have salvation.

But Christ is not only a Saviour. I might save a man from drowning and rescue him from an untimely grave; but I might probably not be able to do any more for him. Christ is something more than a Saviour. When the children of Israel were placed behind the blood, that blood was their salvation; but they would still have heard the crack of the slave-driver's whip if they had not been delivered from the Egyptian yoke of bondage: then it was that God delivered them from the hand of the king of Egypt. I have little sympathy with the idea that God comes down to save us, and then leaves us in prison, the slaves of our besetting sins. No; He has come to deliver us, and to give us victory over our evil tempers, our passions, and our lusts. Are you a professed Christian but one who is a slave to some besetting sin? If you want to get victory over that temper or that lust, go on to know Christ more intimately. He brings deliverance for the past, the present, and the future. "Who delivered; who doth deliver; who will yet deliver." (2 Cor. i. 10.)

How often, like the children of Israel when they came to the Red Sea, have we become discouraged because everything looked dark before us, behind us, and around us, and we knew not which way to turn. Like Peter we have said, "To whom shall we go?" But God has appeared for our deliverance. He has brought us through the Red Sea right out into the wilderness, and opened up the way into the Promised Land. But Christ is not only our Deliverer; He is our Redeemer. That is something more than being our Saviour. He has brought us back. "Ye have sold yourselves for nought; and ye shall be redeemed without money." (Isaiah lii. 3.) "We were not redeemed with corruptible things, as silver and gold." (1 Peter i.

18.) If gold could have redeemed us, could He not have created ten thousand worlds full of gold?

When God had redeemed the children of Israel from the bondage of Egypt, and brought them through the Red Sea, they struck out for the wilderness; and then God became to them their Way. I am so thankful the Lord has not left us in darkness as to the right way. There is no living man who has been groping in the darkness but may know the way. "I am the Way," says Christ. If we follow Christ we shall be in the right way, and have the right doctrine. Who could lead the children of Israel through the wilderness like the Almighty God Himself? He knew the pitfalls and dangers of the way, and guided the people through all their wilderness journey right into the promised land. It is true that if it had not been for their accursed unbelief they might have crossed into the land at Kadesh Barnea, and taken possession of it, but they desired something besides God's word; so they were turned back, and had to wander in the desert for forty years. I believe there are thousands of God's children wandering in the wilderness still. The Lord has delivered them from the hand of the Egyptian, and would at once take them through the wilderness right into the Promised Land, if they were only willing to follow Christ. Christ has been down here, and has made the rough places smooth, and the dark places light, and the crooked places straight. If we will only be led by Him, and will follow Him, all will be peace, and joy, and rest.

In the frontier, when a man goes out hunting he takes a hatchet with him, and cuts off pieces from the bark of the trees as he goes along through the forest: this is called "blazing the way." He does it that he may know the way back, as there is no pathway through these thick forests. Christ has come down to this earth; He has "blazed the Way:" and now that He has gone up on high, if we will but follow him, we shall be kept in the right path. I will tell you how you may know if you are following Christ or not. If some one has slandered you, or misjudged you, do you treat them as your master would have done? If you do not bear these things in a loving and forgiving spirit, all the churches and ministers in the world cannot make you right. "If any man have not the Spirit of Christ, he is none of His." (Romans viii. 9.) "If any man be in Christ Jesus he is a new creature: old things are passed away; behold, all things are become new." (2 Cor. v. 17.)

Christ is not only our way; He is the Light upon the way. He says, "I am the Light of the world." (John viii. 12; ix. 5; xii. 46.) He goes on to say, "He that followeth Me shall not walk in darkness, but shall have the light of life." It is impossible for any man or woman who is following Christ to walk in darkness. If your soul is in the darkness, groping around in the fog and mist of earth, let me tell you it is because you have got away from the true light. There is nothing but light that will dispel darkness. So let those who are walking in spiritual darkness admit Christ into their hearts: He is the Light. I call to mind a picture of which I used at one time to think a good deal; but now I have come to look more closely, I would not put it up in my house except I turned the face to the wall. It represents Christ as standing at a door, knocking, and having a big lantern in His hand. Why, you might as well hang up a lantern to the sun as put one into Christ's hand. He is the Sun of Righteousness; and it is our privilege to walk in the light of an unclouded sun.

Many people are hunting after light, and peace, and joy. We are nowhere told to seek after these things. If we admit Christ into our hearts these will all come of themselves. I remember, when a boy, I used to try in vain to catch my shadow. One day I was walking with my face to the sun; and as I happened to look around I saw that my shadow was following me. The faster I went the faster my shadow followed; I could not get away from it. So when our faces are directed to the Sun of Righteousness, the peace and joy are sure to come. A man said to me some time ago, "Moody, how do you feel?" It was so long since I had thought about my feelings I had to stop and consider awhile, in order to find out. Some Christians are all the time thinking about their feelings; and because they do not feel just right they think their joy is all gone. If we keep our faces towards Christ, and are occupied with Him, we shall be lifted out of the darkness and the trouble that may have gathered round our path.

I remember being in a meeting after the war of the great rebellion broke out. The war had been going on for about six months. The army of the North had been defeated at Bull Run, in fact, we had nothing but defeat, and it looked as though the republic was going to pieces. So we were much cast down and discouraged. At this meeting every speaker for awhile seemed as if he had hung his harp upon the willow; and it was one of the gloomiest meetings I ever attended. Finally an old man with beautiful white hair got up to speak, and his face literally shone. "Young men," he said "you do not talk like sons of the King. Though it is dark just here, remember it is light somewhere else." Then he went on to say that if it were dark all over the world, it was light up around the Throne.

He told us he had come from the east, where a friend had described to him how he had been up a mountain to spend the night and see the sun rise. As the party were climbing up the mountain, and before they had reached the summit, a storm came on. This friend said to the guide, "I will give this up; take me back." The guide smiled, and replied, "I think we shall get above the storm soon." On they went; and it was not long before they got up to where it was as calm as any summer evening. Down in the valley a terrible storm raged; they could hear the thunder rolling, and see the lightning's flash; but all was serene on the mountain top. "And so, my young friends," continued the old man, "though all is dark around you, come a little higher and the darkness will flee away." Often when I have been inclined to get discouraged, I have thought of what he said. Now if you are down in the valley amidst the thick fog and the darkness, get a little higher; get nearer to Christ, and know more of Him.

You remember the Bible says, that when Christ expired on the cross, the light of the world was put out. God sent His Son to be the light of the world; but men did not love the light because it reproved them of their sins. When they were about to put out this light, what did Christ say to His disciples? "Ye shall be witnesses unto Me." (Acts i. 8.) He has gone up yonder to intercede for us; but He wants us to shine for Him down here. "Ye are the light of the world." (Matt. v. 14.) So our work is to shine; not to blow our own trumpet so that people may look at us. What we want to do is to show forth Christ. If we have any light at all it is borrowed light. Some one said to a young Christian: "Converted! it is all moonshine!" Said he: "I thank you for the illustration; the moon borrows its light from the sun; and we borrow ours from the Sun of Righteousness." If we are Christ's, we are here to shine for Him: by and by he will call us home to our reward.

I remember hearing of a blind man who sat by the wayside with a lantern near him. When he was asked what he had a lantern for, as he could not see the light, he said it was that people should not stumble ever him. I believe more people stumble over the inconsistencies of professed Christians than from any other cause. What is doing more harm to the cause of Christ than all the scepticism in the world is this cold, dead formalism, this conformity to the world, this professing what we do not possess. The eyes of the world are upon us. I think it was George Fox who said every Quaker ought to light up the country for ten miles around him. If we were all brightly shining for the Master, those about us would soon be reached, and there would be a shout of praise going to heaven.

People say: "I want to know what is the truth." Listen: "I am the truth," says Christ. (John xiv. 5.) If you want to know what the truth is, get acquainted with Christ. People also complain that they have not life. Many are trying to give themselves spiritual life. You may galvanize yourselves and put electricity into yourselves, so to speak; but the effect will not last very long. Christ alone is the author of life. If you would have real spiritual life, get to know Christ. Many try to stir up spiritual life by going to meetings. That may be well enough; but it will be of no use, unless they get into contact with the living Christ. Then their spiritual life will not be a spasmodic thing, but will be perpetual; flowing on and on, and bringing forth fruit to God.

Then Christ is our Keeper. A great many young disciples are afraid they will not hold out. "He that keepeth Israel shall neither slumber nor sleep." (Psalm cxxi. 4.) It is the work of Christ to keep us; and if He keeps us there will be no danger of our falling. I suppose if Queen Victoria had to take care of the Crown of England, some thief might attempt to get access to it; but it is put away in the Tower of London, and guarded night and day by soldiers. The whole English army would, if necessary, be called out to protect it. And we have no strength in ourselves. We are no match for Satan; he has had six thousand years' experience. But then we remember that the One who neither slumbers nor sleeps is our keeper. In Isaiah xli. 10, we read, "Fear thou not, for I am with thee; be not dismayed, for I am thy God; I will strengthen thee; yea, I will help thee; yea, I will uphold thee with the right hand of My righteousness." In Jude also, verse 24, we are told that He is "able to keep us from falling." "We have an Advocate with the Father, Jesus Christ the righteous." (1 John ii. 1.)

But Christ is something more. He is our Shepherd. It is the work of the shepherd to care for the sheep, to feed them and protect them. "I am the Good Shepherd;" "My sheep hear My voice." "I lay down My life for the sheep." In that wonderful tenth chapter of John, Christ uses the personal pronoun no less than twenty-eight times, in declaring what He is and what He will do. In verse 28 He says, "They shall never perish; neither shall any [man] pluck them out of My hand." But notice the word "man" is in italics. See how the verse really reads: "Neither shall any pluck them out of My hand"—no devil or man shall be able to do it. In another place the Scripture declares, "Your life is hid with Christ in God." (Col. iii. 3.) How safe and how secure!

Christ says, "My sheep hear My voice . . . and they follow Me." (John x. 27.) A gentleman in the East heard of a shepherd who could call all his sheep to him by name. He went and asked if this was true. The shepherd took him to the pasture where they were, and called one of them by some name. One sheep looked up and answered the call, while the others went on feeding and paid no attention. In the same way he called about a dozen of the sheep around him. The stranger said, "How do you know one from the other? They all look perfectly alike." "Well," said he, "you see that sheep toes in a little; that other one has a squint; one has a little piece of wool off; another has a black spot; and another has a piece out of its ear." The man knew all his sheep by their failings, for he had not a perfect one in the whole flock. I suppose our Shepherd knows us in the same way.

An Eastern shepherd was once telling a gentleman that his sheep knew his voice, and that no stranger could deceive them. The gentleman thought he would like to put the statement to the test. So he put on the shepherd's frock and turban, and took his staff and went to the flock. He disguised his voice, and tried to speak as much like the shepherd as he could; but he could not get a single sheep in the flock to follow him. He asked the shepherd if his sheep never followed a stranger. He was obliged to admit that if a sheep got sickly it would follow any one. So it is with a good many professed Christians; when they get sickly and weak in the faith, they will follow any teacher that comes along; but when the soul is in health, a man will not be carried away by errors and heresies. He will know whether the "voice" speaks the truth or not. He can soon tell that, if he is really in communion with God. When God sends a true messenger his words will find a ready response in the Christian heart.

Christ is a tender Shepherd. You may some time think He has not been a very tender Shepherd to you; you are passing under the rod. It is written, "Whom the Lord loveth He chasteneth, and scourgeth every son whom He receiveth." (Heb. xii. 6.) That you are passing under the rod is no proof that Christ does not love you. A friend of mine lost all his children. No man could ever have loved his family more; but the scarlet fever took one by one away; and so the whole four or five, one after another, died. The poor stricken parents went over to great Britain, and wandered from one place to another, there and on the continent. At length they found their way to Syria. One day they saw an Eastern shepherd come down to a stream, and call his flock to cross. The sheep came down to the brink, and looked at the water; but they seemed to shrink from it, and he could not get them to respond to his call. He then took a little lamb, put it under one arm; he took another lamb and put it under the other arm, and thus passed into the stream. The old sheep no longer stood looking at the water: they plunged in after the shepherd; and in a few minutes the whole flock was on the other side; and he led them away to newer and fresher pastures. The bereaved father and mother, as they looked on the scene, felt that it taught them a lesson. They no longer murmured because the Great Shepherd had taken their lambs one by one into yonder world; and they began to look up and look forward to the time when they would follow the loved ones they had lost. If you have loved ones gone before, remember that your Shepherd is calling you to "set your affection on things above." (Col. iii. 2.) Let us be faithful to Him, and follow Him, while we remain in this world. And if you have not taken Him for your Shepherd, do so this very day.

Christ is not only all these things that I have mentioned: He is also our Mediator, our Sanctifier, our Justifier; in fact, it would take volumes to tell what He desires to be to every individual soul. While looking through some papers I once read this wonderful description of Christ. I do not know where it originally came from; but it was so fresh to my soul that I should like to give it to you:—

"Christ is our Way; we walk in Him. He is our Truth; we embrace Him. He is our Life; we live in Him. He is our Lord; we choose Him to rule over us. He is our Master; we serve Him. He is our Teacher, instructing us in the way of salvation. He is our Prophet, pointing out the future. He is our Priest, having atoned for us. He is our Advocate, ever living to make intercession for us. He is our Saviour, saving to the uttermost. He is our Root; we grow from Him. He is our Bread; we feed upon Him. He is our Shepherd, leading us into green pastures. He is our true Vine; we abide in Him. He is the Water of Life; we slake our thirst from Him. He is the fairest among ten thousand: we admire Him above all others. He is 'the brightness of the Father's glory, and the express image of His person;' we strive to reflect His likeness. He is the upholder of all things;

we rest upon Him. He is our wisdom; we are guided by Him. He is our Righteousness; we cast all our imperfections upon Him. He is our Sanctification; we draw all our power for holy life from Him. He is our Redemption, redeeming us from all iniquity. He is our Healer, curing all our diseases. He is our Friend, relieving us in all our necessities. He is our Brother, cheering us in our difficulties."

Here is another beautiful extract: it is from Gotthold:

"For my part, my soul is like a hungry and thirsty child; and I need His love and consolation for my refreshment. I am a wandering and lost sheep; and I need Him as a good and faithful shepherd. My soul is like a frightened dove pursued by the hawk; and I need His wounds for a refuge. I am a feeble vine; and I need His cross to lay hold of, and to wind myself about. I am a sinner; and I need His righteousness. I am naked and bare; and I need His holiness and innocence for a covering. I am ignorant; and I need His teaching: simple and foolish; and I need the guidance of His Holy Spirit. In no situation, and at no time, can I do without Him. Do I pray? He must prompt, and intercede for me. Am I arraigned by Satan at the Divine tribunal? He must be my Advocate. Am I in affliction? He must be my Helper. Am I persecuted by the world? He must defend me. When I am forsaken, He must be my Support; when I am dying, my life: when mouldering in the grave, my Resurrection. Well, then, I will rather part with all the world, and all that it contains, than with Thee, my Saviour. And, God be thanked! I know that Thou, too, art neither able nor willing to do without me. Thou art rich; and I am poor. Thou hast abundance; and I am needy. Thou hast righteousness; and I sins. Thou hast wine and oil; and I wounds. Thou hast cordials and refreshments; and I hunger and thirst.

Use me then, my Saviour, for whatever purpose, and in whatever way, Thou mayest require. Here is my poor heart, an empty vessel; fill it with Thy grace. Here is my sinful and troubled soul; quicken and refresh it with Thy love. Take my heart for Thine abode; my mouth to spread the glory of Thy name; my love and all my powers, for the advancement of Thy believing people; and never suffer the steadfastness and confidence of my faith to abate—that so at all times I may be enabled from the heart to say. 'Jesus needs me, and I Him; and so we suit each other.'"

CHAPTER IX

BACKSLIDING.

"I will heal their backsliding; I will love them freely: for Mine anger is turned away."—Hosea xiv. 4.

There are two kinds of backsliders. Some have never been converted: they have gone through the form of joining a Christian community and claim to be backsliders; but they never have, if I may use the expression, "slid forward." They may talk of backsliding; but they have never really been born again. They need to be treated differently from real back-sliders—those who have been born of the incorruptible seed, but who have turned aside. We want to bring the latter back the same road by which they left their first love.

Turn to Psalm lxxxv. 5. There you read: "Wilt Thou be angry with us for ever? wilt Thou draw out Thine anger to all generations? wilt Thou not revive us again: that Thy people may rejoice in Thee? Show us Thy mercy, O Lord; and grant us Thy salvation." Now look again: "I will hear what God the Lord will speak: for He will speak peace unto His people, and to His saints; but let them not turn again to folly" (verse 8).

There is nothing that will do back-sliders so much good as to come in contact with the Word of God; and for them the Old Testament is as full of help as the New. The book of Jeremiah has some wonderful passages for wanderers. What we want to do is to get back-sliders to hear what God the Lord will say.

Look for a moment at Jeremiah vi. 10. "To whom shall I speak, and give warning, that they may hear? behold, their ear is uncircumcised, and they cannot hearken: behold, the word of the Lord is unto them a reproach; they have no delight in it." That is the condition of back-sliders. They have no delight whatever in the word of God. But we want to bring them back, and let God get their ear. Read from the 14th verse: "They have healed also the hurt of the daughter of My people slightly, saying, Peace, peace;

when there is no peace. Were they ashamed when they had committed abomination? nay, they were not at all ashamed, neither could they blush: therefore they shall fall among them that fall: at the time that I visit them they shall be cast down, saith the Lord. Thus saith the Lord, Stand ye in the ways, and see, and ask for the old paths, where is the good way, and walk therein; and ye shall find rest for your souls. But they said, We will not walk therein. Also I set watchmen over you, saying, Hearken to the sound of the trumpet. But they said, We will not hearken."

That was the condition of the Jews when they had backslidden. They had turned away from the old paths. And that is the condition of backsliders. They have got away from the good old book. Adam and Eve fell by not hearkening to the word of God. They did not believe God's word; but they believed the tempter. That is the way backsliders fall—by turning away from the word of God.

In Jeremiah ii. we find God pleading with them as a father would plead with a son. "Thus saith the Lord, What iniquity have your fathers found in Me, that they are gone from Me, and have walked after vanity, and are become vain? . . . Wherefore I will yet plead with you, saith the Lord; and with your children's children will I plead . . . For my people have committed two evils: they have forsaken Me, the Fountain of living waters, and hewed them out cisterns, broken cisterns, that can hold no water."

Now there is one thing to which we wish to call the attention of backsliders; and that is, that the Lord never forsook them; but that they forsook Him! The Lord never left them; but they left Him! And this, too, without any cause! He says, "What iniquity have your fathers found in Me, that they are gone far from Me?" Is not God the same to-day as when you came to Him first? Has God changed? Men are apt to think that God has changed; but the fault is with them. Backslider, I would ask you, "What iniquity is there in God, that you have left Him and gone far from Him?" You have, He says, hewed out to yourselves broken cisterns that hold no water. The world cannot satisfy the new nature. No earthly well can satisfy the soul that has become a partaker of the heavenly nature. Honor, wealth and the pleasures of this world will not satisfy those who, having tasted the water of life, have gone astray, seeking refreshment at the world's fountains. Earthly wells will get dry. They cannot quench spiritual thirst.

Again in the 32nd verse: "Can a maid forget her ornaments, or a bride her attire? yet My people have forgotten Me, days without number." That is the charge which God brings against the backslider. They "have forgotten Me, days without number."

I have often startled young ladies when I have said to them, "My friend, you think more of your ear-rings than of the Lord." The reply has been, "No, I do not." But when I have asked, "Would you not be troubled if you lost one; and would you not set about seeking for it?" the answer has been, "Well, yes, I think I should." But though they had turned from the Lord, it did not give them any trouble; nor did they seek after Him that they might find Him.

How many once in fellowship and in daily communion with the Lord now think more of their dresses and ornaments than of their precious souls! Love does not like to be forgotten. Mothers would have broken hearts if their children left them and never wrote a word or sent any memento of their affection; and God pleads over backsliders as a parent over loved ones who have gone astray. He tries to woo them back. He asks: "What have I done that you should have forsaken Me?"

The most tender and loving words to be found in the whole of the Bible are from Jehovah to those who have left Him without a cause. Jer. ii. 19.

Hear how He argues with such: (Jer. xi. 19.) "Thine own wickedness shall correct thee, and thy backslidings shall reprove thee; know, therefore, and see, that it is an evil thing and bitter, that thou hast forsaken the Lord thy God, and that My fear is not in thee, saith the Lord God of hosts."

I do not exaggerate when I say that I have seen hundreds of backsliders come back; and I have asked them if they have not found it an evil and a bitter thing to leave the Lord. You cannot find a real backslider, who has known the Lord, but will admit that it is an evil and a bitter thing to turn away from Him; and I do not know of any one verse more used to bring back wanderers than that very one. May it bring you back if you have wandered into the far country.

Look at Lot. Did not he find it an evil and a bitter thing? He was twenty years in Sodom, and never made a convert. He got on well in the sight of the world. Men would have told you that he was one of the most influential and worthy men in all Sodom. But alas! alas! he ruined his family. And it is a pitiful sight to see that old backslider going through the streets of Sodom at midnight, after he has warned his children, and they have turned a deaf ear.

I have never known a man and his wife backslide, without its proving utter ruin to their children. They will make a mockery of religion and will deride their parents: "Thine own wickedness shall correct thee; and thy backsliding shall reprove thee!" Did not David find it so? Mark him, crying, "O my son Absalom, my son, my son Absalom! would God I had died for thee; O Absalom, my son, my son!" I think it was the ruin, rather than the death of his son that caused this anguish.

I remember being engaged in conversation some years ago, till past midnight, with an old man. He had been for years wandering on the barren mountains of sin. That night he wanted to get back. We prayed, and prayed, and prayed, till light broke in upon him; and he went away rejoicing. The next night he sat in front of me when I was preaching, and I think that I never saw any one look so sad and wretched in all my life. He followed me into the enquiry-room. "What is the trouble?" I asked. "Is your eye off the Saviour? Have your doubts come back?" "No; it is not that," he said. "I did not go to business, but spent all this day in visiting my children. They are all married and in this city. I went from house to house, but there was not one but mocked me. It is the darkest day of my life. I have awoke up to what I have done. I have taken my children into the world; and now I cannot get them out." The Lord had restored unto him the joy of His salvation; yet there was the bitter consequence of his transgression. You can run through your experience; and you can find just such instances repeated again and again. Many who came to your city years ago serving God, in their prosperity have forgotten Him: and where are their sons and daughters? Show me the father and mother who have deserted the Lord and gone back to the beggarly elements of the world; and I am mistaken if their children are not on the high road to ruin.

As we desire to be faithful we warn these backsliders. It is a sign of love to warn of danger. We may be looked upon as enemies for a while; but the truest friends are those who lift up the voice of warning. Israel had no truer friend than Moses. In Jeremiah God gave His people a weeping prophet to bring them back to Him; but they cast off God. They forgot the God who brought them out of Egypt, and who led them through the desert into the promised land. In their prosperity they forget Him and turned away. The Lord had told them what would happen. (Deut. xxviii.) And see what did happen. The king who make light of the word of God was taken captive by Nebuchadnezzar, and his children brought up in front of him and every one slain: his eyes were put out of his head; and he was bound in fetters of brass and cast into a dungeon in Babylon. (2 Kings xxv. 7.) That is the way he reaped what he had sown. Surely it is an evil and a bitter thing to backslide, but the Lord would win you back with the message of His Work.

In Jeremiah viii. 5, we read: "Why then is this people of Jerusalem slidden by a perpetual backsliding? They hold fast deceit; They refuse to return." That is what the Lord brings against them. "They refuse to return." "I hearkened and heard; but they spake not aright: no man repented him of his wickedness, saying, What have I done? Every one turned to his course, as the horse rusheth into the battle. Yea, the stork in the heaven knoweth her appointed times; and the turtle and the crane and the swallow observe the time of their coming; but My people know not the judgment of the Lord."

Now look: "I hearkened and heard; but they spake not aright." No family altar! No reading the Bible! No closet devotion! God stoops to hear; but His people have turned away! If there be a penitent backslider, one who is anxious for pardon and restoration, you will find no words more tender than are to be found in Jeremiah iii. 12: "Go, and proclaim these words toward the north, and say, Return, thou backsliding Israel, saith the Lord; and I will not cause Mine anger to fall upon you: for I am merciful, saith the Lord, and I will not keep anger forever." Now notice: "Only acknowledge thine iniquity, that thou hast transgressed against the Lord thy God, and hast scattered thy ways to the stranger under every green tree, and ye have not obeyed My voice, saith the Lord. Turn, O backsliding children, saith the Lord; for I am married unto you"—think of God coming and saying, "I am married unto you!—and I will take you one of a city, and two of a family, and I will bring you to Zion."

"Only acknowledge thine iniquity." How many times have I held that passage up to a backslider! "Acknowledge" it; and God says I will forgive you. I remember a man asking, "Who said that? Is that there?" And I held up to him the passage, "Only acknowledge thine iniquity;" and the man went down on his knees, and cried, "My God, I have sinned"; and the Lord restored him there and then. If you have wandered, He wants you to come back.

He says in another place, "O Ephraim, what shall I do unto thee? O Judah, what shall I do unto thee? for your goodness is as a morning cloud, and as the early dew it goeth away" (Hosea vi. 4). His compassion and His love is wonderful!

In Jeremiah iii. 22; "Return, ye backsliding children, and I will heal your backslidings. Behold, we come unto Thee; Thou art the Lord our God." He just puts words into the mouth of the backslider. Only come; and, if you will come, He will receive you graciously and love you freely.

In Hosea xiv. 1, 2, 4: "O Israel, return unto the Lord thy God; for thou hast fallen by thine iniquity. Take with you words, and turn to the Lord (He puts words into your mouth): say unto Him, Take away all iniquity, and receive us graciously; so will we render the calves of our lips . . . I will heal their backsliding, I will love them freely, for Mine auger is turned away from him." Just observe that, Turn! Turn!! Turn!!! rings all through these passages.

Now, if you have wandered, remember that you left Him, and not He you. You have to get out of the backslider's pit just in the same way you got in. And if you take the same road as when you left the Master you will find Him now, just where you are.

If we were to treat Christ as any earthly friend we should never leave Him; and there would never be a backslider. If I were in a town for a single week I should not think of going away without shaking hands with the friends I had made, and saying "Good bye" to them. I should be justly blamed if I took the train and left without saying a word to any one. The cry would be, "What's the matter?" But did you ever hear of a backslider bidding the Lord Jesus Christ "Good bye"; going into his closet and saying "Lord Jesus, I have known Thee ten, twenty, or thirty years: but I am tired of Thy service; Thy yoke is not easy, nor Thy burden light; so I am going back to the world, to the flesh-pots of Egypt. Good bye, Lord Jesus! Farewell"? Did you ever hear that? No; you never did, and you never will. I tell you, if you get into the closet and shut out the world and hold communion with the Master you cannot leave Him. The language of your heart will be, "To whom shall we go," but unto Thee? "Thou hast the words of eternal life" (John vi. 68). You could not go back to the world if you treated Him in that way. But you left Him and ran away. You have forgotten Him days without number. Come back to-day; just as you are! Make up your mind that you will not rest until God has restored unto you the joy of His salvation.

A gentleman in Cornwall once met a Christian in the street whom he knew to be a backslider. He went up to him, and said: "Tell me, is there not some estrangement between you and the Lord Jesus?" The man hung his head, and said, "Yes." "Well," said the gentleman, "what has He done to you?" The answer to which was a flood of tears.

In Revelation ii. 4, 5, we read: "Nevertheless I have somewhat against thee, because thou hast left the first love. Remember therefore from whence thou art fallen; and repent, and do the first works: or else I will come unto thee quickly, and will remove thy candlestick out of his place, except thou repent." I want to guard you against a mistake which some people make with regard to "doing the first works." Many think that they are to have the same experience over again, That has kept thousands for months without peace; because they have been waiting for a renewal of their first experience. You will never have the same experience as when you first came to the Lord. God never repeats himself. No two people of all earth's millions look alike or think alike. You may say that you cannot tell two people apart; but when you get well acquainted with them you can very quickly distinguish differences. So, no one person will have the same experience a second time. If God will restore His joy to your soul let Him do it in His way. Do not mark out a way for God to bless you. Do not expect the same experience that you had two or twenty years ago. You will have a fresh experience, and God will deal with you in His own way. If you confess your sins and tell Him that you have wandered from the path of His commandments He will restore unto you the joy of His salvation.

I want to call your attention to the manner in which Peter fell; and I think that nearly all fall pretty much in the same way. I want to lift up a warning note to those who have not fallen. "Let him that thinketh he standeth, take heed lest he fall" (1 Cor. x. 12). Twenty-five years ago—and for the first five years after I was converted—I used to think that if I were able to stand for twenty years I need fear no fall. But the nearer you get to the Cross the fiercer the battle. Satan aims high. He went amongst the twelve; and singled out the Treasurer—Judas Iscariot, and the Chief Apostle—Peter. Most men who have fallen have done so on the strongest side of their character. I am told that the only side upon which Edinburgh Castle was successfully assailed was where the rocks were steepest, and where the garrison thought themselves secure. If any man thinks that he is strong enough to resist the devil at any one point he needs special watch there, for the tempter comes that way.

Abraham stands, as it were, at the head of the family of faith; and the children of faith may be said to trace their descent to Abraham: and yet down in Egypt he denied his wife. (Gen. xii.) Moses was noted for his meekness; and yet he was kept out of the promised land because of one hasty act and speech, when he was told by the Lord to speak to the rock so that the congregation and their beasts should have water to drink. "Hear now, ye rebels; must we fetch you water out of this rock?" (Num. xx. 10).

Elijah was remarkable for his boldness: and yet he went off a day's journey into the wilderness like a coward and hid himself under a juniper tree, requesting for himself that he might die, because of a message he received from a woman. (1 Kings xix.) Let us be careful. No matter who the man is—he may be in the pulpit—but if he gets self-conceited he will be sure to fall. We who are followers of Christ need constantly to pray to be made humble, and kept humble. God made Moses' face so to shine that other men could see it; but Moses himself wist not that his face shone, and the more holy in heart a man is the more manifest to the outer world will be his daily life and conversation. Some people talk of how humble they are; but if they have true humility there will be no necessity for them to publish it. It is not needful. A lighthouse does not have a drum beaten or a trumpet-blown in order to proclaim the proximity of a lighthouse: it is its own witness. And so if we have the true light in us it will show itself. It is not those who make the most noise who have the most piety. There is a brook, or a little "burn" as the Scotch call it, not far from where I live; and after a heavy rain you can hear the rush of its waters a long way off: but let there come a few days of pleasant weather, and the brook becomes almost silent. But there is a river near my house, the flow of which I never heard in my life, as it pours on in its deep and majestic course the year round. We should have so much of the love of God within us that its presence shall be evident without our loud proclamation of the fact.

The first step in Peter's downfall was his self-confidence. The Lord warned him. The Lord said: "Simon, Simon, behold, Satan hath desired to have you, that he may sift you as wheat: but I have prayed for thee, that thy faith fail not" (Luke xxii. 31, 32). But Peter said: "I am ready to go with Thee, both into prison and to death." "Though all shall be offended because of Thee, yet will I never be offended." (Matt. xxvi. 23.) "James and John, and the others, may leave You; but You can count on me!" But the Lord warned him: "I tell thee, Peter, the cock shall not crow this day, before that thou shalt thrice deny that thou knowest Me." (Luke xxii. 24.)

Though the Lord rebuked him, Peter said he was ready to follow Him to death. That boasting is too often a forerunner of downfall. Let us walk humbly and softly. We have a great tempter; and, in an unguarded hour, we may stumble and fall and bring a scandal on Christ.

The next step in Peter's downfall was that he went to sleep. If Satan can rock the Church to sleep he does his work through God's own people. Instead of Peter watching one short hour in Gethsemane, he fell asleep, and the Lord asked him, "What, could ye not watch with Me one hour?" (Matt. xxvi. 40.) The next thing was that he fought in the energy of the flesh. The Lord rebuked him again and said, "They that take the sword shall perish with the sword." (Matt. xxvi. 52.) Jesus had to undo what Peter had done. The next thing, he "followed afar off." Step by step he gets away. It is a sad thing when a child of God follows afar off. When you see him associating with worldly friends, and throwing his influence on the wrong side, he is following afar off; and it will not be long before disgrace will be brought upon the old family name, and Jesus Christ will be wounded in the house of his friends. The man, by his example, will cause others to stumble and fall.

The next thing—Peter is familiar and friendly with the enemies of Christ. A damsel says to this bold Peter: "Thou also wast with this Jesus of Galilee." But he denied before them all, saying, "I know not what thou sayest." And when he was gone out into the porch another maid saw him and said unto them that were there, "This fellow was also with Jesus of Nazareth." And again he denied with an oath. "I do not know the Man." Another hour passed; and yet he did not realize his position; when another confidently affirmed that he was a Galilean, for his speech betrayed him. And he was angry and began to curse and to swear, and again denied his Master: and the cock crew. (Matt. xxvi. 69-74.)

He commences away up on the pinacle of self-conceit, and goes down step by step until he breaks out into cursing, and swears that he never knew his Lord.

The Master might have turned and said to him, "Is it true, Peter, that you have forgotten Me so soon? Do you not remember when your wife's mother lay sick of a fever that I rebuked the disease and it left her? Do you not call to mind your astonishment at the draught of fishes so that you exclaimed, 'Depart from me; for I am a sinful man, O Lord?' Do you remember when in answer to your cry, 'Lord, save me, or I perish,' I stretched out My hand and kept you from drowning in the water? Have you forgotten when, on the Mount of Transfiguration, with James and John, you said to Me, 'Lord, it is good to be here: let us make three tabernacles?' Have you forgotten being with Me at the supper-table, and in Gethsemane? Is it true that you have forgotten Me so soon?" The Lord might have upbraided him with questions such as these: but He did nothing of the kind. He cast one look on Peter: and there was so much love in it that it broke that bold disciple's heart: and he went out and wept bitterly.

And after Christ rose from the dead see how tenderly He dealt with the erring disciple. The angel at the sepulchre says, "Tell His disciples, and Peter." (Mark xvi. 7.) The Lord did not forget Peter, though Peter had denied Him thrice; so He caused this kindly special message to be conveyed to the repentant disciple. What a tender and loving Saviour we have!

Friend, if you are one of the wanderers, let the loving look of the Master win you back; and let Him restore you to the joy of His salvation.

Before closing, let me say that I trust God will restore some backslider reading these pages, who may in the future become a useful member of society and a bright ornament of the Church. We should never have had the thirty-second Psalm if David had not been restored: "Blessed is he whose transgression is forgiven, whose sin is covered"; or that beautiful fifty-first Psalm which was written by the restored backslider. Nor should we have had that wonderful sermon on the day of Pentecost when three thousand were converted—preached by another restored backslider.

May God restore other backsliders and make them a thousand times more used for His glory than they ever were before.

MEN OF THE BIBLE

CONTENTS

Abraham's Four Surrenders	277
The Call of Moses	290
Naaman the Syrian	297
The Prophet Nehemiah	311
Herod and John the Baptist	323
The Man Born Blind and Joseph of Arimathea	336
The Penitent Thief	350

ABRAHAM'S FOUR SURRENDERS

A great many people are afraid of the will of God, and yet I believe that one of the sweetest lessons that we can learn in the school of Christ is the surrender of our wills to God, letting Him plan for us and rule our lives. If I know my own mind, if an angel should come from the throne of God and tell me that I could have my will done the rest of my days on earth, and that everything I wished should be carried out, or that I might refer it back to God, and let God's will be done in me and through me, I think in an instant I would say:

"Let the will of God be done."

I cannot look into the future. I do not know what is going to happen to-morrow; in fact, I do not know what may happen before night; so I cannot choose for myself as well as God can choose for me, and it is much better to surrender my will to God's will. Abraham found this out, and I want to call your attention to four surrenders that he was called to make. I think that they give us a pretty good key to his life.

I

In the first place, Abraham was called to give up his kindred and his native country, and to go out, not knowing whither he went.

While men were busy building up Babylon, God called this man out of that nation of the Chaldeans. He lived down near the mouth of the Euphrates, perhaps three hundred miles south of Babylon, when he was called to go into a land that he perhaps had never heard of before, and to possess that land.

In the twelfth chapter of Genesis, the first four verses, we read:

"Now the Lord had said unto Abram, Get thee out of thy country, and from thy kindred, and from thy father's house, unto a land that I will shew thee." Now notice the promise: "And I will make of thee a great nation, and I will bless thee, and make thy name great; and thou shalt be a blessing: and I will bless them that bless thee, and curse him that curseth thee: and in thee shall all families of the earth be blessed. So Abram departed, as the Lord had spoken unto him; and Lot went with him: and Abram was seventy five years old and when he departed out of Haran."

It was several years before this that God first told him to leave Ur of the Chaldees. Then he came to Haran, which is about half-way between the valley of the Euphrates and the valley of the Jordan. God had called him into the land of the Canaanite, and HE CAME HALF-WAY, and stayed there—we do not know just how long, but probably about five years.

Now, I believe that there are a great many Christians who are what might be called Haran Christians. They go to Haran, and there they stay. They only half obey. They are not out-and-out. How was it that God got him out of Haran? His father died. The first call was to leave Ur of the Chaldees and go into Canaan, but instead of going all the way they stopped half-way, and it was affliction that drove Abram out of Haran. A great many of us bring afflictions on ourselves, because we are not out-and-out for the Lord. We do not obey Him fully. God had plans He wanted to work out through Abram, and He could not work them out as long as he was there at Haran. Affliction came, and then we find that he left Haran, and started for the Promised Land.

There is just one word there about Lot—"and Lot went with Abram." That is the key, you might say, to Lot's life. He was a weaker character than Abram, and he followed his uncle.

When they got into the land that God had promised to give him, Abram found it already inhabited by great and warlike nations—not by one nation, but by a number of nations. What could he do, a solitary man, in that land? Not only was his faith tested by finding the land preoccupied by other strong and hostile nations, but he had not been there a great while before a great famine came upon him. No doubt a great conflict was going on in his breast, and he said to himself:

"What does this mean? Here I am, thirteen hundred miles away from my own land, and surrounded by a warlike people. And not only that, but a famine has come, and I must get out of this country."

Now, I don't believe that God sent Abram down to Egypt. I think that He was only testing him, that he might in his darkness and in his trouble be DRAWN NEARER TO GOD.

I believe that many a time trouble and sorrow are permitted to come to us that we may see the face of God, and be shut up to trust in Him alone. But Abram went down into Egypt, and there he got into trouble by denying his wife. That is the blackest spot on Abram's character. But when we get into Egypt we will always be getting into trouble.

II

Abram became rich; but we don't hear of any altar—in fact, we hear of no altar at Haran, and we hear of no altar in Egypt. When he came up with Lot out of Egypt, they had great possessions, and they increased in wealth, and their herds had multiplied, until there was a strife among their herdsmen.

Now it is that Abram's character shines out again. He might have said that he had a right to the best of everything, because he was the older, and because Lot would probably not have been worth anything if it had not been for Abram's help. But instead of standing up for his rights, to choose the best of the land, he surrenders them, and says to the nephew:

"Take your choice. If you go to the right hand, I will take the left; or if you prefer the left hand, then I will go to the right."

Here is where Lot made his mistake. If there was a man under the sun that needed Abram's counsel, and Abram's prayers, and Abram's influence, and to have been surrounded by the friends of Abram, it was Lot. He was just one of those weak characters that NEEDED BOLSTERING UP.

But his covetous eye looked upon the well-watered plains of the valley of the Jordan that reached out towards Sodom, and he chose them. He was influenced by what he saw, He walked by sight, instead of by faith. I think that is where a great many Christian people make their mistake—walking by sight, instead of by faith. If he had stopped to think, Lot might have known that it would be disastrous to him and his family to go anywhere near Sodom. Abram and Lot must both have known about the wickedness of those cities on the plains, and although they were rich, and there was chance of making money, it was better for Lot to keep his family out of that wicked city. But his eyes fell upon the well watered plains, and he pitched his tent towards Sodom, and separated from Abram.

Now, notice that after Abram had let Lot have his choice, and Lot had gone off to the plains, for the first time God had Abram alone. His father had died at Haran, and he had left his brother there. Now, after his nephew had left him, he moved down to Hebron, and there built an altar. "Hebron" means communion. Here it is that God came to him and said:

"Abram, look around as far as your eye can reach—it is all yours. Look from the place where thou art northward, and southward, and eastward, and westward: for all the land which thou seest, to thee will I give it, and to thy seed for ever. And I will make thy seed as the dust of the earth: so that if a man can number the dust of the earth, then shall thy seed also be numbered. Arise, walk through the land in the length of it and in the breadth of it; for I will give it unto thee."

"Then Abram removed his tent, and came and dwelt in the plain of Mamre, which is in Hebron, and built there an altar unto the Lord."

It is astonishing how far you can see in that country. God took Moses up on Pisgah and showed him the Promised Land. In Palestine, a few years ago, I found that on Mount Olivet I could look over and see the Mediterranean. I could look into the valley of the Jordan, and see the Dead Sea. And on the plains of Sharon I could look up to Mount Lebanon, and up at Mount Hermon, away beyond Nazareth. You can see with the naked eye almost the length and breadth of that country. So when God said to Abram that he might look to the north, and that as far as he could see he could have the land; and then look to the south, with its well-watered plains that Lot coveted, and to the east and the west, from the sea to the Euphrates—then God gave His friend Abram a clear title, no conditions whatever, saying:

"I will give it all to you."

Lot chose all he could get, but it was not much. Abram let God choose for him, and was given all the land. Lot had no security for his choice, and soon lost all. Abram's right was maintained undisputed by God the giver.

Do you know that the children of Israel never had faith enough to take possession of all that land as far as the Euphrates? If they had, probably Nebuchadnezzar would never have come and taken them captives. But that was God's offer; He said to Abram, "Unto your seed I will give it forever, clear to the valley of the Euphrates."

From that time on God enlarged Abram's tents. He enriched His promises, and gave him much more that He had promised down there in the valley of the Euphrates when He first called him out. It is very interesting to see how God kept ADDING TO THE PROMISE for the benefit of His friend Abram.

Let us go back a moment to Lot, and see what Lot gained by making that choice. I believe that you can find five thousand Lots to one Abram to-day. People are constantly walking by sight, lured by the temptations of men and of the world. Men are very anxious to get their sons into lucrative positions, although it way be disastrous to their character; it may ruin them morally and religiously, and in every other way. The glitter of this world seems to attract them. Some one has said that Abram was a far-sighted man, and Lot was a short-sighted man; his eye fell on the land right around him. There is the one thing that we are quite sure of—he was so short-sighted that his possessions soon left him. And you will find that these people who are constantly building for time are disappointed.

I have no doubt that the men of Sodom said that Lot was A MUCH SHREWDER MAN than his uncle Abram, and that if he lived twenty-five years he would be the richer of the two, and that by coming into Sodom he could sell his cattle and sheep and goats and whatever else he had for large sums, and could get a good deal better market than Abram could back there on the plains of Mamre.

For awhile Lot did make money very fast, and became a very successful man. If you had gone into Sodom a little while before destruction came, you would have found that Lot owned some of the best corner lots in town, and that Mrs. Lot moved in what they called the bon-ton society or upper ten; and you would have found that she was at the theatre two or three nights in the week. If they had progressive euchre, she could play as well as anybody; and her daughters could dance as well as any other Sodomites. We find Lot sitting in the gates, he was getting on amazingly well. He might have been one of the principal men in the city; Judge Lot, or the Honorable Lot of Sodom. If there had been a Congress in those days, they would have run him for a seat in Congress. They might have elected him MAYOR OF SODOM.

He was getting on amazingly well; wonderfully prosperous.

But by and by there comes a war. If you go into Sodom, you must take Sodom's judgment when it comes, for it is bound to come. The battle turned against those five cities of the plain and they took Lot and his wife and all that they had, and one man escaped and ran off to Hebron and told Abram what had taken place. Abram took his servants,—three hundred and eighteen of them,—went after these victorious kings, and soon returned with all the booty and all the prisoners.

III

On Abram's way back with the spoils one of the strangest scenes of history occurs. Whom should he meet but Melchizedek, who brought out bread and wine; and the priestly king blessed the Father of the Faithful. After the old king of peace had blest him, he met the King of Sodom, and the King of Sodom said, "You take the money, and I will take the people"; but Abram replied:

"Not a thing will I take, not even the shoe-latchets, lest thou shouldst say, I have made Abram rich."

There is another surrender. There was a temptation to get rich at the hands of the King of Sodom. But the King of Salem had blessed him, and this world did not tempt him. It tempted Lot, and no doubt Lot thought Abram made a great mistake when he refused to take this wealth; but Abram would not touch a thing; he spurned it and turned from it. He had the world under his feet; he was living for another world. He would not be enriched from such a source.

Every one of us is met by the prince of this world and the Prince of Peace. The one tempts us with wealth, pleasure, ambition: but our Prince and Priest is ready to succor and strengthen us in the hour of temptation.

A friend of mine told me some years ago that his wife was very fond of painting, but that for a long time he never could see any beauty in her paintings; they all looked like a daub to him. One day his eyes troubled him and he went to see an oculist. The man looked in amazement at him and said:

"You have what we call a short eye and a long eye, and that makes everything a blur."

He gave him some glasses that just fitted him, and then he could see clearly. Then, he said, he understood why it was that his wife was so carried away with art, and he built an art gallery, and filled it full of beautiful things; because everything looked so beautiful after he had had his eyes straightened out.

Now there are lots of people that have A LONG EYE AND A SHORT EYE, and they make miserable work of their Christian life. They keep one eye on the eternal city and the other eye on the well-watered plains of Sodom. That was the way it was with Lot: he had a short eye and a long eye. It would be pretty hard work to believe that Lot was saved if it were not for the New Testament. But there we read that "Lot's righteous soul was vexed,"—so he had a righteous soul, but he had a stormy time. He didn't have peace and joy and victory like Abram.

After Abram had given up the wealth of Sodom that was offered him, then God came and enlarged his borders again—enlarged the promise. God said:

"I will be your exceeding great reward; I will protect you."

Abram might have thought that these kings that he had defeated might get other kings and other armies to come, and he might have thought of himself as a solitary man, with only three hundred and eighteen men, so that he might have feared lest he be swept from the face of the earth. But the Lord came and said:

"Abram, fear not."

That is the first time those oft-repeated words, "fear not," occur in the Bible.

"Fear not, for I will be your shield and your reward."

I would rather have that promise than all the armies of earth and all the navies of the world to protect me—to have the God of heaven for my Protector! God was teaching Abram that He was to be his Friend and his Shield, if he would surrender himself wholly to His keeping, and trust in His goodness. That is what we want—to surrender ourselves up to God, fully and wholly.

In Colorado the superintendent of some works told me of a miner that was promoted, who came to the superintendent, and said:

"There is a man that has seven children, and I have only three, and he is having a hard struggle. Don't promote me, but promote him."

I know of nothing that speaks louder for Christ and Christianity than to see a man or woman giving up what they call their rights for others, and "in honor preferring one another."

We find that Abram was constantly surrendering his own selfish interests and trusting to God. What was the result? Of all the men that ever lived he is the most renowned. He never did anything the world would call great. The largest army he ever mustered was three hundred and eighteen men. How Alexander would have sneered at such an army as that! How Cæsar would have looked down on such an army! How Napoleon would have curled his lip as he thought of Abram with an army of three hundred and eighteen! We are not told that he was a great astronomer; we are not told that he was a great scientist; we are not told that he was a great statesman, or anything the world calls great; but there was one thing he could do—he could live an unselfish life, and in honor could waive his rights, and in that way he became the friend of God; in that way he has become immortal. There is NO NAME IN HISTORY so well known as the name of Abram. Even Christ is not more widely known, for the Mohammedans, the Persians, and the Egyptians make a great deal of Abram. His name has been for centuries and centuries favorably known in Damascus. God promised him that great men, and warriors, and kings, and emperors, should spring from his loins. Was there ever a nation that has turned out such men? Think of Moses, and Joseph, and Joshua, and Caleb, and Samuel, and David, and Solomon, and Elisha. Think of Elijah, and Daniel, and Isaiah, and all the other wonderful Bible characters that have sprung from this man! Then think of Peter, of James, and John, and Paul, and John the Baptist, a mighty army. No man can number the multitude of wonderful men that have sprung from this one man called out of the land of the Chaldeans, unknown and an idolater, probably, when God called him; and yet how literally God has fulfilled His promise that through him He would bless all the nations of the earth. All because he surrendered himself fully and wholly to let God bless him.

IV

The last surrender is perhaps the most touching and the hardest of all to understand. Perhaps he could not have borne it until the evening of life. God had been taking him along, step by step, until now he had reached a place where he had learned to obey fully whatever God told him to do. I believe the world has yet to see what God will do with the man who is perfectly surrendered. Next to God's own Son, Abraham was perhaps the man who came nearest to this standard.

FOR TWENTY-FIVE YEARS Abraham had been in the Promised Land without the promised heir. God had promised that He would bless all the nations of the earth through him, and yet He did not give him a son. Abraham's faith almost staggered a number of times. Ishmael was born, but God set aside the son of the bondwoman, for he was not to be the ancestor of the Son of God. God was setting Abram apart simply that He might prepare the way for His own Son, and now, at last, a messenger comes down from heaven to Hebron, and tells Abraham in his old age that he should have a son.

It seemed too good to be true. He had hard work to believe it; but at the appointed time Isaac was born into that family. I don't believe there was ever a child born into the world that caused so much joy in the home as in Abraham's heart and home. How Abraham and that old mother, Sarah, must have doted on that child! How their eyes feasted on him!

But just when the lad was growing up into manhood Abraham received another very strange command, and there was another surrender—his only son. Perhaps he was making an idol of that boy, and thought more of him than he did of the God that gave him. There must be no idol in the heart if we are going to do the will of God on earth.

I can imagine that one night the old patriarch retired worn out and weary. The boy had gone fast to sleep, when suddenly a heavenly messenger came and told him that he must take that boy off on to a mountain that God was to show him, and offer him up as a sacrifice. No more sleep that night! If you had looked into that tent the next morning I can imagine that you would have seen the servants flying round and making preparations for the master's taking a long journey. He perhaps keeps the secret locked up in his heart, and he doesn't tell even Sarah or Isaac. He doesn't tell the servants, even the faithful servant Eliezer, what is to take place. About nine o'clock you might have seen those four men—Abraham, Isaac and the two young men with them—start off on the long journey. Once in a while Abraham turns his head aside and wipes away the tear. He doesn't want Isaac to see what a terrible struggle is going on within. It is a hard battle to give up his will and to surrender that boy, the idol of his life. Oh, how he loved him!

I can imagine the first night. The boy soon falls asleep, tired and weary with the hot day's journey, but the old man doesn't sleep. I can see him look into the face of the innocent boy, and say:

"Soon my boy will be gone, and I will be returning without him."

Perhaps most of the night his voice could have been heard in prayer, as he cries to God to help him; and as God had helped him in the past so God was helping him that night.

The next day they journeyed on, and again a terrible conflict goes on. Again he brushes away the tear. Perhaps Isaac sees it, and says:

"Father is going away to meet his God, and the angels may come down and talk with him as at Hebron. That is what he is so agitated about."

The second night comes, and the old man looks into that face every hour of the night. He sleeps a little, but not much, and the next morning at family worship he breaks down. He cannot finish his prayer.

They journey on that day—it is a long day—and the old patriarch say: "This is the last day I am to have my boy with me. To-morrow I must offer him up; to-morrow I shall be without the son of my bosom."

The third night comes, and what a night it must have been! I can imagine he didn't eat or sleep that night. Nothing is going to break his fast, and every hour of the night he goes to look into the face of that boy, and once in a while he bends over and kisses him, and he says:

"O Isaac, how can I give thee up?"

Morning breaks. What a morning it must have been for that father! He doesn't eat; he tries to pray, but his voice falters. After breakfast they start on their journey again. He has not gone a great way before he lifts up his eyes, and yonder is Mount Moriah. His heart begins to beat quickly. He says to the two young men:

"You stay here, and I will go yonder with my son."

Then, as father and son went up Mount Moriah, with the wood, and the fire, and the knife, the boy turns suddenly to the father, and says:

"Father, where is the lamb? We haven't any offering, father."

It was a common thing for Isaac to see his father offer up a victim, but there is no lamb now.

Did you ever think HOW PROPHETIC THAT ANSWER WAS when Abraham turned and said to the son, "God will provide Himself a sacrifice?" I don't know that Abraham understood the full meaning of it, but a few hundred years after God did provide a sacrifice right there. Mount Moriah and Mount Calvary are close together, and God's Son was provided as a sacrifice for the world.

On Mount Moriah this father and son begin to roll up the stones, and together they build the altar; then they lay on the wood and everything is ready for the victim. Isaac looks around to see where the lamb is and then the father can keep it from the son no longer, and he says:

"My boy, sit down here close to the altar, and let me tell you something."

Then perhaps that old, white-haired patriarch puts his arm around the lad, and tells how God came to him in the land of the Chaldeans, and the story of his whole life, and how, by one promise after another, God had kept enlarging the promised blessings, and that He would bless all the nations of the earth through him. Isaac was to be the heir. But he says:

"My son, the last night I was at home God came to me in the hours of the night and told me to bring you here and offer you up as a sacrifice. I don't understand what it means, but I can tell you one thing: it is much harder for me to offer you up than it would be for me to be sacrificed myself."

There was a time when I used to think more of the love of Jesus Christ than of God the Father. I used to think of God as a stern judge on the throne, from whose wrath Jesus Christ had saved me. It seems to me now I could not have A FALSER IDEA OF GOD than that. Since I have become a father I have made this discovery: that it takes more love and self-sacrifice for the father to give up the son than it does for the son to die. Is a father on earth a true father that would not rather suffer than to see his child suffer? Do you think that it did not cost God something to redeem this world? It cost God the most precious possession He ever had. When God gave His Son, He gave all, and yet He gave Him freely for you and me.

I can imagine that Abraham talks to Isaac and tells him how hard it is to offer him up. "But God has commanded it," he says, "and I surrender my will to God's will. I don't understand it, but I believe that God will be able to raise you up, and maybe He will."

They fell on their faces, and prayed together. After prayer I can see that old father take his boy to his bosom, and embrace him for the last time. He kisses and kisses him. Then he takes those hands that are so innocent, and binds them, and he binds the feet, and he ties him up, and lays him on the altar, and gives him a last kiss. Then he takes the knife, and raises his hand. No sooner is the hand lifted than a voice calls from heaven:

"Abraham, Abraham, spare thy son!"

You remember that Christ said, "Abraham saw my day, and was glad." I have an idea that God then and there just LIFTED THE CURTAIN OF TIME for Abraham. He looked down into the future, saw God's Son coming up Calvary, bearing his sins and the sins of all posterity. God gave him that secret, and told him how His Son was to come into the world and take away his sins.

Now, my friends, notice: whenever God has been calling me to higher service, there has always been a conflict with my will. I have fought against it, but God's will has been done instead of mine. When I came to Jesus Christ, I had a terrible battle to surrender my will, and to take God's will. When I gave up business, I had another battle for three months; I fought against it. It was a terrible battle. But oh! how many times I have thanked God that I gave up my will and took God's will. Then there was another time when God was calling me into higher service, to go out and preach the gospel all over the land, instead of staying in Chicago. I fought against it for months; but the best thing I ever did was when I surrendered my will, and let the will of God be done in me. Because Abraham obeyed God and held back not even his only child, God enlarged his promises once again:

"And the angel of the Lord called unto Abraham out of heaven the second time, and said, By myself have I sworn, saith the Lord, for because thou hast done this thing, and hast not withheld thy son, thine only son: that in blessing I will bless thee, and in multiplying I will multiply thy seed as the stars of the heaven, and as the sand which is upon the sea shore; and thy seed shall possess the gate of his enemies; and in thy seed shall all the nations of the earth be blessed; because thou hast obeyed my voice."

If you take my advice, you will have no will other than God's will. Make a full and complete surrender, and the sweet messages of heaven will come to you. God will whisper into your soul THE SECRETS OF HEAVEN.

After Abraham did what God told him, then it was that God told His friend all about His Son. If we make a full surrender, God will give us something better than we have ever known before. We will get a new vision of Jesus Christ, and will thank God not only in this life but in the life to come. May God help each and every one of us to make a full and complete and unconditional surrender to God, fully and wholly, now and forever.

THE CALL OF MOSES

There is a great deal more room given in Scripture to the call of men to God's work than there is to their end. For instance, we don't know where Isaiah died, or how he died, but we know a great deal about the call God gave him, when he saw God on high and lifted up on His throne. I suppose that it is true to-day that hundreds of young men and women who are listening for a call and really want to know what their life's mission is, perhaps find it the greatest problem they ever had. Some don't know just what profession or work to take up, and so I should like to take the call of Moses, and see if we cannot draw some lessons from it.

You remember when God met Moses at the burning bush and called him to do as great a work as any man has ever been called to in this world, that HE THOUGHT THE LORD HAD MADE A MISTAKE, that he was not the man. He said, "Who am I?" He was very small in his own estimation. Forty years before he had started out as a good many others have started. He thought he was pretty well equipped for service. He had been in the schools of the Egyptians, he had been in the palaces of Egypt, he had moved in the bon ton society. He had had all the advantages any man could have when he started out, undoubtedly, without calling on the God of Abraham for wisdom and guidance, yet he broke down.

How many men have started out in some profession and made a failure of it! They haven't heard the voice of God, they haven't waited upon God for instruction.

I suppose Moses thought that the children of Israel would be greatly honored to know that a prince of the realm was going to take up their cause, but you remember how he lost his temper and killed the Egyptian, and next day, when he interfered in a quarrel between two Hebrews, they wanted to know who had made him judge and ruler over them, and he had to flee into the desert, and was there for forty years hidden away. He killed the Egyptian and lost his influence thereby. Murder for liberty; wrong for right; it was a poor way to reform abuses, and Moses needed training.

It was a long time for God to keep him in His school, a long time for a man to wait in the prime of his life, from forty to eighty. Moses had been brought us with all the luxuries that Egypt could give him, and now he was a shepherd, and in the sight of the Egyptians a shepherd was an abomination. I have an idea that Moses started out with a great deal bigger head than heart. I believe that is the reason so many fail; they have BIG HEADS AND LITTLE HEARTS.

If a man has a shriveled-up heart and a big head he is a monster. Perhaps Moses looked down on the Hebrews. There are many people who start out with the idea that they are great and other people are small, and they are going to bring them up on the high level with themselves. God never yet used a man of that stamp. Perhaps Moses was a slow scholar in God's school, and so He had to keep him there for forty years.

But now he is ready; he is just the man God wants, and God calls him. Moses said, "Who am I?" He was very small in his own eyes—just small enough so that God could use him. If you had asked the Egyptians who he was, they would have said he was THE BIGGEST FOOL IN THE WORLD.

"Why," they would say, "look at the opportunity that man had! He might have been commander of the Egyptian army, he might have been on the throne, swaying the scepter over the whole world, if he hadn't identified himself with those poor, miserable Hebrews! Think what an opportunity he has lost, and what a privilege he has thrown away!"

He had dropped out of the public mind for forty years, and they didn't know what had become of him, but God had His eye upon him. He was the very man of all others that God wanted, and when he met God with that question, "Who am I?" it didn't matter who he was but who his God was. When men learn the lesson that they are nothing and God is everything, then there is not a position in which God cannot use them. It was not Moses who accomplished that great work of redemption, for he was only the instrument in God's hand. God could have spoken to Pharaoh without Moses. He could have spoken in a voice of thunder, and broken the heart of Pharaoh with one speech, if He had wanted to, but He condescended to take up a human agent, and to use him. He could have sent Gabriel down, but he knew that Moses was the man wanted above all others, so He called him. God uses men to speak to men: He works through mediators. He could have accomplished the exodus of the children of Israel in a flash, but instead He chose to send a lonely and despised shepherd to work out His purpose through pain and disappointment. That was God's way in the Old Testament, and also in the New. He sent His own Son in the likeness of sinful flesh to be the mediator between God and man.

Moses went on making excuses and said, "When I go down there, who shall I say has sent me?" I suppose he remembered how he went before he was sent that other time, and he was afraid of a failure again. A man who has made a failure once is always afraid he will make another. He loses confidence in himself. It is a good thing to lose confidence in ourselves so as to gain confidence in God.

The Lord said, "Say unto them, 'I AM hath sent me.'"

Some one has said that God gave him A BLANK CHECK, and all he had to do was to fill it out from that time on. When he wanted to bring water out of the rock, all he had to do was to fill out the check; when he wanted bread, all he had to do was to fill out the check and the bread came; he had a rich banker. God had taken him into partnership with Himself. God had made him His heir, and all he had to do was to look up to Him, and he got all he wanted.

And yet he seemed to draw back, and began to make another excuse, and said:

"They will not believe me."

He was afraid of the Israelites as well as of Pharaoh: he knew how hard it is to get even your friends to believe in you.

Now, if God has sent you and me with a message it is not for us to say whether others will believe it or not. We cannot make men believe. If I have been sent by God to make men believe, He will give me power to make them believe. Jesus Christ didn't have that power; it is the work of the Holy Ghost; we cannot persuade men and overcome skepticism and infidelity unless we are baptized with the Holy Ghost and with power.

God told Moses that they would believe him, that he would succeed, and bring the children of Israel out of bondage. But Moses seemed to distrust even the God who had spoken to him.

Then the Lord said, "What is that in thy hand?"

He had a rod or staff, a sort of shepherd's crook, which he had cut haphazard when he had wanted something that would serve him in the desert.

"It is only a rod."

"With that you shall deliver the children of Israel; with that rod you shall make Israel believe that I am with you."

When God Almighty linked Himself to that rod, it was worth more than all the armies the world had ever seen. Look and see how that rod did its work. It brought up the plagues of flies, and the thunder storm, and turned the water into blood. It was not Moses, however, nor Moses' rod that did the work, but it was the God of the rod, the God of Moses. As long as God was with him, he could not fail.

Sometimes it looks as if God's servants fail. When Herod beheaded John the Baptist, it looked as if John's mission was a failure. But was it? The voice that rang through the valley of the Jordan rings through the whole world to-day. You can hear its echo upon the mountains and the valleys yet, "I must decrease, but He must increase." He held up Jesus Christ and introduced Him to the world, and Herod had not power to behead him until his life work had been accomplished. Stephen never preached but one sermon that we know of, and that was before the Sanhedrim; but how that sermon has been preached again and again all over the world! Out of his death probably came Paul, the greatest preacher the world has seen since Christ left this earth. If a man is sent by Jehovah, there is no such thing as failure. Was Christ's life a failure? See how His parables are going through the earth to-day. It looked as if the apostles had made a failure, but see how much has been accomplished. If you read the book of Acts, you will see that every seeming failure in Acts was turned into a great victory. Moses wasn't going to fail, although Pharaoh said with contempt, "Who is God that I should obey Him?" He found out who God was. He found out that there was a God.

But Moses made another excuse, and said, "I am slow of speech, slow of tongue." He said he was NOT AN ORATOR.

My friends, we have too many orators. I am tired and sick of your "silver-tongued orators." I used to mourn because I couldn't be an orator. I thought, Oh, if I could only have the gift of speech like some men! I have heard men with a smooth flow of language take the audience captive, but they came and they went, their voice was like the air, there wasn't any power back of it; they trusted in their eloquence and their fine speeches. That is what Paul was thinking of when he wrote to the Corinthians:—"My speech and my preaching was not with enticing words of man's wisdom, but in demonstration of the Spirit and of power: that your faith should not stand in the wisdom of men, but in the power of God."

Take a witness in court and let him try his oratorical powers in the witness-box, and see now quickly the judge will rule him out. It is the man who tells the plain, simple truth that has the most influence with the jury.

Suppose that Moses had prepared a speech for Pharaoh, and had got his hair all smoothly brushed, and had stood before the looking-glass or had gone to an elocutionist to be taught how to make an oratorical speech and how to make gestures. Suppose that he had buttoned his coat, put one hand in his chest, had struck an attitude and begun:

"The God of our fathers, the God of Abraham, Isaac, and Jacob, has commanded me to come into the presence of the noble King of Egypt."

I think they would have taken his head right off! They had Egyptians who could be as eloquent as Moses. It was not eloquence they wanted. When you see a man in the pulpit trying to show off his eloquence he is making a fool of himself and trying to make a fool of the people. Moses was slow of speech, but he had a message, and what God wanted was to have him deliver the message. But he insisted upon having an excuse. He didn't want to go; instead of being eager to act as heaven's messenger, to be God's errand boy, he wanted to excuse himself. The Lord humored him and gave him an interpreter, gave him Aaron.

Now, if there is a stupid thing in the world, it is to talk through an interpreter. I tried it once in Paris. I got up into a little box of a pulpit with the interpreter—there was hardly room enough for one. I said a sentence while he leaned away over to one side, and then I leaned over while he repeated it in French. Can you conceive of a more stupid thing than Moses going before Pharaoh and speaking through Aaron!

But this slow-of-speech man became eloquent. Talk about Gladstone's power to speak! Here is a man one hundred and twenty years old, and he waxed eloquent, as we see in Deuteronomy xxxii:1-4:

Give ear, O ye heavens, and I will speak;

And hear, O earth, the words of my mouth.

My doctrine shall drop as the rain,

My speech shall distil as the dew,

As the small rain upon the tender herb,

And as the showers upon the grass:

Because I will publish the name of the Lord:

Ascribe ye greatness unto our God.

He is the Rock, His work is perfect:

For all His ways are judgment:

A God of truth and without iniquity,

Just and right is He.

He turned out to be one of the most eloquent men the world has ever seen. If God sends men and they deliver His message He will be with their mouth. If God has given you a message, go and give it to the people as God has given it to you. It is a stupid thing for a man to try to be eloquent. Make YOUR MESSAGE, AND NOT YOURSELF, the most prominent thing. Don't be self-conscious Set your heart on what God has given you to do, and don't be so foolish as to let your own difficulties or your own abilities stand in the way. It is said that people would go to hear Cicero and would come away and say, "Did you ever hear anything like it? wasn't it sublime? wasn't it grand?" But they would go and hear Demosthenes, and he would fire them so with the subject that they would want to go and fight at once. They forgot all about Demosthenes, but were stirred by his message; that was the difference between the two men.

Next Moses said: "O my Lord, send, I pray thee, by the hand of him whom thou wilt send."

Did you ever stop to think what Moses would have lost if God had taken him at his word, and said:

"Very well, Moses; you may stay here in the desert, and I will send Aaron, or Joshua, or Caleb!"

Don't seek to be excused if God calls you to some service. What would the twelve disciples have lost if they had declined the call of Jesus! I have always pitied those other disciples of whom we read that they went back, and walked no more with Jesus. Think what Orpah missed and what Ruth gained by cleaving to Naomi's God!

Her story has been TOLD THESE THREE THOUSAND YEARS.

Father, mother, sisters, brothers, the grave of her husband—she turned her back on them all. Ruth, come back, and tell us if you regret your choice! No: her name shines one of the brightest among all the women that have ever lived. The Messiah was one of her descendants.

Moses, you come back and tell us if you were afterwards sorry that God had called you? I think that when he stood in glorified body on the Mount of Transfiguration with Jesus and Elijah, he did not regret it.

My dear friends, God is not confined to any one messenger. We are told that He can raise up children out of stones. Some one has said that there are three classes of people, the "wills," the "won'ts," and the "can'ts"; the first accomplish everything, the second oppose everything, and the third fail in everything. If God calls you, consider it a great honor. Consider it a great privilege to have partnership with Him in anything. Do it cheerfully, gladly. Do it with all your heart, and He will bless you. Don't let false modesty or insincerity, self-interest, or any personal consideration turn you aside from the path of duty and sacrifice. If we listen for God's voice, we shall hear the call; and if He calls and sends us, there will be no such thing as failure, but success all along the line. Moses had glorious success because he went forward and did what God called him to do.

NAAMAN THE SYRIAN

I wish to call your attention to one who was a great man in his own country, and very honorable; one whom the king delighted to honor. He stood high in position; he was captain of the host of the King of Syria; but he was a leper, and that threw a blight over his whole life. As Bishop Hall quaintly puts it, "The meanest slave in Syria would not have changed skins with him."

Now you cannot have a better type of a sinner than Naaman was. I don't care who or what he is, or what position he holds—all men alike have sinned, and all have to bear the same burden of death. "All have sinned, and come short of the glory of God." All men must stand in judgment before God. What a gloom that throws over our whole life!

"But he was a leper." There was NO PHYSICIAN who could help him in Syria. None of the eminent doctors in Damascus could do him any good. If he was to get rid of the leprosy, the power must come from on high. It must be some one unknown to Naaman, for he did not know God.

But I will tell you what they had in Syria—they had one of God's children there, and she was a little girl, a simple captive maid, who waited on Mrs. Naaman. Naaman knew nothing about this little Israelite, though she was one of his household.

I can imagine that one day, as she was waiting on the general's wife, she noticed her weeping. Her heart was breaking because of the dark cloud that rested over her home. So she told her mistress that there was a prophet in her country that could cure her master of his leprosy. "Would to God," she said, "my lord were with the prophet in Samaria! for he would recover him of his leprosy."

There's faith for you!

She boasted of God that He would do more for this heathen than He had done for any in Israel; and GOD HONORED HER FAITH.

"What do you say? A prophet in Israel that can cure leprosy?"

"Yes."

"Why, did you ever know any one that was cured?"

"No."

"Well, then, what makes you think there is a prophet that can cure leprosy?"

"Oh, that isn't anything to what Elisha can do. There was a little child that lived near us that died, and he raised him to life. He has done many wonderful things."

She must have had a reputation for truthfulness. If she hadn't, her testimony would not have been taken.

Some one told the general of it, and he made it known to the king. Now, Naaman stood high in the king's favor, for he had recently won a great victory. He stood near the throne. So the king said:

"You had better go down to Samaria, and see if there is anything in it. I will give you letters of introduction to the King of Israel."

Yes, he would give Naaman letters of introduction to the king. That's just man's idea. The notion was, that if anybody could help him it was the king, and that the king had power both with God and man. Oh, my friends, it is a good deal better to know a man that knows God! A man acquainted with God has more power than any earthly potentate. Gold can't do everything.

Away goes Naaman down to Samaria with his kingly introduction. What a stir it must have made when the commander of the Syrian army drove up! He has brought with him a lot of gold and silver. That is man's idea again; he is going to pay for a great doctor, and he took about five hundred thousand dollars to pay for the doctor's bill. There are a good many men who would willingly pay that sum if with it they could buy the favor of God, and get rid of the curse of sin. Yes, if money could do it, HOW MANY WOULD BUY SALVATION!

But, thank God, it is not in the market for sale. You must buy it at God's price, and that is "without money and without price." Naaman found that out.

My dear friends, did you ever ask yourselves which is the worse— the leprosy of sin, or the leprosy of the body? For my own part, I would a thousand times sooner have the leprosy of the body eating into my eyes, and feet, and arms! I would rather be loathsome in the sight of my fellow-men than die with the leprosy of sin in my soul, and be banished from God forever! The leprosy of the body is bad, but the leprosy of sin is a thousand times worse. It has cast angels out of heaven. It has ruined the best and strongest men that ever lived in the world. Oh, how it has pulled men down! The leprosy of the body could not do that.

There is one thing about Naaman that I like specially, and that is his earnestness of purpose. He was THOROUGHLY IN EARNEST.

He was quite willing to go one hundred and fifty miles, and to take the advice of this little maid. A good many people say:

"Oh, I don't like such and such a minister; I should like to know where he comes from, and what he has done, and whether any bishop has laid his hands on his head."

My dear friends, never mind the minister; it is the message you want. If some one were to send me a telegraph message, and the news were important, I shouldn't stop to ask about the messenger who brought it. I should want to read the news. I should look at the message, and not at the boy who brought it.

And so it is with God's message. The good news is everything, the minister nothing. The Syrians looked down with contempt on the Israelites, and yet this great man was willing to take the good news at the hands of this little maiden, and listened to the words that fell from her lips. If I got lost in New York, I should be willing to ask anybody which way to go, even if it were only a shoeblack; and, in point of fact, a boy's word in such a case is often better than a man's. It is the way I want, not the person who directs me.

But there was one drawback in Naaman's case. Though he was willing to take the advice of the little girl, he was not willing to take the remedy. The stumbling-block of pride stood in his way. The remedy the prophet offered him was a terrible blow to his pride. I have no doubt he expected a grand reception from the King of Israel, to whom he brought letters of introduction. He had been victorious on many a field of battle, and held high rank in the army; perhaps we may call him Major-General Naaman of Syria, or he might have been higher in rank even than that; and bearing with him kingly credentials, he expected no doubt a distinguished reception. But instead of the king rushing out to meet him, he, when he heard of Naaman's arrival and his object, simply rent his mantle, and said:

"Am I God, to kill and to make alive, that this man doth send unto me to recover a man of his leprosy? Wherefore consider, I pray you, and see how he seeketh a quarrel against me."

Elisha heard of the king's trouble, and sent him a message, saying:

"Wherefore hast thou rent thy clothes? Let him come now to me, and he shall know that there is a prophet in Israel."

I can imagine Naaman's pride reasoning thus: "Surely, the prophet will feel very much exalted and flattered that I, the great Syrian general, should come and call upon him."

And so, probably, full of those proud thoughts, he drives up to the prophet's humble dwelling with his chariot and his splendid retinue. Yes, Naaman drove up in grand style to the prophet's abode, and as nobody seemed to be coming out to greet him, he sent in his message:

"Tell the prophet that Major-General Naaman of Syria has arrived, and wishes to see him."

Elisha takes it very coolly. He does not come out to see him, but as soon as he learns his errand he sends his servant to tell him to dip seven times in the river Jordan, and he shall be clean.

That was a terrible blow to his pride. I can imagine him saying to his servant:

"What did you say? Did I understand you aright? Dip seven times in the Jordan! Why, we call the river Jordan a ditch in our country."

But the only answer he got was, "The prophet says, Go and dip seven times in the Jordan, and thy flesh shall become like the flesh of a little child."

I can fancy Naaman's indignation as he asks, "Are not Abana and Pharpar, rivers of Damascus, better than all the waters of Israel? May I not wash in them and be clean? Haven't I bathed myself hundreds of times, and has it helped me? Can water wash away leprosy?"

So he turned and went away in a rage.

It isn't a bad sign when a man gets mad if you tell him the truth. Some people are afraid of getting other people mad. I have known wives afraid to talk to their husbands, afraid of getting them mad. I have known mothers who were afraid to talk to their sons because they were AFRAID THEY WOULD GET MAD.

Don't be afraid of getting them mad, if it is the truth that makes them mad. If it is our foolishness that makes them mad, then we have got reason to mourn over it. If it is the truth, God sent it, and it is a good deal better to have a man get mad than it is to have him go to sleep. I think the trouble with a great many nowadays is that they are sound asleep, and it is a good deal better to rouse them even if they do wake up mad.

The fact was, the Jordan never had any great reputation as a river. It flowed into the Dead Sea, and that sea never had a harbor to it, and its banks were not half so beautiful as those of the rivers of Damascus. Damascus was one of the most beautiful cities in the world. It is said that when Mahomet beheld it he turned his head aside for fear it should divert his thoughts from heaven.

Naaman turned away in a rage. "Ah," he said, "here am I, a great conqueror, a successful general on the battlefield, holding the very highest rank in the army, and yet this prophet does not even come out to meet me; he simply sends a message. Why, I thought he would surely come out to me, and stand and call on the name of the Lord his God, and strike his hand over the place and recover the leper."

There it is. I hardly ever knew a man yet who, when talked to about his sins, didn't say:

"Yes, but I thought so and so."

"Mr. Moody," they say, "I will tell you what I think; I will tell you my opinion."

In the 55th chapter of Isaiah it says that God's thoughts are not our thoughts, nor His ways our ways. And so it was with Naaman. In the first place, he thought a good big doctor's fee would do it all, and settle everything up. And besides that there was another thing he thought; he thought going to the king with his letters of introduction would do it. Yes, those were Naaman's first thoughts. I thought. Exactly so. He turned away in rage and disappointment. He thought the prophet would have come out to him very humble and very subservient, and BID HIM DO SOME GREAT THINGS.

Instead of that, Elisha, who was perhaps busy writing, did not even come to the door or the window. He merely sent out the message:

"Tell him to dip seven times in the Jordan."

And away went Naaman, saying, I thought, I thought, I thought.

I have heard that tale so often that I am tired of it. Give it up, and take God's words, God's thoughts, God's ways. I never yet knew a man converted just in the time and manner he expected to be. I have heard people say, "Well, if ever I am converted, it won't be in a Methodist church; you won't catch me there." I never knew a man say that but, at last, if converted at all, it was in a Methodist church.

In Scotland a man was converted at one of our meetings—an employer. He was very anxious that all his employees should be reached, and he used to send them one by one to the meetings. But there was one man that wouldn't come. We are all more or less troubled with stubbornness; and the moment this man found that his employer wanted him to go to the meetings he made up his mind he wouldn't go. If he was going to be converted, he said, he was going to be converted by some ordained minister; he was not going to any meeting that was conducted by Americans that were not ordained. He believed in conversion, but he was going to be CONVERTED THE REGULAR WAY.

He believed in the regular Presbyterian Church of Scotland, and that was the place for him to be converted.

The employer tried every way he could to get him to attend the meetings, but he wouldn't come.

After we left that town and went away up to Inverness, the employer had some business up there, and he sent this employee to attend to it in the hope that he would attend some of our meetings.

One night as I was preaching on the banks of a river I happened to take this for my text: "I thought; I thought." I was trying to take men's thoughts up and to show the difference between their thoughts and God's thoughts. This man happened to be walking along the banks of the river. He saw a great crowd, and heard some one talking, and he wondered to himself what that man was talking about. He didn't know who was there, so he drew up to the crowd, and listened. He heard the sermon, and became convicted and converted right there. Then he inquired who was the preacher, and he found out it was the very man that he said he would not hear—the man he disliked. The very man he had been talking against was the very man God used to convert him.

Whilst Naaman was thus wavering in his mind, and thinking on what was best to be done, one of his servants drew near and made a very sensible remark:

"My lord, if the prophet had bid thee do some great thing, wouldest thou not have done it? How much rather then, when he saith to thee, Wash, and be clean?"

There is a great deal of truth in that.

If Elisha had told him to go back to Syria on his hands and knees, one hundred and fifty miles, he would have done it and thought it was all right. If he had told him to go into some cave and stay there a year or two, he would have done it and thought it was all right. If he had told him that it was necessary to have some surgical operation performed, and that he had to go through all the torture incident to it, that would have suited him. Men like to have something to do about their salvation; they don't like to give up the idea that they can't do anything; that God must do it all. If you tell them to take bitter herbs every morning and every night for the next five years, they think that's all right, and if he had told Naaman to do that he would have done it. But to tell him merely to dip in the river Jordan seven times, why, it seemed absurd on the face of it! But this servant suggested to him that he had better go down to the Jordan and try the remedy, as it was A VERY SIMPLE ONE.

Now, don't you see yourselves there? How many men there are who are waiting for some great thing; waiting for some sudden feeling to come stealing over them; waiting for some shock to come upon them. That is not what the Lord wants. There is a man that I have talked to about his soul for a number of years, and the last time I had a talk with him, he said:

"Well, the thing hasn't struck me yet."

I said: "What?"

"Well," says he, "the thing hasn't struck me yet."

"Struck you; what do you mean?"

"Well," said he, "I go to church, and I hear you preach, and I hear other men preach, but the thing hasn't struck me yet; it strikes some people, but it hasn't struck me yet."

That was all that I could get out of him. There are a good many men who reason in that way. They have heard some young converts tell how light dawned upon them like the flash of a meteor; how they experienced a new sensation; and so they are waiting for something of the kind. But you can't find any place in Scripture where you are told to wait for anything of the kind. You are just to obey what God tells you to do, and let your feelings take care of themselves. I can't control my feelings. I can't make myself feel good and bad when I want to, but I can obey God. God gives me the power. He doesn't command me to do something and not give me the power to do it. With the command comes the power.

Now, Naaman could do what the prophet told him; he could go down to the Jordan, and he could dip seven times; and that is what the Lord had for him to do; and if we are going to get into the kingdom of God, right at the threshold of that kingdom we have to learn this doctrine of obedience, to do whatsoever He tells us.

I can fancy Naaman still reluctant to believe in it, saying, "Why, if there is such cleansing power in the waters of Jordan, would not every leper in Israel go down and dip in them, and be healed?"

"Well, but you know," urges the servant, "now that you have come a hundred and fifty miles, don't you think you had better do what he tells you? After all, you can but try it. He sends word distinctly, my lord, that your flesh shall come again as that of a little child."

Naaman accepts this word in season. His anger is cooling down. He has got over the first flush of his indignation. He says:

"Well, I think I might as well try it."

That was THE STARTING-POINT OF HIS FAITH, although still he thought it a foolish thing, and could not bring himself to believe that the result would be what the prophet had said.

At last Naaman's will was conquered, and he surrendered. When General Grant was besieging a town which was a stronghold of the Southern Confederacy, some of the officers sent word that they would leave the city if he would let them go with their men. But General Grant sent word:

"No, nothing but an unconditional surrender!"

Then they sent word that they would go if he would let them take their flag with them. But the answer was: "No, an unconditional surrender."

At last the beleagured walls were broken down, and the city entered, and then the enemy made a complete and unconditional surrender. Well, it was so with Naaman; he got to that point when he was willing to obey, and the Scripture tell us, "To obey is better than to sacrifice."

God wants obedience. Naaman had to learn this lesson. There was no virtue, probably, in going down to the Jordan, any more than in obeying the voice of God. He had to obey the word, and IN THE VERY ACT OF OBEDIENCE he was blessed.

Look at those ten New Testament lepers who came to Christ. He said to them: "Go show yourselves to the priests."

"Well," they might have said, "what good is that going to do us? Here we are all full of leprosy, and if we go and show ourselves to the priests they will order us back again into exile. That is not going to help us."

But those ten men started off, and did just what the Lord Jesus Christ told them to do, and in the very act of doing it they were blessed; their leprosy left them.

He said to that man that had the palsy, whom they brought to Him upon a bed: "Take up thy bed and walk."

The man might have said: "Lord, I have been trying for years to take that bed up, but I can't. I haven't got the power. I have been shaking with the palsy for the last ten years. Do you think that if I could have rolled up that bed that I would have been brought here and let down through the roof? I haven't the power."

But when the Lord commanded him He gave the power. Power came with the command, and that man stood up, rolled up his bed, and started off home. He was blessed in the very act of obedience.

My friends, if you want God to bless you, obey Him. Do whatsoever He calls upon you to do, and then see if He will not bless you.

Christ went to a Pharisee's house one day while He was down here upon earth, to be entertained. They wanted to get Him to do something to break the law of Moses, that they might condemn Him to death, and so they put a man right opposite to Him at the table with a withered hand, to see if He would heal upon the Sabbath day. He said to the man:

"Stretch out thy hand."

Now, the man might have said, "Lord, that is a very strange command. I haven't got the power. That hand has been withered for the last twenty years. I haven't stretched it out for the last twenty years; and you say, 'Stretch it out.'"

But when He told him to do it He gave him the power, and out went that old withered hand, and before it came out straight, right in the very act, it was made whole. He was blessed in the very act of obedience.

Now, Naaman had to be taught the lesson that he had to obey; and so, finally, he went down to the Jordan just as he was told to do. And if you will do just what the Lord tells you the Lord will bless you as He did Naaman.

You may ask, "What does He tell me?"

"Believe on the Lord Jesus Christ and thou shalt be saved."

The word of God to Naaman was to go and wash; and the word of God to every soul out of Christ is to believe on His Son. "Verily, verily, I say unto you, he that heareth My word and believeth on Him that sent Me hath everlasting life, and shall not come into condemnation, but is passed from death unto life." If a man believes with all his heart on the Lord Jesus Christ, God will never bring him to judgment for sin; that is all passed—that is all gone. Take Him at His word; believe Him; believe what He says, and you shall enter into life eternal. "He came unto His own, and His own received Him not." Him—mark you—not a dogma, not a creed, NOT A MYTH, BUT A PERSON.

"He came to His own, and His own received Him not. But as many as received Him, to them gave He power to become the sons and daughters of God." That is the way you get the power.

Naaman goes down to the river and takes the first dip. As he comes up I can imagine him looking at himself, and saying to his servant:

"There! there I am, no better than I was when I went in! If one-seventh of the leprosy was gone, I should be content."

The servant says: "The man of God told you to dip seven times. Do just as he told you. There is no discount on God's word."

Well, down he goes a second time, and he comes up puffing and blowing, as much a leper as ever; and so he goes down again and again, the third, fourth, fifth, and sixth time, with the same result, as much a leper as ever. Some of the people standing on the banks of the river probably said, as they certainly would in our day:

"Why, that man has gone clean out of his mind!"

When he comes up the sixth time, he looks at himself, and says:

"Ah, no better! What a fool I have made of myself! How they will all laugh at me! I wouldn't have the generals and aristocracy of Damascus know that I have been dipping in this way in Jordan for all the world. However, as I have gone so far, I'll make the seventh plunge."

He has not altogether lost faith, and down he goes the seventh time, and comes up again. He looks at himself, and shouts aloud for joy.

"Lo, I am well! My leprosy is all gone, all gone! My flesh has come again as that of a little child."

If one speck of leprosy had remained, it would have been a reflection on God.

Ask him now how he feels.

"Feel? I feel that this is the happiest day of my life. I thought when I won a great victory upon the battlefield that that was the most joyful day of my life; I thought I should never be so happy again; but that wasn't anything; it didn't compare with this hour; my leprosy is all gone, I am whole, I am cleansed."

First he lost his temper; then he lost his pride; then his leprosy. That is generally the order in which proud, rebellious sinners are converted.

So he comes up out of Jordan and puts on his clothes, and goes back to the prophet. He was very mad with Elisha in the beginning, but when he was cleansed his anger was all gone too. He wants to pay him. That's just the old story; Naaman WANTS TO GIVE MONEY for his cure. How many people want to do the same nowadays. Why it would have spoiled the story of grace if the prophet had taken anything! You may give a thank-offering to God's cause, not to purchase salvation, but because you are saved. The Lord doesn't charge anything to save you. It is "without money and without price." The prophet Elisha refused to take anything, and I can imagine no one felt more rejoiced than he did.

Naaman starts back to Damascus a very different man than he was when he left it. The dark cloud has gone from his mind; he is no longer a leper, in fear of dying from a loathsome disease. He lost the leprosy in Jordan when he did what the man of God told him; and if you obey the voice of God, even while I am speaking to you, the burden of your sins will fall from off you, and you shall be cleansed. It is all done through faith and obedience.

Let us see what Naaman's faith led him to believe. "And he returned to the man of God, he and all his company, and came, and stood before him: and he said, Behold, now I know that there is no God in all the earth, but in Israel: now therefore, I pray thee, take a blessing of thy servant."

What I want particularly to call your attention to is the words I KNOW.

There is no hesitation about it, no qualifying the expression. Naaman doesn't now say, "I think"; no, he says, "I know there is a God who has power to cleanse the leprosy."

Then there is another thought. Naaman left only one thing in Samaria, and that was his leprosy; and the only thing God wishes you to leave with Him is your sin. And yet it is the only thing you seem not to care about giving up.

"Oh," you say, "I love leprosy, it is so delightful, I can't give it up; I know God wants it, that He may make me clean. But I can't give it up."

Why, what downright madness it is for you to love leprosy; and yet that is your condition.

"Ah," says someone, "I don't believe in sudden conversions."

Don't you? How long did it take Naaman to be cured? The seventh time he went down, away went the leprosy. Read the great conversions recorded in the Bible. Saul of Tarsus, Zacchæus, and a host of others; how long did it take the Lord to bring them about? They were effected in a minute. We are born in iniquity, shapen in it, dead in trespasses and sins; but when spiritual life comes it comes in a moment, and we are free both from sin and death.

You may be sure when he got home there was no small stir in Naaman's house. I can see his wife, Mrs. Naaman, when he gets back. She has been watching and looking out of the window for him with a great burden on her heart. And when she asks him, "Well, husband, how is it?" I can see the tears running down his cheeks as he says:

"Thank God, I am well."

They embrace each other, and pour out mutual expressions of rejoicing and gladness. The servants are just as glad as their master and mistress, as they have been waiting eagerly for the news. There never was a happier household than Naaman's, now that he has got rid of the leprosy. And so, my friends, it will be with your own households if you will only get rid of the leprosy of sin to-day. Not only will there be joy in your own hearts and at home, but there will also be JOY AMONG THE SAINTS IN HEAVEN.

Once, as I was walking down the street, I heard some people laughing and talking aloud. One of them said:

"Well, there will be no difference, it will be all the same a hundred years hence."

The thought flashed across my mind, "Will there be no difference? Where will you be a hundred years hence?"

Young man, just ask yourself the question, "Where shall I be?" Some of you who are getting on in years may be in eternity ten years hence. Where will you be, on the left or the right hand of God? I cannot tell your feelings, but I can my own. I ask you, "Where will you spend eternity? Where will you be a hundred years hence?"

I heard once of a man who went to England from the Continent, and brought letters with him to eminent physicians from the Emperor. The letters said:

"This man is a personal friend of mine, and we are afraid he is going to lose his reason. Do all you can for him."

The doctor asked him if he had lost any dear friend in his own country, or any position of importance, or what it was that was weighing on his mind.

The young man said, "No; but my father and grandfather and myself were brought up infidels, and for the last two or three years this thought has been haunting me, Where shall I spend eternity? And the thought of it follows me day and night."

The doctor said, "You have come to THE WRONG PHYSICIAN, but I will tell you of one who can cure you"; and he told him of Christ, and read to him the 53d chapter of Isaiah, "With His stripes we are healed."

The young man said, "Doctor, do you believe that?"

The doctor told him he did, and prayed and wrestled with him, and at last the clear light of Calvary shone on his soul. He had settled the question in his own mind at last, where he would spend eternity. I ask you, sinner, to settle it now. It is for you to decide. Shall it be with the saints, and martyrs, and prophets, or in the dark caverns of hell, amidst blackness and darkness forever? Make haste to be wise; for "how shall we escape if we neglect so great salvation?"

At our church in Chicago I was closing the meeting one day, when a young soldier got up and entreated the people to decide for Christ at once. He said he had just come from a dark scene. A comrade of his, who had enlisted with him, had a father who was always entreating him to become a Christian, and in reply he always said he would when the war was over. At last he was wounded, and was put into the hospital, but got worse and was gradually sinking. One day, a few hours before he died, a letter came from his sister, but he was too far gone to read it. Oh, it was such an earnest letter! The comrade read it to him, but he did not seem to understand it, he was so weak, till it came to the last sentence, which said:

"Oh, my dear brother, when you get this letter, will you not accept your sister's Savior?"

The dying man sprang up from his cot, and said, "What do you say? what do you say?" and then, falling back on his pillow, feebly exclaimed, "It is too late! It is too late!"

My dear friends, thank God it is not too late for you to-day. The Master is still calling you. Let every one of us, young and old, rich and poor, come to Christ at once, and He will put all our sins away. Don't wait any longer for feeling, but obey at once. You can believe, you can trust, you can lay hold on eternal life, if you will. Will you not do it now?

THE PROPHET NEHEMIAH

I should like to call your attention to the prophet Nehemiah. We may gain some help from that distinguished man who accomplished a great work. He was one of the last of the prophets, was supposed to be contemporary with Malachi, and perhaps his book was one of the last of the Old Testament books that was written. He might have known Daniel, for he was a young man in the declining years of that very eminent and godly statesman. We are sure of one thing at least—he was a man of sterling worth. Although he was brought up in the Persian court among idolaters, yet he had a character that has stood all these centuries.

Notice his prayer in which he made confession of Israel's apostasy from God. There may be some confessions we need to make to be brought into close fellowship with God. I have no doubt that numbers of Christians are hungering and thirsting for a personal blessing, and have a great desire to get closer to God. If that is the desire of your heart, keep in mind that if there is some obstacle in the way which you can remove, you will not get a blessing until you remove it. We must cooperate with God. If there is any sin in my heart that I am not willing to give up then I need not pray. You may take a bottle and cork it up tight, and put it under Niagara, and not a drop of that mighty volume of water will get into the bottle. If there is any sin in my heart that I am not willing to give up, I need not expect a blessing. The men who have had power with God in prayer have always begun by confessing their sins. Take the prayers of Jeremiah and Daniel. You find Daniel confessing his sin, when there isn't a single sin recorded against him; but he confesses his sin and the sins of the people. Notice how David confessed his sins and what power he had with God. So it is a good thing for us to begin as Nehemiah did.

It seems that some men had come down from his country to the Persian court, perhaps to see the king on business. This man, who was in high favor with the king, met them, and finding that they had come from Jerusalem he began to inquire about his country. He not only loved his God, but he LOVED HIS COUNTRY.

I like to see a patriotic man. He began to inquire about his people and about the city that was very near to his heart, Jerusalem. He had never seen the city. He had no relations back there in Jerusalem that he knew of. Nehemiah was not a Jewish prince, although it is supposed he had royal blood in his veins. He was born in captivity. It was about one hundred years after Jerusalem was taken that he appeared upon the horizon. He was in the court of Artaxerxes, a cupbearer to the king, and held a high position. Yet he longed to hear from his native land. When these men told him the condition of the city, that the people were in great want and distress and degradation, and that the walls of the city were still down, that the gates had been burned and never restored, his patriotic heart began to burn. We are told he fasted and prayed and wept, and not only did he pray for one week, or one month, but he kept on praying. He prayed "day and night." Having many duties to perform, of course he was not always on his knees, but in heart he was ever before the throne of grace. It was not hard for him to understand and obey the precept, "Pray without ceasing." He began the work in prayer, continued in prayer, and the last recorded words of Nehemiah are a prayer.

It was in November or December when those men arrived at that court, and this man prayed on until March or April before he spoke to the king. If a blessing doesn't come to-night, pray harder to-morrow, and if it doesn't come to-morrow, pray harder, and then, if it doesn't come keep right on, and you will not be disappointed. God in heaven will hear your prayers, and will answer them. He has never failed, if a man has been honest in his petitions and honest in his confessions. Let your faith beget patience. God is never in a hurry, said St. Augustine, because He has all eternity to work.

In the first chapter of Nehemiah is THE PRAYER of this wonderful man, his cry which has been on record all these years, and a great help to many people:

"I beseech thee, O Lord God of heaven, the great and terrible God, that keepeth covenant and mercy for them that love him and observe his commandments: let thine ear now be attentive, and thine eyes open, that thou mayest hear the prayer of thy servant, which I pray before thee now, day and night, for the children of Israel thy servants, and confess the sins of the children of Israel, which we have sinned against thee: both I and my father's house have sinned. We have dealt very corruptly against thee, and have not kept the commandments, nor the statutes, nor the judgments, which thou commandedst thy servant Moses. Remember, I beseech thee, the word that thou commandedst thy servant Moses, saying, If ye transgress, I will scatter you abroad among the nations: but if ye turn unto me, and keep my commandments, and do them; though there were of you cast out unto the uttermost part of the heaven, yet will I gather them from thence, and will bring them unto the place that I have chosen to set my name there. Now these are thy servants and thy people, whom thou hast redeemed by thy great power, and by thy strong hand. O Lord, I beseech thee, let now thine ear be attentive to the prayer of thy servant, and to the prayer of thy servants, who desire to fear thy name: and prosper, I pray thee, thy servant this day, and grant him mercy in the sight of this man."

When he began to pray I have no idea that he thought he was to be the instrument in God's hand of building the walls of Jerusalem. But when a man gets into sympathy and harmony with God, then God prepares him for the work He has for him. No doubt he thought the Persian king might send one of his great warriors and accomplish the work with a great army of men, but after he had been praying for months, it may be the thought flashed into his mind:

"Why should not I go to Jerusalem myself and build those walls?"

Prayer for the work will soon arouse your own sympathy and effort.

Now mark, it meant a good deal for Nehemiah to give up the palace of Shushan and his high office, and identify himself with the despised and captive Jews. He was among the highest in the whole realm. Not only that, but he was a man of wealth, lived in ease and luxury, and had great influence at court. For him to go to Jerusalem and lose caste was like Moses turning his back on the palace of Pharaoh and identifying himself with the Hebrew slaves. Yet we might NEVER HAVE HEARD OF either of them if they had not done this. They stooped to conquer; and when you get ready to stoop God will bless you. Plato, Socrates, and other Greek philosophers lived in the same century as Nehemiah. How few have heard of them and read their words compared with the hundreds of thousands who have heard and read of Nehemiah during the last two thousand years!

If you and I are to be blessed in this world, we must be willing to take any position into which God puts us. So, after Nehemiah had prayed a while, he began to pray God to send him, and that he might be the man to rebuild the walls of Jerusalem.

After he had been praying some time, he was one day in the banqueting hall, and the king noticed that his countenance was sad. We might not have called the face sad; but much prayer and fasting CHANGE THE VERY COUNTENANCE of a man. I know some godly men and women, and they seem to have the stamp of heaven on them. The king noticed a strange look about this cupbearer, and he began to question him. Then the thought came to Nehemiah that he would tell the king what caused his sorrow,—how his own nation was degraded, and how his heart was going out for his own country. After he had told the king, the king said:

"What is your request?"

Now, some men tell us they don't have time to pray, but I tell you if any man has God's work lying deep in his heart he will have time to pray. Nehemiah SHOT UP A PRAYER to heaven right there in the king's dining hall that the Lord would help him to make his request in the right way. He first looked beyond Artaxerxes to the King of Kings. You need not make a long prayer. A man who prays much in private will make short prayers in public. The Lord told Nehemiah what to ask for, that he might be sent to his own country, that some men might go with him, and that the king would give him letters to the governors through whose provinces he would pass so that he might have a profitable journey and be able to rebuild the walls of his city. God had been preparing the king, for the king at once granted the request, and before long this young prince was on his way to Jerusalem.

When he reached the city he didn't have a lot of men go before him blowing trumpets and saying that the cupbearer of the great Persian king, THE CONVERTED CUPBEARER, had arrived from the Persian court, and was going to build the walls of Jerusalem. There are some men who are always telling what they are going to do. Man, let the work speak for itself. You needn't blow any horns; go and do the work, and it will advertise itself. Nehemiah didn't have any newspapers writing about him, or any placards. However, there was no small stir. No doubt every one in town was talking about it, saying that a very important personage had arrived from the Persian court; but he was there three days and three nights without telling anyone why he had come.

One night he went out to survey the city. He couldn't ride around;

even now you cannot ride a beast around the walls of Jerusalem. He tried to ride around, but he couldn't, so he walked. It was a difficult task which he had before him, but he was not discouraged. That is what makes character. Men who can go into a hard field and succeed, they are the men we want. Any quantity of men are looking for easy places, but the world will never hear of them. We want men who are looking for hard places, who are willing to go into the darkest corners of the earth, and make those dark places bloom like gardens. They can do it if the Lord is with them.

Everything looked dark before Nehemiah. The walls were broken down. There was not a man of influence among the people, not a man of culture or a man of wealth. The nations all around were looking down upon these weak, feeble Jews. So it is in many churches today, the walls are down, and people say it is no use, and their hands drop down by their side. Everything seemed against Nehemiah, but he was a man who had the fire of God in his soul; he had come to build the walls of Jerusalem. If you could have bored a hole into his head, you would have found "Jerusalem" stamped on his brain. If you could have looked into his heart you would have found "Jerusalem" there. He was a fanatic; he was terribly in earnest; he was an enthusiast. I like to see a man take up some one thing and say, "I will do it; I live for this thing; this one thing I am bound to do." We spread out so much, and try to do so many things, that WE SPREAD SO THIN the world never hears of us.

After he had been in the city three days and nights, he called the elders of Israel together, and told them for what he had come. God had been preparing them, for the moment he told them they said:

"Let us rise up and build."

But there has not been a work undertaken for God since Adam fell which has not met with opposition. If Satan allows us to work unhindered, it is because our work is of no consequence. The first thing we read, after the decision had been made to rebuild the walls, is:

"When Sanballat the Horonite, and Tobiah the servant, the Ammonite, and Geshem the Arabian, heard it, they laughed us to scorn, and despised us, and said, What is this thing that ye do? will ye rebel against the king?"

These men were very indignant. They didn't care for the welfare of Jerusalem. Who were they? A mixed multitude who had no portion nor right nor memorial in Jerusalem. They didn't like to see the restoration of the ruins, just as people nowadays do not like to see the cause of Christ prospering. The offence of the cross has not ceased.

It doesn't take long to build the walls of a city if you can only get the whole of the people at it. If the Christians of this country would only rise up, we could evangelize America in twelve months. All the Jews had a hand in repairing the walls of Jerusalem. Each built over against his own house, priest and merchant, goldsmith and apothecary, and even the women. The men of Jericho and other cities came to help. The walls began to rise.

This stirred up Nehemiah's enemies, and they began to ridicule. RIDICULE is a mighty weapon.

"What do these feeble Jews?" said Sanballat. "Will they fortify themselves? Will they sacrifice? Will they make an end in a day? Will they revive the stones out of the heaps of the rubbish which are burned?"

"Even that which they build, if a fox go up, he shall even break down their stone wall," said Tobiah the Ammonite.

But Nehemiah was wise. He paid no attention to them. He just looked to God for grace and comfort:

"Hear, O our God; for we are despised: and turn their reproach upon their own head, and give them for a prey in the land of captivity: and cover not their iniquity, and let not their sin be blotted out from before: for they have provoked thee to anger before the builders."

Young man, if you wish to be successful in this world, don't mind Sanballat or Tobiah. Don't be kept out of the kingdom of God or out of active Christian work by the scorn and laughter and ridicule of your godless neighbors and companions.

Next, these enemies conspired to come and fight against Jerusalem.

Nehemiah was warned, and took steps to guard against them. Half of the people were on the watch, and the other half held a sword in one hand and a trowel in the other. There was NO EIGHT-HOUR WORKING DAY then; they were on duty from the rising of the morning till the stars appeared. They did not take off their clothes except to wash them. Fancy, this man who came from the Persian court with all its luxury, living and sleeping in his clothes for those fifty-two days! But he was in earnest. Ah, that is what we want! men who will set themselves to do one thing, and keep at it day and night.

All the people were bidden to lodge within the city, so that they should always be on hand to work and fight. Would to God that we could get all who belong inside the church to come in and do their share. "Happy is the church," says one, "whose workers are well skilled in the use of the Scripture, so that while strenuously building the Gospel Wall, they can fight too, if occasion require it." We ought all be ready to use the Sword of the Spirit.

By and by the men wrote a friendly letter, and wanted Nehemiah to go down on the plain of Ono and have a friendly discussion. It is A MASTERPIECE OF THE DEVIL to get men into friendly discussions. I don't know whether Nehemiah had a typewriter in those days or not; I don't know whether he had a printed form of letters, but he always sent back the same reply:

"I am doing a great work, so that I cannot come down."

How many a church has turned aside for years to discuss "questions of the day," and has neglected the salvation of the world because they must go down to the "plain of Ono" and have a friendly discussion! Nehemiah struck a good keynote—"I am doing a great work, so that I cannot come down." If God has sent you to build the walls of Jerusalem, you go and do it.

They sent him another letter, and again he sent word back, "I am doing a great work, so that I cannot come down." He did not believe in "coming down." They sent him another, and he sent back the same word. They sent him a fourth letter, with the same result. They could not get him down; they wanted to slay him on the way.

I have seen many Christian men on the plain of Ono, men who were doing a splendid work but had been switched off. Think how much work has been neglected by temperance advocates in this country because they have gone into politics and into discussing woman's rights and woman's suffrage. How many times the Young Men's Christian Association has been switched off by discussing some other subject instead of holding up Christ before a lost world! If the church would only keep right on and build the walls of Jerusalem they would soon be built. Oh, it is a wily devil that we have to contend with! Do you know it? If he can only get the church to stop to discuss these questions, he has accomplished his desire.

His enemies wrote him one more letter, AN OPEN LETTER, in which they said that they had heard he was going to set up a kingdom in opposition to the Persians, and that they were going to report him to the king. Treason has an ugly sound, but Nehemiah committed himself to the Lord, and went on building.

Then his enemies hired a prophet, one of his friends. A hundred enemies outside are not half so hard to deal with as one inside—a false friend. When the devil gets possession of a child of God he will do the work better than the devil himself. Temptations are never so dangerous as when they come to us in a religious garb. So Tobiah and Sanballat bought up one of the prophets, and hired him to try to induce Nehemiah to go into the temple, that they might put him to death there.

"Now, Nehemiah, there is a plan to kill you, come into the temple. Let's go in and stay for the night."

He came near being deceived, but he said, "Shall I, such a man as I, be afraid of my life, and do that to save my life?"

After he had refused their invitation he saw that this man was a false prophet; and so by his standing his ground he succeeded in fifty-two days in building the walls of Jerusalem. Then the gates were set up and the work was finished.

Now during all these centuries that story has been told. If Nehemiah had remained at court, he might have died a millionaire, but he never would have been heard of twenty years after his death. Do you know the names of any of Nineveh's millionaires? This man stepped out of that high position and took a low position, one that the world looked down upon and frowned upon, and his name has been associated with the walls of Jerusalem all these centuries. Young man, if you want to be immortal, become identified with God's work, and pay no attention to what men outside say. Nehemiah and his associates began at sunrise and worked until it grew so dark they could not see. A man who will take up God's work, and work summer and winter right through the year, will have a harvest before the year is over, and the record of it will shine after he enters the other world.

The next thing we learn of Nehemiah is that he got up a great OPEN-AIR MEETING for the reading of the law of Moses in the hearing of the people. A pulpit of wood, large enough to hold Ezra the Scribe and thirteen others, was built. The people wept when they heard the words of the law, but Nehemiah said:

"Mourn not, nor weep. Go your way, eat the fat, and drink the sweet, and send portions unto them for whom nothing is prepared: for this day is holy unto our Lord: neither be ye sorry; for the joy of the Lord is your strength."

He did not forget the poor. Reading the Bible and remembering the poor—a combination of faith and works—will always bring joy.

Nehemiah then began to govern the city, and correct the abuses he found existing. He gathered about fifty priests and scribes together and made them sign and seal a written covenant. There were five things in that covenant I want to call attention to.

First, they were not to give their daughters to the heathen.

They had been violating the law of God, and had been marrying their daughters to the ungodly. God had forbidden them to intermarry with the heathen nations in the land of Canaan; "for they will turn away thy son from following me, that they may serve other gods: so will the anger of the Lord be kindled against you and destroy thee suddenly." I have known many a man who has lost his power by being identified with the ungodly. If you want to have the blessing of God rest upon you, you must be very careful about your alliances. The Jews always got into trouble when they married with the nations round about. The houses of Ahab and of Solomon lost their kingdom by that sin. That was the cause of the overthrow of David's kingdom. Families who marry for wealth, and marry the godly to the ungodly, always bring distress into the family.

Then he made them sign a covenant that they would keep the Sabbath, that they would not buy upon the Sabbath.

Think of a man going from a heathen court where they had no Sabbath, a man brought up in that atmosphere, coming up to Jerusalem and enforcing the law of Moses! It is recorded that they brought up fish, and he would not let them into the city on the Sabbath, and the fish spoiled. After they had tried that a few times, they gave it up. If you will take your stand for God, even if you stand alone, it will not be very long before you will get other men to stand with you. God stood with this man, and he carried everything before him.

I don't believe we shall have the right atmosphere in this country until we can get men who have backbone enough to stand up against the thing they believe is wrong. If it is a custom rooted and grounded for a hundred years, never mind; you take your stand against it if you believe it is wrong. If you have gatherings, and it is fashionable to have wine and champagne, and you are a teetotaler; if they ask you anywhere and you know that they are to have drink, tell them you are not going. A man said to me some years ago:

"Mr. Moody, now that I am converted, must I give up the world?"

I said: "No, you haven't got to give up the world. If you give a good ringing testimony for the Son of God, the world will give you up pretty quick; they won't want you around."

They were going to have a great celebration at the opening of a saloon and billiard hall in Chicago, in the northern part of the city, where I lived. It was to be a gateway to death and to hell, one of the worst places in Chicago. As a joke they sent me an invitation to go to the opening. I took the invitation and went down and saw the two men who had the saloon, and I said:

"Is that a genuine invitation?"

They said it was.

"Thank you," I said, "I will be around; if there is anything here I don't like I may have something to say about it."

They said: "You are not going to preach?"

"I may."

"We don't want you. We won't let you in."

"How are you going to keep me out?" I asked; "there is the invitation."

"We will put a policeman at the door."

"What is the policeman going to do with that invitation?"

"We won't let you in."

"Well," I said, "I will be there."

I gave them a good scare, and then I said, "I will compromise the matter; if you two men will get down here and let me pray with you, I will let you off."

I got those two rum sellers down on their knees, one on one side of me, and the other on the other side, and I prayed God to save their souls and smite their business. One of them had a Christian mother, and he seemed to have some conscience left. After I had prayed, I said:

"How can you do this business? How can you throw this place open to ruin young men of Chicago?"

Within three months the whole thing smashed up, and one of them was converted some time after. I have never been invited to a saloon since.

You won't have to give up the world, not by a good deal. If you go to reunions, and there is drinking, get up and go away. Don't you be party to it. That is the kind of men we want. When you find anything that is ruining your fellow men, fight it to its bitter end.

Nehemiah said, "We will not have desecration of the Sabbath." Not sell the Sunday paper? Not buy a Sunday paper? How many read the Sunday newspapers?

I suppose that if you had Nehemiah as mayor of New York, he would stop that sort of thing. Here we have boys who are kept away from the Sunday school to sell papers on the streets—trains running in order that the papers can be distributed. I don't believe a man is in a fit state to hear a sermon whose mind is full of such trash as the Sunday newspaper is filled with. Men break the Sabbath and wonder why it is they have not spiritual power. The trouble nowadays is that it doesn't mean anything to some people to be a Christian. What we must have is a higher type of Christianity in this country. We must have a Christianity that has in it the principle of self-denial. We must deny ourselves. If we want power, we must be separate.

The next thing they were to do—(and bear in mind this was a thing they had to sign)—was to give their land rest.

For four hundred and ninety years they had not let their land rest, so God took them away to Babylon for seventy years, and let the land rest. A man that works seven days in the week right along is cut off about five or ten years earlier. You cannot rob God. Why is it that so many railroad superintendents and physicians die early? It is because they work seven days in the week. So Nehemiah made them covenant to keep the law of Moses. If the nations of the earth had kept that law, the truth would have gone to the four corners of the earth before this time.

Then he made them sign a covenant that they would not charge usury.

They were just grinding the poor down. I believe that the reason we are in such a wretched state in this country to-day is on account of crowding the poor, and getting such a large amount of money for usury. People evade the law, and pay the interest, and then they give a few hundred dollars to negotiate the loan. There is a great amount of usury, and see where we are to-day! See what a wretched state of things we are having, not only in this country, but all over the world!

The fifth thing he made them do was to bring their first fruits to the sons of Levi.

They were to give God a tenth, the first and best. As long as Israel did that they prospered, and when they turned away from that law they did not prosper. You can look through history and look around you and see the same thing to-day. As long as men keep God's law and respect God's testimony, they are going to prosper, but when they turn aside, like Samson, they lose their strength; they have no power.

If you take these five things and carry them out, you will have prosperity. Let us all do it personally. If it was good for those men it is good for us. The moment we begin to rob God of time or talents then darkness and misery and wretchedness will come.

HEROD AND JOHN THE BAPTIST

If some one had told me a few years ago that he thought Herod at one time came near the kingdom of God, I should have been inclined to doubt it. I would have said, "I do not believe that the bloodthirsty wretch who took the life of John the Baptist ever had a serious thought in his life about his soul's welfare." I held that opinion because there is one scene recorded in Herod's life that I had overlooked. But some years ago, when I was going through the gospel of Mark, making a careful study of the book, I found this verse:

"Herod feared John, knowing that he was a just man and an holy, and observed him; and when he heard him, he did many things, and heard him gladly." (Mark vi, 20).

This caused me to change my views about Herod. I saw that he was not only brought within the sound of John's voice, but under the power of the Spirit of God; his heart was touched and his conscience awakened. We are not told under what circumstances he heard John; but the narrative plainly states that he was brought under the influence of the Baptist's wonderful ministry.

Let me first say a word or two about THE PREACHER.

I contend that John the Baptist must have been one of the grandest preachers this world has ever had. Almost any man can get a hearing nowadays in a town or a city, where the people live close together; especially if he speaks in a fine building where there is a splendid choir, and if the meetings have been advertised and worked up for weeks or months beforehand. In such circumstances any man who has a gift for speaking will get a good audience. But it was very different with John. He drew the people out of the towns and cities away into the wilderness. There were no ministers to back him; no business men interested in Christ's cause to work with him; no newspaper reporters to take his sermons down and send them out. He was an unknown man, without any title to his name. He was not the Right-Rev. John the Baptist, D. D., or anything of the kind, but plain John the Baptist. When the people went to inquire of him if he were Elias or Jeremiah come back to life, he said he was not.

"Who are you then?"

"I am the Voice of one crying in the wilderness."

He was nothing but a voice—to be heard and not seen; he was Mr. Nobody. He regarded himself as a messenger who had received his commission from the eternal world.

How he began his ministry, and how he gathered the crowds together we are not informed. I can imagine that one day this strange man makes his appearance in the valley of the Jordan, where he finds a few shepherds tending their flocks. They bring together their scattered sheep, and the man begins to preach to these shepherds. The kingdom of heaven, he says, is about to be set up on the earth; and he urges them to set their houses in order—to repent and turn away from their sins. Having delivered his message, he tells them that he will come back the next day and speak again.

When he had disappeared in the desert, I can suppose one of the shepherds saying to another:

"Was he not a strange man? Did you ever hear a man speak like that? He did not talk as the rabbis or the Pharisees or the Sadducees do. I really think he must be one of the old prophets. Did you notice that his coat was made of camel's hair, and that he had a leathern girdle round his loins? Don't the Scriptures say that Elijah was clothed like that?"

Says another: "You remember how Malachi says that before the great and dreadful day of the Lord, Elijah should come? I really believe this man is the old prophet of Carmel."

What could stir the heart of the Jewish people more than the name of Elijah?

The tidings of John's appearance spread up and down the valley of the Jordan, and when he returned the next day, there was great excitement and expectation as the people listened to the strange preacher. Perhaps till Christ came he had only that ONE TEXT:

"Repent, for the kingdom of heaven is at hand." Day after day you could hear his voice ringing through the valley of the Jordan:

"Repent! repent! repent! The King is at the door. I do not know the day or the hour, but He will be here very soon."

By and by some of the people who flocked to hear him wanted to be baptized, and he took them to the Jordan and baptized them.

The news spread to the surrounding villages and towns, and it was not long before it reached Jerusalem. Then the people of the city began to flock into the desert to hear this prince among preachers. His fame soon reached Galilee, and the people in the mountains began to flock down to hear him. Men left their fishing-smacks on the lake, that they might listen to this wonderful preacher. When he was in the zenith of his popularity, as many as twenty or thirty thousand people perhaps flocked to his ministry day after day.

No doubt there were some old croakers who said it was ALL SENSATION.

"Catch me there! No, sir; I never did like sensational preaching."

Just as some people speak nowadays when any special effort is made to reach the people!

"Great harm will be done," they say.

I wish all these croakers had died out with that generation in Judea; but we have plenty of their descendants still. I venture to say you have met with them. Why, my dear friends, there is more excitement in your whisky shops and beer saloons in one night than in all the churches put together in twelve months. What a stir there must have been in Palestine under the preaching of John the Baptist, and of Christ! The whole country reeled and rocked with intense excitement. Don't be afraid of a little excitement in religious matters; it won't hurt.

One might hear those old Pharisees and Scribes grumbling about John being such a sensational preacher. "It won't last." And when Herod had John the Baptist beheaded, they would say, "Didn't I tell you so?"

Do not let us be in a hurry in passing judgment. John the Baptist lives to-day more than ever he did; his voice goes ringing through the world yet. He only preached a few months, but for more than eighteen hundred years his sermons have been repeated and multiplied, and the power of his words will never die as long as the world lasts.

I can imagine that just when John was at the height of his popularity, as Herod sat in his palace in Jerusalem looking out towards the valley of the Jordan, he could see great crowds of people passing day by day. He began to make inquiries as to what it meant, and the news came to him about this strange and powerful preacher. Some one, perhaps, reported that John was preaching treason. He was telling of a king who was at hand, and who was going to set up his kingdom.

"A king at hand! If Cæsar were coming, I should have heard of it. There is no king but Cæsar. I must look into the matter. I will go down to the Jordan, and hear this man for myself."

So one day, as John stood preaching, with the eyes of the whole audience upon him, the people being swayed by his eloquence like tree-tops when the wind passes over them, all at once he lost their attention. All eyes were suddenly turned in the direction of the city. One cries:

"Look, look! Herod is coming!"

Soon the whole congregation knows it, and there is great excitement.

"I believe he will stop this preaching," says one.

And if they had in those days some of the compromising weak-kneed Christians we sometimes meet, they would have said to John:

"Don't talk about a coming King; Herod won't stand it. Talk about repentance, but any talk about a coming King will be high treason in the ears of Herod."

I think if any one had dared to give John such counsel, he would have replied: "I have received my message from heaven; what do I care for Herod or any one else?"

As he stood thundering away and calling on the people to repent, I can see Herod, with his guard of soldiers around him, listening attentively to find anything in the preacher's words that he can lay hold of. At last John says:

"The King is just at the door. He will set up His kingdom, and will separate the wheat from the chaff."

I can imagine Herod then saying to himself: "I will have that man's head off inside of twenty-four hours. I would arrest him here and now if I dared. I will catch him to-morrow before the crowd gathers."

By and by, as Herod listens, some of the people begin to press close up to the preacher, and to question him. Some soldiers are among them, and they ask John:

"What shall we do?"

John answers: "Do violence to no man, neither accuse any falsely; and be content with your wages."

"That is pretty good advice," Herod thinks; "I have had a good deal of trouble with these men, but if they follow the preacher's advice, it will make them better soldiers."

Then he hears the publicans ask John, as they come to be baptized:

"What shall we do?"

The answer is: "Exact no more than that which is appointed you."

"Well," says Herod, "that is excellent advice. These publicans are all the time overtaxing the people. If they would do as the preacher tells them, the people would be more contented."

Then the preacher addresses himself to the Pharisees and the Sadducees in the crowd, and cries:

"O generation of vipers! Who hath warned you to flee from the wrath to come? Bring forth fruits worthy of repentance."

Says Herod within himself: "I like that. I am glad he is giving it pretty strong to these men. I do not think I will have him arrested just yet."

So he goes back to his palace. I can imagine he was NOT ABLE TO SLEEP MUCH that night; he kept thinking of what he had heard. When the Holy Ghost is dealing with a man's conscience, very often sleep departs from him. Herod cannot get this wilderness preacher and his message out of his mind. The truth had reached his soul; it echoed and re-echoed within him: "Repent, for the kingdom of heaven is at hand." He says:

"I went out to-day to hear for the Roman Government; I think I will go to-morrow and hear for myself."

So he goes back again and again. My text says that he heard him gladly, that he observed him, and feared him, knowing that he was a just man and a holy. He must have known down in his heart that John was A HEAVEN-SENT MESSENGER.

Had you gone into the palace in those days, you would have heard Herod talking of nobody but John the Baptist. He would say to his associates:

"Have you been out into the desert to hear this strange preacher?"

"No; have you?"

"Yes."

"What! you, the Roman Governor, going to hear this unordained preacher?"

"Yes, I have been quite often. I would rather hear him than any man I ever knew. He does not talk like the regular preachers. I never heard any one who had such influence over me."

You would have thought that Herod was a very hopeful subject. "He did many things." Perhaps he stopped swearing. He may have stopped gambling and getting drunk. A wonderful change seemed to have passed over him. Perhaps he ceased from taking bribes for a time; we catch him at it afterwards, but just then he refrained from it. He became quite virtuous in certain directions. It really looked as if he were near the kingdom of heaven.

I can imagine that one day, as John stands preaching, the truth is going home to the hearts and consciences of the people, and the powers of another world are falling upon them, one of John's disciples stands near Herod's chariot, and sees the tears in the eyes of the Roman Governor. At the close of the service he goes to John and says:

"I stood close to Herod today, and no one seemed more impressed. I could see the tears coming, and he had to brush them away to keep them from falling."

Have you ever seen a man in a religious meeting trying to keep the tears back? You noticed that his forehead seemed to itch, and he put up his hand; you may know what it means—he wants to conceal the fact that the tears are there. He thinks it is a weakness. It is no weakness to get drunk and abuse your family, but it is weakness to shed tears. So this disciple of John may have noticed that Herod put his hand to his brow a number of times; he did not wish his soldiers, or those standing near, to observe that he was weeping. The disciple says to John:

"It looks as if he were coming near the kingdom. I believe you will have him as an inquirer very soon."

When a man enjoys hearing such a preacher, it certainly seems a hopeful sign.

Herod might have been present that day when Christ was baptized. Was there ever a man lifted so near to heaven as Herod must have been if he were present on that occasion? I see John standing surrounded by a great throng of people who are hanging on his words. The eyes of the preacher, that never had quailed before, suddenly began to look strange. He turned pale and seemed to draw back as though something wonderful had happened, and right in the middle of a sentence he ceased to speak. If I were suddenly to grow pale, and stop speaking, you would ask:

"Has death crept onto the platform? Is the tongue of the speaker palsied?"

There must have been quite a commotion among the audience when John stopped. The eyes of the Baptist were fixed upon a Stranger who pushed His way through the crowd, and coming up to the preacher, requested to be baptized. That was a common occurrence; it had happened day after day for weeks past. John listened to the Stranger's words, but instead of going at once to the Jordan and baptizing Him, he said:

"I need to be baptized of Thee!"

What a thrill of excitement must have shot through the audience! I can hear one whispering to another:

"I believe that is the Messiah!"

Yes, it was the long-looked-for One, for whose appearing the nation had been waiting these thousands of years. From the time God had made the promise to Adam, away back in Eden, every true Israelite had been looking for the Messiah; and there He was in their midst!

He insisted that John should baptize Him, and the forerunner recognized His authority as Master, took Him to the Jordan, and baptized Him. As He came up from the water, lo! the heavens opened, and the Spirit of God in the form of a dove descended and rested on Him. When Noah sent forth the dove from the Ark, it could find no resting-place; but now the Son of God had come to do the will of God, and the dove found its resting-place upon Him. The Holy Ghost had found a home. Now God broke the silence of four thousand years. There came a voice from heaven, and Herod may have heard it if he was there that day:

"This is my beloved Son, in whom I am well pleased."

Even if he had not witnessed this scene and heard the voice, he must have heard about it; for the thing was not done in a corner.

There were thousands to witness it, and the news must have been taken to every corner of the land.

Yet Herod, living in such times, and hearing such a preacher, missed the kingdom of heaven at last. He did many things because he feared John. Had he feared God he would have done everything. "He did many things"; but there was one thing he would not do—HE WOULD NOT GIVE UP ONE DARLING SIN.

The longer I preach, the more I am convinced that that is what keeps men out of the kingdom of God. John knew about Herod's private life, and warned him plainly.

If those compromising Christians of whom I have spoken had been near John, one of them would have said:

"Look here, John, it is reported that Herod is very anxious about his soul, and is asking what he must do to be saved. Let me give you some advice; don't touch on Herod's secret sin. He is living with his brother's wife, but don't you say anything about it, for he won't stand it. He has the whole Roman Government behind him, and if you allude to that matter it will be more than your life is worth. You have a good chance with Herod; he is afraid of you. Only be careful, and don't go too far, or he will have your head off."

There are those who are willing enough that you should preach about the sins of other people, so long as you do not come home to them. My wife was once teaching my little boy a Sabbath-school lesson; she was telling him to notice how sin grows till it becomes habit. The little fellow thought it was coming too close to him, so he colored up, and finally said:

"Mamma, I think you are getting a good way from the subject."

John was a preacher of this uncompromising kind, for he drove the message right home. I do not know when or how the two were brought together at that time, but John kept nothing back; he boldly said:

"Herod, it is not lawful for thee to have thy brother's wife."

The man was breaking the law of God, and living in the cursed sin of adultery. Thank God, John did not spare him! It cost the preacher his head, but the Lord had got his heart, and he did not care what became of his head. We read that Herod feared John, but John did not fear Herod.

I want to say that I do not know of a quicker way to hell than by the way of adultery. Let no one flatter himself that he is going into the kingdom of God who does not repent of this sin in sackcloth and ashes. My friend, do you think God will never bring you into judgment? Does not the Bible say that no adulterer shall inherit the kingdom of God?

Do you think John the Baptist would have been a true friend of Herod if he had spared him, and had covered up his sin? Was it not a true sign that John loved him when he warned him, and told him he must quit his sin? Herod had before done many things, and heard John gladly; but he did not like him then. It is one thing to hear a man preach down other people's sins. Men will say, "That is splendid," and will want all their friends to go and hear the preacher. But let him touch on their individual sin as John did, and declare (as Nathan did to David), "Thou art the man," and they say, "I do not like that." The preacher has touched a sore place.

When a man has broken his arm, the surgeon must find out the exact spot where the fracture is. He feels along and presses gently with his fingers.

"Is it there?"

"No"

"Is it there?"

"No."

Presently, when the surgeon touches another spot, "Ouch!" says the man.

He has found the broken part, and it hurts. John placed his finger on the diseased spot, and Herod winced under it. He put his hand right on it:

"Herod, it is not lawful for thee to have thy brother Philip's wife!"

Herod did not want to give up his sin.

Many a man would be willing to enter into the kingdom of God, if he could do it without giving up sin. People sometimes wonder why Jesus Christ, who lived six hundred years before Mohammed, has got fewer disciples than Mohammed to-day. There is no difficulty in explaining that. A man may become a disciple of Mohammed, and continue to live in the foulest, blackest, deepest sin; but a man cannot be a disciple of Christ without giving up sin. If you are trying to make yourself believe that you can get into the kingdom of God without renouncing your sin, may God tear the mask from you! Can Satan persuade you that Herod will be found in the kingdom of God along with John the Baptist, with the sin of adultery and of murder on his soul?

And now, let me say this to you. If your minister comes to you frankly, tells you of your sin, and warns you faithfully, thank God for him. He is your best friend; he is a heaven-sent man. But if a minister speaks smooth, oily words to you; tells you it is all right, when you know, and he knows, that it is all wrong, and that you are living in sin, you may be sure that he is a devil-sent man. I want to say I have a contempt for a preacher that will tone his message down to suit some one in his audience; some Senator, or big man whom he sees present. If the devil can get possession of such a minister and speak through him, he will do the work better than the devil himself. You might be horrified if you knew it was Satan deceiving you, but if a professed minister of Jesus Christ preaches this doctrine and says that God will make it all right in the end, that though you go on living in sin, it is just the same. Don't be deluded into believing such doctrine—it is as false as any lie that ever came from the pit of hell. All the priests and ministers of all the churches cannot save one soul that will not part with sin.

There is an old saying that, "Every man has his price." Esau sold his birthright for a mess of pottage; pretty cheap, was it not? Ahab sold out for a garden of herbs. Judas sold out for thirty pieces of silver—less than $17 of our money. Pretty cheap, was it not? Herod sold out for adultery.

WHAT IS THE PRICE that you put upon your soul? You say you do not know. I will tell you. It is the sin that keeps you from God. It may be whisky; there is many a man who will give up the hope of heaven and sell his soul for whisky. It may be adultery; you say:

"Give me the harlot, and I will relinquish heaven with all its glories. I would rather be damned with my sin than saved without it."

What are you selling out for, my friend? You know what it is.

Do you not think it would have been a thousand times better for Herod to-day if he had taken the advice of John the Baptist instead of that vile, adulterous woman? There was Herodias pulling one way, John the other, and Herod was in the balance. It's the same old battle between right and wrong; heaven pulling one way, hell the other. Are you going to make the same mistake yourself? We have ten thousand-fold more light than Herod had. He lived on the other side of the cross. The glorious gospel had not shone out as it has done since. Think of the sermons you have heard, of the entreaties addressed to you to become a Christian. Some of you have had godly mothers who have prayed for you. Many of you have godly wives who have pleaded with you, and with God, on your behalf. You have been surrounded with holy influences from year to year, and how often you have been near the kingdom of God! Yet here you are to-day, further off than ever!

It may be true of you, as it was of Herod, that you hear your preacher gladly. You attend church, you contribute liberally, you do many things. Remember that none of these avail to cleanse your soul from sin. They will not be accepted in the place of what God demands—repentance and the forsaking of every sin.

A child was once playing with a vase, and put his hand in and could not draw it out again. His father tried to help him, but in vain. At last he said:

"Now, make one more try. Open your fingers out straight, and let me pull your arm."

"Oh, no, papa," said the son, "I'd drop the penny if I opened my fingers like that!"

Of course he couldn't get his hand out when his fist was doubled. He didn't want to give up the penny. Just so with the sinner. He won't cut loose from his sins.

Your path and mine will perhaps never cross again. But if I have any influence with you, I beseech and beg of you to break with sin now, let it cost you what it will. Herod might have been associated with Joseph of Arimathea, and with the twelve apostles of the Lamb, if he had taken the advice of John. There might have been a fragrance around his name all these centuries. But alas! when we speak of Herod, we see a sneer on the faces of those who hear us. If one had said to Herod in those days, "Do you know that you are going to silence that great preacher, and have him beheaded?" he would have replied, "Is thy servant a dog that he should do such a thing? I never would take the life of such a man." He would probably have thought he could never do it. Yet it was only a little while after that he had the servant of God beheaded.

Do you know that the Gospel of Jesus Christ proves either a savor of life unto life, or of death unto death? You sometimes hear people say: "We will go and hear this man preach. If it does us no good, it will do us no harm." Don't you believe it, my friend! Every time you hear the Gospel and reject it, the hardening process goes on. The same sun that melts the ice hardens the clay. The sermon that would have moved you a few years ago would make no impression now. Do you not recall some night when you heard some sermon that shook the foundations of your skepticism and unbelief? But you are indifferent now.

I believe Herod was seven times more a child of hell after his conviction had passed away than he was before. There is not a true minister of the Gospel who will not say that the hardest people to reach are those who have been impressed, and whose impressions have worn away. It is a good deal easier to commit a sin the second time than it was to commit it the first time, but it is a good deal harder to repent the second time than the first.

If you are near the kingdom of God now, take the advice of a friend and step into it. Don't be satisfied with just getting near to it. Christ said to the young ruler, "Thou art not far from the kingdom," but he failed to get there. Don't run any risks. Death may overtake you before you have time to carry out your best intentions, if you put off a decision.

It is sad to think that men heard Jesus and Paul, and were moved under their preaching, but were not saved. Judas must many times have come near the kingdom, but he never entered in. I saw it in the army—men who had ALMOST DECIDED to become Christians cut down in battle without having taken the step that would have made them sure of eternal life. I confess there is something very sad about it.

In one of the tenement houses in New York city, a doctor was sent for. He came, and found a young man very sick. When he got to the bedside the young man said:

"Doctor, I don't want you to deceive me; I want to know the worst. Is this illness to prove serious?"

After the doctor had made an examination, he said: "I am sorry to tell you you cannot live out the night."

The young man looked up and said: "Well, then, I have missed it at last!"

"Missed what?"

"I have missed eternal life. I always intended to become a Christian some day, but I thought I had plenty of time, and put it off."

The doctor, who was himself a Christian man, said: "It is not too late. Call on God for mercy."

"No; I have always had a great contempt for a man who repents when he is dying; he is a miserable coward. If I were not sick I would not have a thought about my soul, and I am not going to insult God now."

The doctor spent the day with him, read to him out of the Bible, and tried to get him to lay hold of the promises. The young man said he would not call on God, and in that state of mind he passed away. Just as he was dying the doctor saw his lips moving. He reached down, and all he could hear was the faint whisper:

"I have missed it at last!"

Dear friend, make sure that you do not miss eternal life at last. Will you go with Herod or with John? Bow your head now and say:

"Son of God, come into this heart of mine. I yield myself to Thee, fully, wholly, unreservedly."

He will come to you, and will not only save you, but will keep you to the end.

THE MAN BORN BLIND AND JOSEPH OF ARIMATHEA

There were two extraordinary men living in the city of Jerusalem when Christ was on earth. One of them has come down through history nameless—we do not know who he was; the name of the other is given. One was not only a beggar, but blind from his birth; the other was one of the rich men of Jerusalem. Yet in the Gospel of John, there is more space given to this blind beggar than to any other character. The reason why so much has been recorded of this man is because he took his stand for Jesus Christ.

Look at the account given in John ix., beginning at the fifth verse. In the previous chapter Christ had been telling them that He was the Light of the world, and that if any man would follow Him he should not walk in darkness, but should have the light of life. After making a statement of that kind, Christ often gave

AN EVIDENCE OF THE TRUTH of what He said by performing some miracle. If He had said He was the Light of the world, He would show them in what way He was the Light of the world. If He had said He was the Life of the world, He would prove Himself to be such by quickening and raising the dead; just as He did, after telling them that He was the Resurrection and the Life, by going to the graveyard of Bethany and calling Lazarus forth. When Lazarus heard the voice of his friend saying, "Lazarus, come forth!" he came forth immediately.

The Son of God does not ask men to believe Him without a reason for so doing. We need to keep this in mind. You might as well ask a man to see without light or eyes, as to believe without testimony.

He gave them good reason for believing in Him, and proved His Messiahship and authority. He not only told them that He had the power, but He showed them that He had.

These two men, then, were both at Jerusalem. One held as high a position, and the other as low a position, as any in the city. One was at the top of the social ladder, and the other at the bottom.

And yet they both made a good confession; and one was as acceptable to Jesus as the other.

I

The man mentioned in this chapter was born blind. We find the Lord's disciples asking Him:

"Master, who did sin, this man or his parents, that he was born blind?"

Jesus answered, "Neither hath this man sinned, nor his parents; but that the works of God should be manifest in him."

When He had thus spoken, He spat on the ground, and made clay of the spittle; and He anointed the eyes of the blind man with the clay, and said unto him:

"Go wash in the pool of Siloam."

The blind man went his way and washed, and his eyesight was restored.

Observe what that man did. He did just what Christ told him to do. The Savior's command to him was to go to the pool of Siloam and wash; and "he went his way therefore, and came seeing." He was blessed in the very act of obedience.

Another thought: God does not generally repeat Himself. Of all the blind men who were healed while Christ was on earth, no two were healed in exactly the same way. Jesus met blind Bartimeus near the gates of Jericho, and called him to Him and said:

"What wilt thou that I should do unto thee?"

The answer was: "Lord, that I might receive my sight."

Now, see what He did. He did not send Bartimeus off to Jerusalem twenty miles away to the pool of Siloam to wash. He did not spit on the ground, and make clay, and anoint his eyes; but with a word He wrought the cure, saying:

"Go thy way; thy faith hath made thee whole."

Suppose Bartimeus had gone from Jericho and had met the other blind beggar at the gate of the city of Jerusalem, and asked him how it was he got his sight; suppose they began to compare notes—one telling his experience, and the other telling his. Imagine the first saying:

"I do not believe that you have got your sight, because you did not get it in the same way that I got mine."

Would the different ways the Lord Jesus had in healing them make their cases the less true? Yet there are some people who talk just that way now. Because God does not deal with some exactly as He does with others, people think that God is not dealing with them at all. God seldom repeats Himself. No two persons were ever converted exactly alike, so far as my experience goes. Each one must have an experience of his own. Let the Lord give sight in His own way.

There are thousands of people who KEEP AWAY FROM CHRIST because they are looking for the experience of some dear friend or relative. They should not judge of their conversion by the experiences of others. They have heard some one tell how he was converted twenty years ago, and they expect to be converted in the same way. Persons should never count upon having an experience precisely similar to that of some one else of whom they have heard or read. They must go right to the Lord Himself, and do what He tells them to do. If He says, "Go to the pool of Siloam and wash," then they must go. If He says, "Come just as you are," and promises to give sight, then they must come, and let Him do His own work in His own way, just as this blind man did. It was a peculiar way by which to give a man sight; but it was the Lord's way; and the man's sight was given him. We might think it was enough to make a man blind to fill his eyes with clay. True, he was now doubly blind; for if he had been able to see before, the clay would have deprived him of his sight. But the Lord wanted to show the people that they were not only spiritually blind by nature, but that they had also allowed themselves to be blinded by the clay of this world, which had been spread over their eyes. But God's ways are not our ways. If He is going to work, we must let Him act as He pleases.

Shall we dictate to the Almighty? Shall the clay say to the potter, "Why hast thou made me thus?" Who art thou, O man, that repliest against God? Let God work in His own way; and when the Holy Ghost comes, let Him mark out a way for Himself. We must be willing to submit, and to do what the Lord tells us, without any questioning whatever.

"He went his way, therefore, and washed, and came seeing. The neighbors, therefore, and they which before had seen him that he was blind, said, 'Is not this he that sat and begged?' "

"Some said, 'This is he'; others said, 'He is like him.' "

Now, if he had been like a good many at the present time, I am afraid he would have remained silent. He would have said:

"Well, now I have got my sight, and I will just keep quiet about it. It is not necessary for me to confess it. Why should I say anything? There is a good deal of opposition to this man Jesus Christ. There are a great many bitter things said in Jerusalem against Him. He has a great many enemies. I think there will be trouble if I talk about Him; so I will say nothing."

Some said, "This is he"; others said, "He is like him." But he said, "I am he." He not only got his eyes opened, but, thank God, he got his mouth open too!

Surely, the next thing after we get our eyes opened is for us to open our lips and begin to testify for Him.

The people asked him, "How were thine eyes opened?"

He answered: "A man that is called Jesus made clay and anointed mine eyes, and said unto me, Go to the pool of Siloam and wash: and I went and washed, and I received sight."

He told a straightforward story, just what the Lord had done for him. That is all. That is what a witness ought to do—tell what he knows, not what he does not know. He did not try to make a long speech. It is not the most flippant and fluent witness who has the most influence with a jury.

This man's testimony is what I call "experience." One of the greatest hindrances to the progress of the Gospel to-day is that the narration of the experience of the Church is not encouraged. There are a great many men and women who come into the Church, and we never hear anything of their experiences, or of the Lord's dealings with them. If we could, it would be a great help to others. It would stimulate faith and encourage the more feeble of the flock.

THE APOSTLE PAUL'S EXPERIENCE has been recorded three times. I have no doubt that he told it everywhere he went: how God had met him; how God had opened his eyes and his heart; and how God had blessed him. Depend upon it, experience has its place; the great mistake that is made now is in the other extreme. In some places and at some periods there has been too much of it—it has been all experience; and now we have let the pendulum swing too far the other way.

I think it is not only right, but exceedingly useful, that we should give our experience. This man bore testimony to what the Lord had done for him.

"And it was the Sabbath day when Jesus made the clay, and opened his eyes; Then again the Pharisees also asked him how he had received his sight. He said unto them, 'He put clay upon mine eyes; and I washed, and do see.' Therefore said some of the Pharisees, 'This man is not of God, because he keepeth not the Sabbath day.' Others said, 'How can a man that is a sinner do such miracles?' And there was a division among them.

They say unto the blind man again, 'What sayest thou of Him, that He hath opened thine eyes?'"

What an opportunity he had for evading the questions! He might have said: "Why, I have never seen Him. When He met me I was blind; I could not see Him. When I came back I could not find Him; and I have not formed any opinion yet." He might have put them off in that way, but he said:

"He is a prophet."

He gave them his opinion. He was a man of backbone. He had moral courage. He stood right up among the enemies of Jesus Christ, the Pharisees, and told them what he thought of Him—

"He is a prophet."

If you can get young Christians to talk, not about themselves, but about Christ, their testimony will have power. Many converts talk altogether about their own experience—"I," "I," "I," "I." But this blind man got away to the Master, and said, "He is a prophet." He believed, and he told them what he believed.

"But the Jews did not believe concerning him, that he had been blind, and received his sight, until they called the parents of him that had received his sight. And they asked them, saying, 'Is this your son, who ye say was born blind? How then doth he now see?' His parents answered them, and said, 'We know that this is our son, and that he was born blind: but by what means he now seeth, we know not: or who hath opened his eyes, we know not: he is of age; ask him: he shall speak for himself.' These words spake his parents, because they feared the Jews; for the Jews had agreed already that if any man did confess that He was Christ, he should be put out of the synagogue. Therefore said his parents, 'He is of age; ask him.'"

I have always had great contempt for those parents. They had a noble son, and their lack of moral courage then and there to confess what the Lord Jesus Christ had done for their son, makes them unworthy of him. They say, "We do not know how he got it," which looks as if they did not believe their own son. "He is of age; ask him."

It is sorrowfully true to-day that we have hundreds and thousands of people who are professed disciples of Jesus Christ, but when the time comes that they ought to take their stand, and give a clear testimony for Him, they testify against Him. You can always tell those who are really converted to God. The new man always takes his stand for God; and the old man takes his stand against Him. These parents had an opportunity to confess the Lord Jesus Christ, and to do great things for Him; but they neglected their golden opportunity.

If they had but stood up with their noble son, and said, "This is our son. We have tried all the physicians, and used all the means in our power, and were unable to do anything for him; but now, out of gratitude, we confess that he received his sight from the prophet of Galilee, Jesus of Nazareth," they might have led many to believe on Him. But, instead of that, they said, "We know that this is our son, and that he was born blind: but by what means he now seeth, we know not."

Do you know why they did not want to tell how he got his sight? Simply because it would COST THEM TOO MUCH.

They represent those Christians who do not want to serve Christ if it is going to cost them anything; if they have to give up society, position, or worldly pleasures. They do not want to come out. This is what keeps hundreds and thousands from becoming Christians.

It was a serious thing to be put out of the synagogue in those days. It does not amount to much now. If a man is put out of one church, another may receive him; but when he went out of the synagogue there was no other to take him in. It was the State church: it was the only one they had. If he were cast out of that, he was cast out of society, position, and everything else; and his business suffered also.

Then again the Jews called the man that was blind, "and said unto him, 'Give God the praise; we know that this man is a sinner.'"

It looks now as if they were trying to prejudice him against Christ:

but he "answered and said, 'Whether He be a sinner or no, I know not; one thing I know, that whereas I was blind, now I see.'"

There were no infidels or philosophers there who could persuade him out of that. There were not men enough in Jerusalem to make him believe that his eyes were not opened. Did he not know that for over twenty years he had been feeling his way around Jerusalem; that he had been led by children and friends; and that during all those years he had not seen the sun in its glory, or any of the beauties of nature? Did he not know that he had been feeling his way through life up to that very day?

And do we not know that we have been born of God, and that we have got the eyes of our souls opened? Do we not know that old things have passed away and all things have become new, and that the eternal light has dawned upon our souls? Do we not know that the chains that once bound us have snapped asunder, that the darkness is gone, and that the light has come? Have we not liberty where we once had bondage? Do we not know it? If so, then let us not hold our peace. Let us testify for the Son of God, and say, as the blind man did in Jerusalem, "One thing I know, that whereas I was blind, now I see. I have a new power. I have a new light. I have a new love. I have a new nature. I have something that reaches out toward God. By the eye of faith I can see yonder heaven. I can see Christ standing at the right hand of God. By and by, when my journey is over, I am going to hear that voice saying, 'Come hither,' when I shall sit down in the kingdom of God."

"Then said they to him again, 'What did He do to thee? how opened He thine eyes?' But he answered them, 'I have told you already, and ye did not hear; wherefore would ye hear it again? Will ye also be His disciples?'"

This was a most extraordinary man. Here was a young convert in Jerusalem, not a day old, TRYING TO MAKE CONVERTS of these Pharisees—men who had been fighting Christ for nearly three years! He asked them if they would also become His disciples. He was ready to tell his experience to all who were willing to hear it. If he had covered it up at the first, and had not come out at once, he would not have had the privilege of testifying in that way, neither would he have been a winner of souls. This man was going to be a soul-winner.

I venture to say he became one of the best workers in Jerusalem. I have no doubt he stood well to the front on the day of Pentecost, when Peter preached, and when the wounded were around him; he went to work and told how the Lord had blessed him, and how He would bless them. He was a worker, not an idler, and he kept his lips open.

It is a very sad thing that so many of God's children are dumb; yet it is true. Parents would think it a great calamity to have their children born dumb; they would mourn over it, and weep; and well they might; but did you ever think of the many dumb children God has? The churches are full of them; they never speak for Christ. They can talk about politics, art, and science; they can speak well enough and fast enough about the fashions of the day; but they have NO VOICE FOR THE SON OF GOD.

Dear friend, if He is your Savior, confess Him. Every follower of Jesus should bear testimony for Him. How many opportunities each one has in society and in business to speak a word for Jesus Christ! How many opportunities occur daily wherein every Christian might be "instant in season and out of season" in pleading for Jesus! In so doing we receive blessing for ourselves, and also become a means of blessing to others.

This man wanted to make converts of those Pharisees, who only a little while before had their hands full of stones, ready to put the Son of God to death, and even now had murder in their hearts. They reviled him, saying, "Thou art His disciple, but we are Moses' disciples. We know that God spake unto Moses. As for this fellow, we know not from whence He is."

Well, now the once blind man might have said, "There is a good deal of opposition, and I will say no more; I will keep quiet, and walk off and leave them." But, thank God, he stood right up with the courage of a Paul! He answered and said unto them:

"Why, herein is a marvellous thing, that ye know not from whence He is, and yet He hath opened mine eyes! Now we know that God heareth not sinners; but if any man be a worshiper of God, and doeth His will, him He heareth."

Now, I call that logic. If he had been through a theological seminary he could not have given a better answer. It is sound doctrine, and was a good sermon for those who were opposed to the work of Christ. "If this man were not of God He could do nothing." This is very strong proof of the man's conviction as to who the Lord Jesus was. It is as though he said: "I, a man born blind, and He can give me sight. He a sinner!" Why, it is unreasonable! If Jesus Christ were a man only, how could He give that man sight?

Let philosophers, skeptics, and infidels answer the question,

Neither had he to wear glasses. He received good sight, not short sight, or weak sight, but as good sight as any man in Jerusalem, and perhaps a little better. They could all look at him and see for themselves. His testimony was beyond dispute.

After his splendid confession of the divinity and power of Christ, "they answered and said unto him, 'Thou wast altogether born in sin, and dost thou teach us?' And they cast him out." They could not meet his argument, and so they cast him out. So it is now. If we give a clear testimony for Christ, the world will cast us out. It is a good thing to give our testimony so clearly for Christ that the world dislikes it; it is a good thing when such testimony for Christ causes the world to cast us out.

Let us see what happened when they cast him out. "Jesus heard," that is the next thing. No sooner did they cast him out than Jesus heard of it. No man was ever cast out by the world for the sake of Jesus Christ but He heard of it; indeed, He will be the first one to hear of it. "Jesus heard that they had cast him out; and when He found him He said unto him, 'Dost thou believe in the Son of God?' He answered and said, 'Who is He, Lord, that I might believe on Him?' And Jesus said unto him, 'Thou hast both seen Him, and it is He that talketh with thee.' And he said, 'Lord, I believe!' And he worshiped Him."

That was A GOOD PLACE TO LEAVE HIM —at the feet of Jesus. We shall meet him by and by in the kingdom of God.

His testimony has been ringing down through the ages these last nineteen hundred years. It has been talked about wherever the Word of God has been known. It was a wonderful day's work that man did for the Son of God; doubtless there will be many in eternity who will thank God for his confession of Christ.

By thus showing his gratitude in coming out and confessing Christ, he has left a record that has stirred the Church of God ever since. He is one of the characters that always stirs one up, imparting new life and fire, new boldness and courage when one reads about him. This is what we need to-day as much as ever—to stand up for the Son of God. Let the Pharisees rage against us; let the world go on mocking, and sneering, and scoffing; we will stand up courageously for the Son of God. If they cast us out, they will cast us right into His own bosom. He will take us to His own loving arms. It is a blessed thing to live so godly in Christ Jesus that the world will not want you—that they will cast you out.

II

Now we come to Joseph of Arimathea.

I do not think he came out quite so nobly as this blind beggar did; but he did come out, and we will thank God for that. We read in John that for fear of the Jews he was kept back from confessing openly.

"And after this, Joseph of Arimathea, being a disciple of Jesus, but secretly, for fear of the Jews, besought Pilate that he might take away the body of Jesus; and Pilate gave him leave. He came, therefore, and took the body of Jesus."

Read the four accounts given in the four Gospels of Joseph of Arimathea. There is very seldom anything mentioned by all four of the Evangelists. If Matthew and Mark refer to an event it is often omitted by Luke and John; and, if it occur in the latter, it may not be contained in the former. John's Gospel is made up of that which is absent from the others in most instances—as in the case of the blind man alluded to. But all four record what Joseph did for Christ. All His disciples had forsaken Him. One had sold Him, and another had denied Him. He was left in gloom and darkness, when Joseph of Arimathea came out and confessed Him.

It was the death of Jesus Christ that brought out Joseph of Arimathea. Probably he was one of the number that stood at the cross when the centurion smote his breast, and cried out, "Truly, this was the Son of God," and he was doubtless convinced at the same time. He was a disciple before, because we read that on the night of the trial he did not give his consent to the death of Christ. There must have been some surprise in the Council-chamber on that occasion, when Joseph of Arimathea, a rich man, stood up and said:

"I will never give my consent to His death."

There were seventy of those men, but we have very good reason to believe that there were two of them that, like Caleb and Joshua of old, had the courage to stand up for Jesus Christ—these were Joseph of Arimathea and Nicodemus: neither of them gave their consent to the death of Christ. But I am afraid Joseph did not come out and say that he was a disciple—for we do not find a word said about his being one until after the crucifixion.

I am afraid there are MANY JOSEPHS TODAY, men of position, of whom it could be said they are secret disciples. Such would probably say to-day, "I do not need to take my stand on Christ's side. What more do I need? I have everything." We read that he was a rich and honorable councillor, a just and a good man, and holding a high position in the government of the nation. He was also a benevolent man, and a devout man too. What more could he need? God wants something more than Joseph's good life and high position. A man may be all Joseph was and yet be without Christ.

But a crisis came in his history. If he was to take his stand, now was the time for him to do it, I consider that this is one of the grandest, the noblest acts that any man ever did, to take his stand for Christ when there seemed nothing, humanly speaking, that Christ could give him. Joseph had no hope concerning the resurrection. It seems that none of our Lord's disciples understood that He was going to rise again even Peter, James, and John, as well as the rest, scarcely believed that He had risen when He appeared to them. They had anticipated that He would set up His kingdom, but He had no sceptre in His hand; and, so far as they could see, no kingdom in view. In fact, He was dead on the cross, with nails through His hands and feet. There He hung until His spirit took its flight; that which had made Him so grand, so glorious, and so noble, had now left the body.

Joseph might have said, "It will be no use my taking a stand for Him now. If I come out and confess Him I shall probably lose my position in society and in the council, and my influence. I had better remain where I am."

There was no earthly reward for him; there was nothing, humanly speaking, that could have induced him to come out; and yet we are told by Mark that he went boldly into Pilate's judgment-hall and begged the body of Jesus. I consider this was ONE OF THE SUBLIMEST, GRANDEST ACTS that any man ever did. In that darkness and gloom, His disciples having all forsaken Him; Judas having sold Him for thirty pieces of silver; the chief apostle Peter having denied Him with a curse, swearing that he never knew Him; the chief priests having found Him guilty of blasphemy; the

Council having condemned him to death; and when there was a hiss going up to heaven over all Jerusalem, Joseph went right against the current, right against the influence of all his friends, and begged the body of Jesus.

Blessed act! Doubtless he upbraided himself for not having been more bold in his defence of Christ when He was tried, and before He was condemned to be crucified. The Scripture says he was an honorable man, an honorable councillor, a rich man, and yet we have only the record of that one thing—the one act of begging the body of Jesus. But I tell you, that what he did for the Son of God, out of pure love for Him, will live for ever; that one act rises up above everything else that Joseph of Arimathea ever did. He might have given large sums of money to different institutions, he might have been very good to the poor, he might have been very kind to the needy in various ways; but that one act for Jesus Christ, on that memorable, that dark afternoon, was one of the noblest acts that a man ever did. He must have been a man of great influence, or Pilate would not have given him the body.

And now you see another secret disciple, Nicodemus. Nicodemus and Joseph go to the cross. Joseph is there first, and while he is waiting for Nicodemus to come, he looks down the hill; and I can imagine his delight as he sees his friend coming with a hundred pounds of ointment. Although Jesus Christ had led such a lowly life, He was to have a kingly anointing and burial. God has touched the hearts of these two noble men and they drew out the nails, and took the body down, washed the blood away from the wounds that had been made on His back by the scourge, and on His head by the crown of thorns; then they took the lifeless form, washed it clean, and wrapped it in fine linen, and Joseph laid Him in his own sepulchre.

When all was dark and gloomy, when His cause seemed to be lost, and the hope of the Church buried in that new tomb, Joseph took his stand for the One "despised and rejected of men." It was the greatest act of his life; and, my reader, if you want to stand with the Lord Jesus Christ in glory; if you want the power of God to be bestowed upon you for service down here, you must not hesitate to take your stand boldly and manfully for the most despised of all men—the Man Christ Jesus. His cause is unpopular. The ungodly sneer at His name. But if you want the blessings of heaven on your soul, and to hear the "Well done, good and faithful servant, enter thou into the joy of thy Lord," take your stand at once for Him;

whatever your position may be, or however much your friends may be against you. Decide for Jesus Christ, the crucified but risen Savior. Go outside the camp and bear His reproach. Take up your cross and follow Him, and by and by you will lay it down and take the crown to wear it for ever.

I remember some meetings being held in a locality where the tide did not rise very quickly, and bitter and reproachful things were being said about the work. But one day, one of the most prominent men in the place rose and said:

"I want it to be known that I am a disciple of Jesus Christ, and if there is any odium to be cast on His cause, I am prepared to take my share of it."

It went through the meeting like an electric current, and a blessing came at once to his own soul and to the souls of others.

Depend upon it, there is NO CROWN WITHOUT A CROSS.

We must take our proper position here, as Joseph did. It cost him something to take up his cross. I have no doubt they put him out of the council and out of the synagogue. He lost his standing, and perhaps his wealth: like other faithful followers of Christ, he became, henceforth, a despised and unpopular man.

The blind man could not have done what Joseph did. Some men can do what others cannot. God will hold us responsible for our own influence. Let each of us do what we can. Even though the conduct of our Lord's professed followers was anything but helpful to those who, like Joseph, had but little courage to come out on the Lord's side, he was not deterred from taking his stand.

Whatever it costs us, let us be true Christians, and take a firm stand. It is like the dust in the balance in comparison to what God has in store for us. We can afford to suffer with Him a little while if we are going to reign with Him for ever. We can afford to take up the cross and follow Him, to be despised and rejected by the world, with such a bright prospect in view. If the glories of heaven are real, it will be to His praise and to our advantage to share in His rejection now.

May the Lord keep us from halting; and may we, when weighed in the balance, not be found wanting! May God help every reader to do all that the poor blind beggar did, and all that Joseph did!

Let us confess Him at all times and in all places. Let us show our friends that we are out and out on His side. Every one has a circle that he can influence, and God will hold us responsible for the influence we possess. Joseph of Arimathea and the blind man had circles in which their influence was powerful. I can influence people that others cannot reach; and they, in their turn, can reach a class that I could not touch. It is only for a little while that we can confess Him and work for Him. It is only for a few months or years; and then the eternal ages will roll on, and great will be our reward in the crowning day that is coming. We shall then hear the Master say to us:

"Well done, good and faithful servant, enter thou into the joy of thy Lord."

God grant it may be so!

THE PENITENT THIEF

It should give us all a great deal of hope and comfort that Jesus saved such a man as the penitent thief just before He went back to heaven. Every one who is not a Christian ought to be interested in this case, to know how he was converted. Any one who does not believe in sudden conversions ought to look into it. If conversions are gradual, if it takes six months, or six weeks, or six days to convert a man, there was no chance for this thief. If a man who has lived a good, consistent life cannot be converted suddenly, how much less chance for him! Turn to the 23d chapter of Luke, and see how the Lord dealt with him. He was a thief, and the worst kind of a thief, or else they would not have punished him by crucifixion. Yet Christ not only saved him, but took him up with Himself into glory.

Let us look at Christ hanging on the cross between the two thieves. The Scribes and Pharisees wagged their heads, and jeered at Him. His disciples had fled. Only His mother and one or two other women remained in sight to cheer Him with their presence among all the crowd of enemies. Hear those spiteful Pharisees mocking among themselves: "He saved others; Himself He cannot save." The account also says that the two thieves "cast the same in his teeth."

REVILING.

The first thing we read, then, of this man is that he was a reviler of Christ.

You would think that he would be doing something else at such a time as that; but hanging there in the midst of torture, and certain to be dead in a few hours, instead of confessing his sins and preparing to meet that God whose law he had broken all his life, he is abusing God's only Son. Surely, he cannot sink any lower, until he sinks into hell!

UNDER CONVICTION.

The next time we hear of him, he appears to be under conviction:

"And one of the malefactors which were hanged railed on Him, saying, If thou be Christ, save Thyself and us. But the other answering rebuked him, saying, Dost not thou fear God, seeing thou art in the same condemnation? And we indeed justly; for we receive the due reward of our deeds: but this Man hath done nothing amiss."

What do you suppose made so great a change in this man in these few hours? Christ had not preached a sermon, had given him no exhortation. The darkness had not yet come on. The earth had not opened her mouth. The business of death was going on undisturbed. The crowd was still there, mocking and hissing and wagging the head. Yet this man, who in the morning was railing at Christ, is now confessing his sins and rebuking the other thief. "We indeed justly!" No miracle had been wrought before his eyes. No angel from heaven had come to place a glittering crown upon His head in place of the bloody crown of thorns.

What was it wrought such a change in him?

I will tell you what I think it was. I think it was the Savior's prayer:

"Father, forgive them, for they know not what they do."

I seem to hear the thief TALKING TO HIMSELF in this way:

"What a strange kind of man this must be! He claims to be king of the Jews, and the superscription over His cross says the same. But what sort of a throne is this! He says He is the Son of God. Why does not God send down His angels and destroy all these people who are torturing His Son to death? If He has all power now, as He used to have when He worked those miracles they talked about, why does He not bring out His vengeance, and sweep all these wretches into destruction? I would do it in a minute if I had the power. I wouldn't spare any of them. I would open the earth and swallow them up! But this man prays to God to forgive them! Strange, strange! He must be different from us. I am sorry I said one word against Him when they first hung us up here.

What a difference there is between Him and me! Here we are, hanging on two crosses, side by side; but all the rest of our lives we have been far enough apart. I have been robbing and murdering, and He has been feeding the hungry, healing the sick, and raising the dead. Now these people are railing at us both! I begin to believe He must be the Son of God; for surely no man could forgive his enemies like that."

Yes, that prayer of Christ's did what the scourge could not do. This man had gone through his trial, he had been beaten, he had been nailed to the cross; but his heart had not been subdued, he had raised no cry to God, he was not sorry for his sins. Yet, when he heard the Savior praying for His murderers, that BROKE HIS HEART.

It flashed into this thief's soul that Jesus was the Son of God, and that moment he rebuked his companion, saying:

"Dost thou not fear God?"

The fear of God fell upon him. There is not much hope of a man's being saved until the fear of God comes upon him. Solomon says, "The fear of God is the beginning of wisdom."

We read in Acts that great fear fell upon the people; that was the fear of the Lord. That was the first sign that conviction had entered the soul of the thief. "Dost thou not fear God?" That was the first sign we have of life springing up.

CONFESSING.

Next, he confessed his sins: "We indeed justly." He took his place among sinners, not trying to justify himself.

A man may be very sorry for his sins, but if he doesn't confess them, he has no promise of being forgiven. Cain felt badly enough over his sins, but he did not confess. Saul was greatly tormented in mind, but he went to the witch of Endor instead of to the Lord. Judas felt so bad over the betrayal of his Master that he went out and hanged himself; but he did not confess to God. True, he went and confessed to the priests, saying, "I have sinned in that I have betrayed innocent blood"; but it was of no use to confess to them— they could not forgive him.

How different is the case of this penitent thief! He confessed his sins, and Christ had mercy on him there and then.

The great trouble is, people are always trying to make out that they are not sinners, that they have nothing to confess. Therefore, there is no chance of reaching them with the Gospel. There is no hope for a man who folds his arms and says: "I don't think God will punish sin; I am going to take the risk." There is no hope for a man until he sees that he is under just condemnation for his sins and shortcomings. God never forgives a sinner until he confesses.

JUSTIFYING CHRIST.

The next thing, he justifies Christ: "This Man hath done nothing amiss."

When men are talking against Christ, they are a great way from becoming Christians. Now he says, "He hath done nothing amiss." There was the world mocking him; but in the midst of it all, you can hear that thief crying out:

"This Man hath done nothing amiss."

FAITH.

The next step is faith.

Talk about faith! I think this is about the most extraordinary case of faith in the Bible. Abraham was the father of the faithful; but God had him in training for twenty-five years. Moses was a man of faith; but he saw the burning bush, and had other evidences of God. Elijah had faith; but see what good reason he had for it. God took care of him, and fed him in time of famine. But here was a man who perhaps had never seen a miracle; who had spent his life among criminals; whose friends were thieves and outlaws; who was now in his dying agonies in the presence of a crowd who were rejecting and reviling the Son of God. His disciples, who had heard His wonderful words, and witnessed His mighty works, had forsaken Him; and perhaps the thief knew this. Peter had denied Him with oaths and cursing; and perhaps this had been told the thief. Judas had betrayed Him. He saw no glittering crown upon His brow; only the crown of thorns. He could see no sign of His kingdom. Where were His subjects? And yet, nailed to the cross, racked with pain in every nerve, overwhelmed with horror, his wicked soul in a tempest of passion, this poor wretch managed to lay hold on Christ and trust Him for a swift salvation. The faith of this thief, how it flashes out amid the darkness of Calvary! It is one of the most astounding instances of faith in the Bible!

When I was a boy I was a poor speller. One day there came a word to the boy at the head of the class which he couldn't spell, and none of the class could spell it. I spelled it; by good luck; and I went from the foot of the class to the head. So the thief on the cross passed by Abraham, Moses and Elijah, and went to the head of the class. He said unto Jesus:

"Lord, remember me when thou comest into Thy kingdom."

Thank God for such a faith! How refreshing it must have been to Christ to have one own Him as Lord, and believe in His kingdom, at that dark hour! How this thief's heart goes out to the Son of God! How glad he would be to fall on his knees at the foot of the cross, and pour out his prayer! But this he cannot do. His hands and feet are nailed fast to the wood, but they have not nailed his eyes and his tongue and his heart. He can at least turn his head and look upon the Son of God, and his breaking heart can go out in love to that One who was dying for him and dying for you and me, and he can say:

"Lord, remember me when Thou comest into Thy kingdom."

WHAT A CONFESSION of Christ that was! He called Him "Lord." A queer Lord! Nails through His hands and feet, fastened to the cross. A strange throne! Blood trickling down His face from the scars made by the crown of thorns. But He was all the more "Lord" because of this.

Sinner, call Him "Lord" now. Take your place as a poor condemned rebel, and cry out:

"Lord, remember me!"

That isn't a very long prayer, but it will prevail. You don't have to add—"when Thou comest into Thy kingdom," because Christ is now at His Father's right hand. Three words; a chain of three golden links that will bind the sinner to his Lord.

Some people think they must have a form of prayer, a prayer-book, perhaps, if they are going to address the Throne of Grace properly; but what could that poor fellow do with a prayer-book up there, hanging on the cross, with both hands nailed fast? Suppose it had been necessary for some priest or minister to pray for him, what could he do? Nobody is there to pray for him, and yet he is going to die in a few hours. He is out of reach of help from man, but God has laid help upon One who is mighty, and that One is close at hand. He prayed out of the heart. His prayer was short, but it brought the blessing. It came to the point: "Lord, remember me when Thou comest into Thy kingdom." He asked the Lord to give him, right there and then, what he wanted.

THE ANSWERED PRAYER.

Now consider the answer to his prayer. He got more than he asked, just as every one does who asks in faith. He only asked Christ to "remember" him; but Christ answered:

"To-day shalt thou be with me in Paradise!"

Immediate blessing—promise of fellowship—eternal rest; this is the way Christ answered his prayer.

DARKNESS.

And now darkness falls upon the earth. The sun hides itself. Worse than all, the Father hides His face from His Son. What else is the meaning of that bitter cry:

"My God! my God! Why hast Thou forsaken me?"

Ah! It had been written, "Cursed is every one that hangeth on a tree." Jesus was made a curse for us. God cannot look upon sin: and so when even His own Son was bearing our sins in His body, God could not look upon Him.

I think this is what bore heaviest upon the Savior's heart in the garden when He prayed:

"If it be possible, let this cup pass from me."

He could bear the unfaithfulness of His friends, the spite of His enemies, the pain of His crucifixion, and the shadow of death; He could bear all these; but when it came to the hiding of His Father's face, that seemed almost too much for even the Son of God to bear. But even this He endured for our sins; and now the face of God is turned back to us, whose sins had turned it away, and looking upon Jesus, the sinless One, He sees us in Him.

In the midst of all His agony, how sweet it must have been to Christ to hear that poor thief confessing Him!

He likes to have men confess Him. Don't you remember His asking Peter, "Whom do men say that I am?" and when Peter answered, "Some people say you are Moses, some people say you are Elias, and some people say you are one of the old Prophets," He asked again, "But, Peter, whom do you say I am?" When Peter said, "Thou art the Son of God," Jesus blessed him for that confession. And now this thief confesses Him—confesses Him in the darkness. Perhaps it is so dark he cannot see Him any longer; but he feels that He is there beside him. Christ wants us to confess Him in the dark as well as in the light; when it is hard as well as when it is easy. For He was not ashamed of us, but bore our sins and carried our sorrows, even unto death.

When a prominent man dies, we are anxious, to get his last words and acts.

THE LAST ACT OF THE SON OF GOD was to save a sinner. That was a part of the glory of His death. He commenced His ministry by saving sinners, and ended it by saving this poor thief. "Shall the prey be taken from the mighty, or the lawful captive delivered? But thus saith the Lord: Even the captives of the mighty shall be taken away, and the prey of the terrible shall be delivered." He took this captive from the jaws of death. He was on the borders of hell, and Christ snatched him away.

No doubt Satan was saying to himself: "I shall have the soul of that thief pretty soon. He belongs to me. He has been mine all these years."

But in his last hours the poor wretch cried out to the Lord, and He snapped the fetters that bound his soul, and set him at liberty. He threw him a passport into heaven. I can imagine, as the soldier drove his spear into our Savior's side, there came flashing into the mind of the thief the words of the prophet Zechariah:

"In that day there shall be a fountain opened to the house of David, and to the inhabitants of Jerusalem, for sin and for uncleanness."

You see, in the conversion of this thief, that SALVATION IS DISTINCT AND SEPARATE FROM WORKS.

Some people tell us we have to work to be saved. What has the man who believes that to say about the salvation of this thief? How could he work, when he was nailed to the cross?

He took the Lord at His word, and believed. It is with the heart men believe, not with their hands or feet. All that is necessary for a man to be saved is to believe with his heart. This thief made a good confession. If he had been a Christian fifty years, he could not have done Christ more service there than he did. He confessed Him before the world; and for nineteen hundred years that confession has been told. Matthew, Mark, Luke and John all recorded it. They felt it so important that they thought we should have it.

See how SALVATION IS SEPARATE AND DISTINCT FROM ALL

ORDINANCES —not but that ordinances are right in their place.

Many people think it is impossible for any one to get into the kingdom of God if he is not baptized into it. I know people who were greatly exercised because little children died unbaptized. I have seen them carry the children through the streets because the pastor could not come. I don't want you to think I am talking against ordinances. Baptism is right in its place; but when you put it in the place of salvation, you put a snare in the way. You cannot baptize men into the kingdom of God. The last conversion before Christ perished on the cross ought to forever settle that question. If you tell me a man cannot get into Paradise without being baptized, I answer, This thief was not baptized. If he had wanted to be baptized, I don't believe he could have found a man to baptize him.

I have known people who had sick relatives, and because they could not get a minister to come to their house and administer the sacrament, they were distressed and troubled. Now, I am not saying anything against the ordinance by which we commemorate the death of our Lord, and remember His return. God forbid! But let me say that it is not necessary for salvation. I might die and be lost before I could get to the Lord's table; but if I get to the Lord I am saved. Thank God, salvation is within my reach always, and I have to wait for no minister. This poor thief certainly never partook of the sacrament. Was there a man on that hill that would have had faith to believe he was saved? Would any church to-day have received him into membership? He had not to wait for this. The moment he asked life, our Savior gave it.

Baptism is one thing; the sacrament of the Lord's Supper is another thing; and salvation through Christ is quite another thing. If we have been saved through Christ, let us confess Him by baptism, let us go to His table, and do whatever else He bids. But let us not make stumbling-blocks out of these things.

That is what I call sudden conversion—men calling on God for salvation and getting it. You certainly won't get it unless you call for it, and unless you take it when He offers it to you. If you want Christ to remember you—to save you—call upon Him.

TWO SIDES.

The cross of Christ divides all mankind. There are only two sides, those for Christ, and those against Him. Think of the two thieves; from the side of Christ one went down to death cursing God, and the other went to glory.

What a contrast! In the morning he is led out, a condemned criminal; in the evening he is saved from his sins. In the morning he is cursing; in the evening he is singing hallelujahs with a choir of angels. In the morning he is condemned by men as not fit to live on earth; in the evening he is reckoned good enough for heaven. In the morning nailed to the cross; in the evening in the Paradise of God, crowned with a crown he should wear through all the ages. In the morning not an eye to pity; in the evening washed and made clean in the blood of the Lamb. In the morning in the society of thieves and outcasts; in the evening Christ is not ashamed to walk arm-in-arm with him down the golden pavements of the eternal city.

The thief was THE FIRST MAN TO ENTER PARADISE after the veil of the Temple was rent. If we could look up yonder, and catch a glimpse of the throne, we would see the Father there, and Jesus Christ at His right hand; and hard by we would see that thief. He is there to-day. Nineteen hundred years he has been there, just because he cried in faith:

"Lord, remember me when Thou comest into Thy kingdom."

You know Christ died a little while before the thief. I can imagine that He wanted to hurry home to get a place ready for His new friend, the first soul brought from the world He was dying to redeem. The Lord loved him because he confessed Him in that dark hour. It was a dark hour for many who reviled the Savior. You have heard of the child who did not want to die and go to heaven because he didn't know anybody there. But the thief would have one acquaintance. I can imagine how his soul leaped within him when he saw the spear thrust into our Savior's side, and heard the cry:

"It is finished!"

He wanted to follow Christ. He was in a hurry to be gone, when they came to break his legs. I can hear the Lord calling:

"Gabriel, prepare a chariot. Make haste. There is a friend of mine hanging on that cross. They are breaking his legs. He will soon be ready to come. Make haste, and bring him to me?"

The angel in the chariot swept down from heaven, took the soul of that penitent thief, and hastened back to glory. The gates of the city swung wide open, and the angels shouted welcome to this poor sinner who had been washed white in the blood of the Lamb.

And that, my friends, is just what Christ wants to do for you. That is the business on which He came down from heaven. That is why He died. And if He gave such a swift salvation to this poor thief on the cross, surely He will give you the same if, like the penitent thief, you repent, and confess, and trust in the Savior.

Somebody says that this man "was saved at the eleventh hour." I don't know about that. It might have been the first hour with him. Perhaps he never knew of Christ until he was led out to die beside Him. This may have been the very first time he ever had a chance to know the Son of God.

How many of you gave your hearts to Christ the very first time He asked them of you? Are you not farther along in the day than even that poor thief?

Some years ago, in one of the mining districts of England, a young man attended one of our meetings and refused to go from the place till he had found peace in the Savior. The next day he went down into the pit, and the coal fell in upon him. When they took him out he was broken and mangled, and had only two or three minutes of life left in him. His friends gathered about him, saw his lips moving, and, bending down to catch his words, heard him say:

"It was a good thing I settled it last night."

Settle it now, my friends, once for all. Begin now to confess your sins, and pray the Lord to remember you. He will make you an heir of His kingdom, if you will accept the gift of salvation. He is just the same Savior the thief had. Will you not cry to Him for mercy?

A cross,—and one who hangs thereon, in sight
Of heaven and earth.
The cruel nails are fast
In trembling hands and feet, the face is white
And changed with agony, the failing head
Is drooping heavily; but still again,
And yet again, the weary eyes are raised
To seek the face of One who hangeth pale

Upon another cross. He hears no shrill
And taunting voices of the crowd beneath,
He marks no cruel looks of all that gaze
Upon the woeful sight. He sees alone
That face upon the cross. Oh, long, long look,
That searcheth there the deep and awful things
Which are of God!
In his first agony
And horror he had joined with them that spake
Against the Lord, the Lamb, who gave Himself
That day for us. But when he met the look
Of those calm eyes,—he paused that instant; pale
And trembling, stricken to the heart, and faint
At sight of Him.

. . . .

At length
The pale, glad lips have breathed the trembling prayer,
"O Lord, remember me!" The hosts of God
With wistful angel-faces, bending low
Above their dying King, were surely stirred
To wonder at the cry. Not one of all
The shining host had dared to speak to Him
In that dread hour of woe, when Heaven and Earth
Stood trembling and amazed. Yet, lo! the voice
Of one who speaks to Him, who dares to pray,
"O Lord, remember me!" A sinful man
May make his pitiful appeal to Christ,
The sinner's Friend, when angels dare not speak.
And sweetly from the dying lips that day
The answer came.
Oh, strange and solemn joy

Which broke upon the fading face of him
Who there received the promise: "Thou shalt be
In Paradise this night, this night, with Me."
. . . .
O Christ, the King!
We also wander on the desert-hills,
Though haunted by Thy call, returning sweet
At morn and eve. We will not come to Thee
Till Thou hast nailed us to some bitter cross,
And made us look on Thine, and driven at last
To call on Thee with trembling and with tears.—
Thou lookest down in love, upbraiding not,
And promising the kingdom!
          . . . .

A throne,—and one
Who kneels before it, bending low in new
And speechless joy.
It is the night on earth.
The shadows fall like dew upon the hills
Around the Holy City, but above,
Beyond the dark vale of the sky, beyond
The smiling of the stars, they meet once more
In peace and glory. Heaven is comforted,—
For that strange warfare is accomplished now,
Her King returned with joy: and one who watches
The far-off morning in a prison dim,
And hung at noonday on the bitter cross,
Is kneeling at His feet, and tasteth now
The sweet, sweet opening of an endless joy.